# Transforming
# Postliberal Theology

# Transforming Postliberal Theology

## George Lindbeck, Pragmatism and Scripture

C.C. PECKNOLD

t&t clark

T&T Clark International
*A Continuum imprint*

The Tower Building, 11 York Road, London SE1 7NX
15 East 26th Street, New York, NY 10010

**British Library Cataloguing-in-Publication Data**
A catalogue record for this book is available from the British Library.

ISBN:     HB: 0-567-03033-4
          PB: 0-567-03034-2

**Library of Congress Cataloging-in-Publication Data**
A catalog record for this book is available from the Library of Congress.

Typeset by Free Range Book Design & Production
Printed and bound in Great Britain by MPG Books Ltd, Cornwall

# Contents

# Abbreviations

| | |
|---|---|
| *Civ. dei* | Augustine, *The City of God* |
| *Conf.* | Augustine, *Confessions* |
| *CP* | Charles Peirce, *Collected Papers of Charles Sanders Peirce* |
| *De doct. chr.* | Augustine, *De doctrina christiana* |
| *De mag.* | Augustine, *De magistro* |
| *De trin.* | Augustine, *De trinitate* |
| *Doctrine* | George Lindbeck, *The Nature of Doctrine: Religion and Theology in a Postliberal Age* |
| *EP* | Charles Peirce, *The Essential Peirce* |
| *PPLS* | Peter Ochs, *Peirce, Pragmatism and the Logic of Scripture* |

# Preface

Hans Frei once subtly and perceptively commented that George Lindbeck offered theology and religion a vision of '*the orthodox Christian as liberal humanist*'.[1] The use of the word 'liberal' may be misleading for the 'postliberal' Lindbeck, but the sense is right. This, Frei thought, was the way to read Lindbeck: as a theologian who combined the hermeneutical and cultural sensitivities of a Schleiermacher with the ecclesial and dogmatic sensitivities of a Barth. This has not always been the way Lindbeck has been read. In fact, Frei's comment is unique. Indeed, a vision of 'the orthodox Christian as liberal humanist' has seemed altogether contradictory to some theologians, who at their least generous will call Lindbeck 'relativistic' and 'sectarian', rather than 'orthodox' and 'humanist'. Much of the burden of this book is to show that Frei was right to read Lindbeck this way. But there is a clarification to be made here. I argue that Lindbeck is not the 'liberal humanist', but the postliberal 'scriptural pragmatist'.[2] But to argue this is also subtly to transform postliberal theology.

This book shows that postliberal theology is not only being transformed through a number of new conversations, but that it also has at heart a tradition-constituted attentiveness to God's transformative power in the real world, especially through particular, communal practices of semiotic or scriptural reasoning. What I present is nothing like an exhaustive account of postliberal theology, or a summary of the changes it has undergone over the past 20 years. Rather, I help readers to appreciate some subtle but profound developments in postliberal theology, and I begin a conversation about some of the philosophical and theological shifts that have encouraged these developments to occur. I hope that one of the outcomes of this book is that it inspires other readers to continue this conversation, and the work of transformation that is at the heart of the postliberal vision.

In the Introduction I provide a very brief assessment of postliberal theology. I then provide a logical reduction of the main areas of postliberal debate into sets of *relata* that require mediation (e.g. language–experience, text–church, church–world, theory–practice, etc.). In light of the methodological third-way that postliberalism proposes, I ask what is theologically at stake in the theory of mediation implicit in postliberal tendencies to see beyond binary pairs. I close the Introduction by forming the hypothesis that 'semiotics' is the most appropriate category for careful assessments of mediation, both in scriptural and philosophical terms, and may help to make explicit the complex relationship between scripture and pragmatism that has always been, I will argue, the transformative but frequently neglected heart of postliberal thought.

Chapter 1 focuses on Lindbeck, who offers a concise critique of modern theology, and also a powerful vision of postliberal methodology in his cultural-linguistic approach to religion and the corresponding regulative view of Christian doctrine. Seldom recognized about Lindbeck, however, is the extent to which his vision of postliberal methodology rediscovers a certain kind of pragmatism. I discuss how critics have or have not recognized his pragmatism, and claim that it is neither irrelevant to his project nor, as some critics have claimed, his greatest weakness. Rather, the kind of pragmatism Lindbeck's work suggests is one of the most underdeveloped, yet promising strengths of postliberalism. I perform a redescription of *The Nature of Doctrine* in order to highlight some of the most pragmatic features of his original argument. I close the chapter by suggesting that the linguistic pragmatism of Wittgenstein that influenced Lindbeck's 1984 description might require supplementation by an Ochsian-type (Peircean) 'semiotic' or 'scriptural pragmatism' which is able to deal with both the linguistic and non-linguistic mediations of truth, especially through attentiveness to the signs of scripture.

In Chapter 2 I engage in work of retrieval and repair, rethinking Lindbeck's 'semiotic universe encoded in holy writ' *through* St Augustine. I begin this chapter by noting the recent turn towards Augustine in semiotics, where his thought has been recognized as foundational to the discipline. I explore the significance of his theory of signs with reference to his life and thought, primarily through close studies of the *Confessions* and his book on biblical hermeneutics, *De Doctrina Christiana*. I argue that Augustine's 'theo-semiotics', shaped by his incarnational and trinitarian Word of God theology, provides an interpretive theological lens which might fund the development of a postliberal 'scriptural pragmatism' in ways that take Christians on a journey of intensification (world-description) that simultaneously enables a transformative effect upon communal reasoning (problem-solving) with those who are different.

Chapter 3 focuses on Peter Ochs, and shifts to more explicitly pragmatic terrain by attending to the persuasive case he makes for relating the semiotic pragmatism of Charles Peirce with the logic of scripture (*Peirce, Pragmatism and the Logic of Scripture*). This chapter is descriptive of the Ochsian development of postliberal pragmatism, and my reading puts his work into conversation with Lindbeck. My reading of Ochs also deals with the church–Israel relation, one of the most interesting new areas of *relata* within recent postliberal discourse. I claim that the reasoning of Lindbeck, Augustine and Ochs is in each case shaped by the scriptural narrative, and as a result, these thinkers have certain pragmatic aims in common, with sociopolitical implications for both Christians and Jews.

In the Conclusion, I review some of the theological themes that emerge in this book, attending especially to the christological and trinitarian dimensions of a scriptural pragmatism that is capable of mediating both the repair and renewal of reading communities. Facing Jesus Christ through the scriptural witness and the practices of the church, the faithful reading community is likewise capable of facing the world with the same transformative generosity that faces it in its worship of the God of Israel.[3] I propose that postliberal theology continue its long-term project of performing communal, biblical reasoning in ways that generate patient, conversational and transformative exchanges within and across cultural-linguistic borders (both religious and secular). This means a subtly different postliberal theology than the one that first emerged in the 1980s. It means a postliberal theology that understands that the witness of the church requires a public, performative mediation of the Word of God, and that requires the church not only to be itself, but to become more itself in seeking the ultimate Kingdom of God whose borders overwhelm those lines of demarcation called church and Israel.

This work is as much the product of communal conversation as it is the work of a scholar writing in isolation. But the debts one happily accrues through conversation become so great that one can only hope for the Jubilee year, for the forgiveness of debts.

First and foremost, I am most deeply indebted to David Ford, Regius Professor of Divinity in the University of Cambridge. He supervised the research and guided the conversations I was having in wise and charitable ways; he gently shaved off many of my roughest edges and made me a better theologian. The expansive, responsible and generous orthodoxy of his own theological vision should be apparent in these pages. Peter Ochs's powerful heart and mind have directed me on countless occasions, and his influence on this book is clearly profound. Daniel Hardy has constantly encouraged me to see just beyond my present horizons. Together, these three giants have taught me to think in community.

My conversation partners in Cambridge have been Rachel Muers, Ben Quash, Susannah Ticciati, Jon Cooley, and a number of colleagues who joined in our biblical reasoning group over the course of four years. I also have to thank Randi Rashkover for reading many drafts of work-in-progress, as well as Curtis Freeman, Frederick van Fleteran, Eugene Rogers, Mark McIntosh, Willie Young, Oliver Davies, Janet Soskice, Robert Cathey and Charles Hefling, all of whom gave me advice and/or feedback at some stage of the research. None of these people are, of course, responsible for the inadequacies and limitations of this study, but they certainly made it better than it would have been without their collegial counsel.

Financial support for this research came from the President and Fellows of Clare Hall in the University of Cambridge, the Bethune-Baker Fund, the Norrissian Prize Fund, the Spalding Trust, the Episcopal Church Foundation, and through Steve Moore's tireless ministrations, from the Wesley Foundation. A very special vote of thanks goes to Elizabeth Jones-Ketner, as well as Rand and Phyllis Michael, who practise the Christian virtue of generosity, giving abundantly, frequently and whenever there is need. I am immensely grateful to my parents, Cliff and Jennifer Pecknold, and my grand-parents, Cliff and Rita Pecknold, for their lifelong investment in me.

Thanks is also due to the community of St Benet's Church, Cambridge, which has been such a happy place to live and worship, bolstered in part by the presence of Franciscan brothers who embody the profound unity of word and sacrament that complicates dyadic ways of thinking about the church. Brother Samuel SSF, and all at St Francis House in Cambridge, have my gratitude for supporting this work with prayer – which as Bonhoeffer once wisely noted, enables theology to begin.

My wife Sara, above all, has emptied herself of her own deepest ambitions and desires in order that this work be brought to completion. This emptying has not been in vain! Our son William was a 'consolation from love' during the writing of this book, and a reminder of our joyful responsibility to care for the next generation. I dedicate this book to Sara and William.

# Introduction

## Postliberalism, pragmatism and scripture

Postliberalism cannot be simply defined. As a diverse movement (or better, an intellectual tendency) within theology and religion in late modern society, it has been famously associated with a community of thinkers at Yale University in the 1980s – most notably Hans Frei and George Lindbeck, whose 1984 book *The Nature of Doctrine: Religion and Theology in a Postliberal Age* first introduced the term. It has also been called 'narrative theology', owing to the tendency of both Frei and Lindbeck to transform the terms of modern theology through a heightened pitch of attention to the narratives of scripture and the practices of the church throughout history.

Taken literally, 'postliberal' implies a critique of modern liberalism – especially the kind that Karl Barth opposed in his theological critiques of Liberal Protestantism, but also those philosophical critiques of liberalism posed in different ways by Ludwig Wittgenstein, Gilbert Ryle and Alasdair MacIntyre, and the sociological and anthropological ones made by Peter Berger and Clifford Geertz. Despite temptations to the contrary, however, the postliberal critique should not be taken as being anti-modern, anti-secular or anti-liberal. If it were anti-liberal, it would have said so. Postliberalism is better seen as a critical conversation with liberal theology, seeking to repair problems through charitable judgments and constructive transformations. Such an appreciation of the corrective role of postliberalism better corresponds to the primary intention of its critique: *to remove obstacles that hinder the repair of a fragmented church*. We should continually remember that the critical task was intended to renew the ecumenical imperative for catholic unity and enable the church to be a more authentic witness to God and neighbour. The theological method for achieving such an ambitious agenda became synonymous with the critical term 'postliberal'. But despite the desire of some to

1

view postliberalism solely as a type of 'negative theology', the critical sense of the term does not exhaust the full range of the postliberal agenda.

Postliberalism may also be understood through its constructive dimensions as a 'return to scripture' that seeks to describe 'best practices' for the enduring church in a complex and pluralist world. The return to the scriptural narrative has been profoundly important. Karl Barth supplied much of the impetus for this return, and his influence is evident in postliberals of the 'Yale school' period, especially in the work of Frei and David Kelsey, and before both of them in the work of H. Richard Niebuhr.[4] But it is also a 'return to the tradition', allied in various ways with *nouvelle théologie*, and the concern in twentieth-century French Catholic thought that *ressourcement* could help constructive theologians in their task of creative faithfulness to the tradition in the face of contemporary challenges.

In light of these various European sources, we might see postliberalism as an Anglo-American variation on this theme of returning to sources; a trend which Jeffrey Stout has recently called 'new traditionalism', and Peter Ochs and Stanley Hauerwas sometimes refer to as 'radical traditionalism'.[5] The radical returns, both to scripture and tradition, remind us that postliberalism is a movement of radical reform. It is not 'returning' to scripture and tradition for no reason: the church faces urgent problems that need repair – and often radical repair. The intention is not to be 'radical' in some political or theological sense (these may or may not be possible outcomes); 'radical' is descriptive of methodology which returns to authoritative sources (more at *radix*, or 'root'). The postliberal intention, so frequently lost amongst critical readers, is to return to the roots of the tradition in order to heal and repair the church. What we think today are 'traditional Christian values' may, on closer inspection of the sources, turn out to be anything but traditional. How would such a return to roots change our minds? Would it change how we perform and practise the Christian faith? This was not a naïve desire to repristinate the past, to return to a primitive church or even a medieval one. It was a desire for a self-critical reflection on contemporary ecclesial practice and also a desire to reconnect the embodied practices to the generative logic of the tradition for the sake of a better future.

Reaching deeply into tradition and scripture may transform contemporary church practices, to be sure. It has already made theologians much more reflexive about ecclesial practices, and this has been one of the great contributions of postliberal theology. But what it also might mean is that such a return to 'roots' transforms postliberal theology itself. Both critics and comrades alike have sometimes missed the subtle evolutions that have been occurring internally within postliberal theology. One critic suggested to me that postliberal theology is like 'nail soup', no matter how much is added, it will still be nail soup! There is not much that can be said in response to such ossified critiques of postliberal theology. But much more can be said to the many constructive criticisms that have been made, and this book responds to these and tries to point to ways forward.

There is no substitute for reading Lindbeck's important book, other assessments of postliberalism, or the many articles available which document the conversations and debates which have steadily appeared over the past 20 years.[6] What I offer in this Introduction is simply a brief outline of some 'postliberal tendencies', some review of the major areas of debate and some theological assessment of what the conversation has achieved thus far. My own introductory assessment of postliberalism is not exhaustive but is intended to be especially sensitive to christological questions of mediation, and I will suggest that the mediation of scriptural signs is a nexus issue around which many of the debates can be reoriented.

## Postliberal tendencies

Postliberal tendencies are available in a concise but tentative way in Lindbeck's *The Nature of Doctrine*. For better or for worse, what began in 1984 as prolegomena to a larger theological project (an aborted 'comparative dogmatics' in ecumenical theology), is now one of the most pedagogically powerful representations of postliberal theology to date. In the North American classroom at least, it has become standard reading for undergraduates, graduates and seminarians alike. Both the profound pedagogical effect of Lindbeck's slim volume, and the representational status it has gained as a contemporary classic of postliberalism, seem to suggest that 20 years on, it is a work of some enduring significance.

Though Hans Frei provided more sustained theological arguments for narrative theology, it was Lindbeck who brought conciseness and precision to the 'pre-theological' argument for postliberalism in theology and religion.[7] It is most likely this conciseness that makes his book so pedagogically useful. In it, Lindbeck spelled out the postliberal critique of two kinds of foundationalism (one premodern and one modern). This postfoundationalist critique makes way for a distinctive approach to religion and theology that he famously called the 'cultural-linguistic' model.

The logic of Lindbeck's argument in *The Nature of Doctrine* runs along the following lines. There are basically two tendencies in theology and religion which either exclude or embrace liberalism and/or modernity. These two tendencies have failed in various ways, and so a third, mediating tendency is required that can repair the failures of the first two tendencies. The triadicity of the logic implicit here is important to note as we will return to it in due course. But let us first briefly describe each of these tendencies before turning to the heated debate which followed Lindbeck's proposal.

The premodern tendency was towards a certain kind of excessive confidence in the foundations of human reason. Lindbeck calls this the 'propositional-cognitivist' approach to theology. It claims that objective realities can be known directly, and that Christian doctrines simply provide 'informative propositions' or 'truth claims' about these objective realities which can then be systematically organized as corresponding to objective reality. In the mode of anecdotal critique, Lindbeck writes about a crusader proclaiming 'Jesus is Lord' as he cleaves the skull of an infidel. Under a 'propositional-cognivist' approach to Christian doctrine, the crusader's utterance ('Jesus is Lord') is 'true', corresponding to objective reality, regardless as to whether or not the *words* 'fit' the *action* of the subject, namely the crusader. This view privileged the 'objective' over the 'subjective', and sought foundations in the knowledge of 'propositions' that adequately corresponded to reality. The problem is that it did violence to the whole subjective dimension of doing descriptive justice to the truth.

The modern 'liberal' tendency was to search for foundations elsewhere, in a universal 'essence' of human experience that was shared by all religions (the Kantian 'categorical imperative' is an ethical instance of making a particular human experience into a universal claim). Contrary to the premodern tendency, it privileged the subjective, 'the noninformative and nondiscursive symbols of inner feelings, attitudes, or existential conditions' which express human experience. Unfortunately, though it did justice to the subject in a way that the prior tendency did not, the 'experiential-expressivist' approach also had the effect of diminishing the particularity of each religion, of smoothing out differences that were, in fact, irreducible. At least one problem with this liberal tendency was that the foundationalist posture of 'essentialism' tended to obliterate 'difference' and therefore, obliterated particular religious identities. In the midst of the extraordinary violence of the twentieth century, where much of the violence was inflicted upon particular religious identities, critics began to reassess the liberal strategy in theology and religion (as well as in other areas of study).

The postliberal tendency is, by contrast, post-foundationalist and particularist to the core (in contrast to the potentially violent implications of the first two tendencies, the postliberal agenda may implicitly involve a methodological pacifism). The search for universal foundations, whether objective or subjective, is relativized against particular traditions of enquiry. The quest for a common core, the 'essence' of religious experience, or the 'general concept' is abandoned (in Barth's criticism, these quests tend towards idolatry). Rather, the postliberal tendency seeks concrete descriptions of lived reality – attending particularly to those practices that constitute the life of the church. Practices are judged on their ability to embody the logic of the scriptures in the church, e.g. through catechesis, scripture study, prayer, preaching, sacraments, etc. It does not offer apologetics for such particularity (though it admits *ad hoc* apologetics under certain contingencies); it celebrates the scandal of it. Taking up the Barthian dictum that 'the best apologetics is a good dogmatics', the postliberal tendency was to remove obstacles to faithfulness, to repair broken practices and empower the church's witness to the world and her service to both God and neighbour by enabling communities better to speak and practise the language of the scriptures.

For biblical communities, the complex relationship between language and culture must be shaped by the 'semiotic universe encoded in holy writ'. For Lindbeck and other postliberals, it is the scriptural narrative that is essential for shaping ecclesial identity and witness. Discovering the relationship between this scriptural language and the culture that is appropriate to Christian community is the central aim. The scriptural narrative provides 'native speakers' with a linguistic field of reference that is generative of a certain kind of culture, a certain way of being and communicating in the world, and there is, as a result, a strong postliberal emphasis upon good performance.

Following this 'cultural-linguistic' approach to religion, Lindbeck extends the analogy further and likens Christian doctrines to grammatical rules in language. Doctrines, like grammars, are second-order reflections upon how this scriptural sign-system is used or performed in this community. They are regulative of the 'semiotic universe' of scripture in the same way that grammars are regulative of other semiotic systems embodied in communal life (the analogy especially holds for religions that derive their coherence from authoritatively inscribed narratives). Doctrines, then, both reflect the actual practices of native speaker, and in turn, also have a subtle influence upon first-order practices. In other words, doctrines are primarily descriptive of the way Christians live and speak the language of scripture (especially in liturgical practice) even if these second-order descriptions cannot be neatly separated from first-order practice at all times.

In Peter Ochs's words, postliberals are interested in 'the logic of scripture', and as such are interested in being guided and directed by this logic for maximizing the mission and service of the church. Whatever the postliberal theologian does, s/he privileges the 'first-order' uses of scripture as embodied by 'native speakers'. Where the need arises to form 'doctrines' (i.e. 'second-order concepts and theories'), these will be in descriptive service to the concrete embodiment of the scriptures in first-order practice (the performance of the faith). These distinctions, between first- and second-order, are not hard-and-fast ones. They simply serve to display the order of the relation between practice and theory, not to force a wedge between them. The key move that is being made here is the semiotic and practical one: turning all eyes towards the performance or embodiment of the scriptural narrative.

Though postliberal theology left the liberal search for experiential foundations behind, it did not leave the concern with 'experience' behind. It simply sought a different kind of relation between language and experience. I argue that Lindbeck transformed the liberal concern with 'universal' experience by attending to descriptions of concrete 'particular' experience as *mediated* through cultural-linguistic signs. The mediatorial move is extremely significant. *Postliberalism transforms liberal theology by a greater descriptive attentiveness to the mediatorial capacity of signs*, that is, to our culturally and linguistically mediated experience of reality (and thus seeks to do justice to 'objective realities' too).

Likewise, though postliberalism had left the conservative search for 'propositional-cognitive' foundations behind, it did not leave behind the realist concern to attend to 'objective realities'. But if such realities are always already mediated through cultural-linguistic signs, a much more modest, even humble 'cognitivism' must be admitted. As in the critique of liberalism, a healthy dose of fallibilism is needed, and rational certainty must be tempered by God's ability to judge all human certainties at the end of time. This is another way of saying that

Christians can never rest easy with a closed discourse of meaning, but must always be open to judgment in seeking the Kingdom of God.

The elegant logic implicit in all of these moves is theological. In both philosophical and theological terms, it concerns mediation. Beginning with the refusal of the *dyad*, of the uncomplicated 'either/or' between 'liberal' or 'conservative', between 'propositional' or 'experiential' knowledge, between 'subjective' or 'objective' knowledge, postliberal theology seeks both to maintain these distinctions and to unite them. Only an adequate theory of mediation can do this, and Lindbeck's 'cultural-linguistic' model provided a provisional and methodological third way aimed at just this kind of mediation. Postliberal theology resists the 'either/or' of these binaries precisely because they are logically resistant to mediation and *to be logically resistant to mediation is also to be resistant to the mediation of Jesus Christ* (in this sense, the Aristotelian 'law of the excluded middle' is challenged by Christian reasoning).

Over the course of this book, readers will revisit postliberal debates in some new ways by attending primarily to these issues of mediation, namely the mediation of signs, of scripture, of church, and in all of these the mediation of the Word of God incarnate in Jesus Christ. The aim is not to provide readers with an overview of postliberal theology, but to gain a certain theological sensibility about what postliberal debates have been about and what transforming them might entail.

## Debates and agendas

In the most influential assessments of postliberal theology in recent years, four central areas of debate are usually identified.

In 1997 William Placher identified the four areas of debate he deemed 'liveliest' as (1) the adequacy of postliberalism to deal with truth in a non-relativistic way; (2) the relationship between texts and their interpretive communities; (3) the coherence of the narratives of scripture and/or the tradition, and the degree to which a pluralism within these narratives is to be embraced; and (4) questions about Lindbeck's 'sociological sectarianism' in the light of non-sectarian responsibilities of Christian communities.[8]

In the new (third) edition of the same volume, Jim Fodor writes the latest assessment of postliberal theology.[9] Nearly a decade apart, the issues remain the same in both accounts but have developed in some subtle and interesting ways. Fodor, likewise, identifies four areas of debate: (1) the primacy of scriptural narrative for theology and the need to differentiate narrative in more precise and systematic ways (e.g. 'semiotics') and to specify the relation of the text to a variety of vital categories; (2) the relationship between texts and their interpretive communities; (3) the ongoing debate about how postliberals deal with truth; and (4) 'sectarianism or sharing Israelhood'. Fodor's fourth category is, however, most substantively a reflection of the way in which postliberal theology has been changing in recent years, transforming the debate about sectarianism into a debate about the way in which Jews and Christians are both shaped by 'Israel's story'. The church's sectarian or 'separated' existence, to the degree that it is shaped by Israel's story, thus entails the 'selfless service of all humankind' and an identity deeply bound up with that of the religious 'other'. This has all sorts of implications for an ecclesial education not only with the religious but also with the secular 'stranger within our gates', without giving up a diaspora-like ecclesial identity (i.e. 'sociologically sectarian' need not mean sectarian in terms of social responsibility).

These accounts of postliberal theology are invaluable and provide students with a welcome assessment of what the philosophical, anthropological, political or hermeneutical stakes are in these debates. What is not always apparent in assessments of postliberal theology is what, exactly, the *theological* stakes are in these same debates.

### Signs, mediation and truth

Following Peter Ochs, Jim Fodor writes that Lindbeck's cultural-linguistic approach 'encourages a certain *pragmatic* tentativeness in the use of philosophical concepts to explicate faith, since rule-following does not compel allegiance to any particular metaphysical outlook or allegiance to particular ontological beliefs, thereby honoring and upholding God's mystery'. This is guaranteed to disappoint those who are rigidly committed to dogmatically held metaphysical commitments abstracted from scripture and community practice. It must be stressed, however, that *postliberal theology has never excluded the possibility of metaphysical or ontological commitments*. Rather, what it encourages is 'a certain pragmatic tentativeness' towards them, especially when dealing with radical returns to scripture and tradition in order to heal a fragmented church.

One of the most important ways that this pragmatic stance takes root in Lindbeck is stated well by Fodor in his recent Ochsian-inspired account of postliberal theology. Fodor writes, 'there is, on the cultural-linguistic account, no *direct* way to judge religious claims "true" or "false" ... One can only judge the truth of religious statements *indirectly* and *holistically* according to a pragmatic criterion of "fruitfulness".' Theories of truth, in other words, stand or fall on their ability to deal with mediation, with that which 'stands between', and enables judgments to be made through indirect and holistic criteria. A few entrenched critics of pragmatism will sniff that this is merely a 'pragmatic theory of truth', but more often than not these same critics betray an ignorance of a highly differentiated field of study, and frequently confuse pragmatism with utilitarianism, relativism, or worst of all to some critics, a kind of 'works-righteousness'.

Lest 'pragmatism' seem like a foreign concept to Christianity, it should be noted that the Bible has its own pragmatic categories. The biblical category of 'fruitfulness' has taken on a special significance. The Ochsian turn in postliberal theology has made Jesus's words in Matthew 7.16 ('By their fruits you will know them') profoundly integral, both for assessments of Peircean pragmatism and for genuinely scriptural forms of pragmatism. This has had the effect of transforming Peircean pragmatism by inserting it into the world of the Bible, but it has also had fructifying effects on postliberal methodology.

With respect to the careful way Placher and Fodor have assessed the debates above, my own view is that there are logically simpler ways of assessing the debate which might bear fruit. What if we consider that these debates have centred around four *powerful relationships*: (1) the relationship between language and experience; (2) between scripture and church practice (and/or between texts and reading communities); (3) between church and Israel; and (4) between church and world. The issue of truth is not so much one debate among others as it is a problematic that inheres in the question of how to mediate these powerful relationships. In my view, these debates hinge on these issues of truth and the mediation of powerful *signs*, increasingly with special reference to the mediation of the signs of scripture.

All of these debates pose the question: What mediates particular kinds of *relata*? For example, one major area of critique has been about Lindbeck's comment that the 'scriptures absorb the world'. The one-way relationship of 'absorbing' is at worst a kind of totalitarianism, critics will say, and at best a kind of insular autism. This is a good critique in the sense that it asks postliberals to clarify how it understands the *relata* in question. And there have been repeated attempts to provide such clarifications. What postliberals clearly need is a pragmatic tentativeness towards their own category of 'absorbing'. Postliberals need a more dynamic word that provides a better description of the relations that obtain between 'inner' and 'outer' distinctions.

This book suggests that semiotics points the way forward, suggesting the dynamic, even sacramental language of 'transformation' for such questions of *relata*. This suggests mutual transformations of all relations through an indwelling and inhabiting of the scriptures that is itself hospitable and conversational, as well as being open to judgment, correction and renewal.

Under all of these issues the category of 'semiotics' has become increasingly critical in the extension and supplementation of postliberal theology because 'semiotics' names a discipline of thinking about the unavoidable mediation of signs. This book claims that this is the powerful implicit claim proposed in Lindbeck's cultural-linguistic theory of religion. Semiotics and pragmatism have always been intrinsically linked, and we know this because they are linked not only in the work of Charles Peirce, the modern progenitor of both semiotics and pragmatism, but also within the Christian tradition through the original semiotic theory of St Augustine. Much of this book works to bring postliberal theology forward through journeys ancient and modern that are conversant about the relation between pragmatism and scripture.

### Scripture, theo-logics and pragmatism

In responding to issues of truth and mediation, the single most important philosophical development in postliberal theology has been the Ochsian move to supplement Wittgenstein with a Peircean-type logic. This extends the semiotic and pragmatic dimensions that were implicit in *The Nature of Doctrine* in significant ways. In Ochsian perspective, Peircean 'semiotic pragmatism' gives theology and religion all the benefits of Wittgensteinian linguistic pragmatism without any of the disadvantages of 'incommensurable' language-games. It does this by a return to scripture, those texts which are authoritative to religious communities (Tanakh, Bible, Qur'an). In Christian terms, this return to scripture entails a return to the Word of God, which is able to sustain, correct, repair and renew a fragmented church and world. It is a return to a theo-logic that embodies this repair in the sign given to the church and the world in Jesus Christ.

The postliberal commitment to ecclesial identity has never been an insular movement; it is neither a form of 'cultural isolationism' nor a 'political quietism'. Rather, postliberal theology senses its profound responsibility to past and future generations of the church. It is a very serious commitment to being theologically, socially and politically responsible with the Christian tradition, enabling Christian witness maximum effectiveness in service to the world's greatest needs at the same time as it attends to the practical life of communities that think and worship God truly. That it does so through a heightened pitch of attention to the 'theo-logic' of scripture means that it is better situated to correct (for 'I know that my Redeemer lives') what has gone wrong between all of us who find ourselves in the church, in Israel, and in a world tearing itself apart.

If it can be agreed that 'scripture' might be the first word to come from the lips of a postliberal theologian, a second word might be 'practices', or arguably better still, 'pragmatism', the study of practical consequences.[10] Interestingly, the early reception of *The Nature of Doctrine* either (1) ignored the pragmatic dimensions of Lindbeck's book; or (2) criticized its 'pragmatism'; or (3) accused Lindbeck of not sufficiently thinking through his implicit pragmatism. But after the early reception of the book in the 1980s, postliberals went 'underground' on the question of 'pragmatism', despite its importance for repairing ecclesial practices. But 'pragmatism' is now beginning to emerge again as a central issue. One important question now being asked is: 'In what way are postliberals pragmatists?' Mainly, this is the search for a tradition-constituted warrant for scripture-centred pragmatism that serves the aims of postliberal theology. In the process, what readers will find is an account of how postliberal theology has been evolving. The transformations take us deeper into the theo-logical heart of postliberalism which, in Jim Fodor's words, is about not only the repair of the church but also 'compassionate healing and repair of the world'.[11]

This turn towards the language of 'healing' and 'repair' owes much to the influence of the Jewish postliberal pragmatist, Peter Ochs. His work on Charles Peirce has done the most to reignite this question about a postliberal pragmatism, and helps readers to ask what a developed form of this postliberal pragmatism might look like, in both Christian and Jewish terms. In Jewish terms, the language of healing and 'repair' comes from theological claims about Israel's mission, *tikkun olam*, 'to repair the world' and to be a light to the nations. But what would this look like in Christian terms? What theological claims could ground a Christian pragmatism? Is there a pragmatism that is native to the Hebrew and Christian scriptures, or must postliberal theologians reach outside of the Christian tradition for help in developing a pragmatism that is appropriate to its own deep purposes?

Intrinsically tied to the relation between scripture and pragmatism are two related theo-political issues that have also led to internal transformations in postliberal theology. These have to do with (a) rethinking the church–Israel relation; and (b) rethinking the church–world relation. What is most remarkable is how deeply bound these issues are to each other, but the scriptural–pragmatic dimension seems primary in this regard.

In this book I explore possibilities for a postliberal 'scriptural pragmatism'. I do not chart the evolution of postliberal theology or seek to direct its future. What follows are three coordinated essays which describe three different ways of moving towards this 'scriptural pragmatism': Lindbeck, Augustine and Ochs. By the end of the book, I hope it will be apparent that postliberal theology seeks a transformation of both the world and the church. But I also hope it will be apparent that to seek this transformation is nothing less than to seek God's face.

It is in the seeking of God that postliberal theology will both have transformative powers, and will itself be transformed. By appreciating the unavoidable mediation of scriptural signs in seeking God's face, postliberal theology rightly recognizes the need for a radical orientation in which facing the Word of God instantiated in scripture simultaneously entails facing our religious and secular neighbours. A transforming postliberal theology does not so much envision the scriptures 'absorbing' the world as it envisions the scriptures providing the mediation most needful in 'conversing' with those who are different.

# 1

# Lindbeck

## A new version of pragmatism

In this chapter I elaborate my understanding of Lindbeck's *The Nature of Doctrine* as a new version of pragmatism. David Tracy's remarkable 1985 claim that Lindbeck's postliberalism was a 'new linguistic version of one side of classical pragmatism' has been largely forgotten in debates about postliberal theology.[12] Few of Lindbeck's readers have recognized the pragmatism implicit in postliberalism, and those who have recognized it have seen it as a burden to the argument. I argue the opposite. The new version of pragmatism implicit in postliberalism significantly strengthens Lindbeck's argument. The more important question to ask is: What is this new version of pragmatism that postliberalism offers to the study of theology and religion? And how might it be developed? The first section assesses postliberal debates and proposes what was theologically and pragmatically at stake in them. The second section redescribes *The Nature of Doctrine* in order to draw attention to the theological and pragmatic contours of the argument. In the third section I articulate what is gained by making Lindbeck's proposal more theologically and pragmatically explicit. In a concluding section, I discuss further the provocative point that a Wittgensteinian linguistic pragmatism will not serve postliberal purposes without some supplementation from a Peircean-inspired 'semiotic' or 'scriptural' pragmatism.

### Background debate

The postliberalism that was once (in 1985), considered a 'minority' opinion against the then 'dominant' liberalism, has, in a relatively short space of time, become a widely and intensively discussed opinion especially in Anglo-American theological discourse.[13] The intense debates that *The Nature of Doctrine* provoked from the outset, in diverse academic journals such as *The Thomist* and *Modern Theology*, were early signs that Lindbeck initiated a paradigm-shift in theology which continues to have far-reaching effects across a spectrum of theological discourse – effects so pervasive that Lindbeck's work is now essential for understanding contemporary theological presuppositions. Re-examining Lindbeck, then, is in some sense to re-examine contemporary presuppositions about how Lindbeck has been read. One basic claim I make is that Lindbeck's work has been misread on a number of levels and that such misreadings have stifled the development of postliberalism.

The four features of debate I highlighted in the Introduction are apparent even in the initial reception that the book received in *The Thomist* as well as in multiple issues of the journal *Modern Theology*. The four categories are abstractions from particular distinctions made about how postliberalism was or was not 'public theology', about whether the implicit theory of truth in Lindbeck's proposal allowed for ontological reference or not, about whether postliberalism was too pragmatic or not pragmatic enough, about the incommensurability of different semiotic systems, or about whether intratextuality also meant 'hermetically sealed' from other world-descriptions, to name only a few prominent lines of debate. The most vigorous and sustained assessments of Lindbeck's postliberal proposal were made before the 1980s were over, and any review of literature will admit that the issues involved resist neat summaries and are frequently so intertwined as to challenge categorization. But the debates clearly had a shape and a mood, and it is worth reflecting not only on the categories of the debate early identified, and my own theological interpretation of the mediatorial significance of these debates, but also on the context in which Lindbeck's book was written and in which these early debates were set.

First we should remember that there was, in the universities at least, a general mood of non-foundationalism in the wake of Wittgenstein, and the turn towards linguistic and cultural particularity in the social sciences. And at least one major antecedent theological debate energized the conversation, the one that hardly requires mention: Barth's strong confessional response to Schleiermacher's correlationist strategy for the church–world relationship. More likely to be overlooked, however, were concurrent debates in political philosophy which also added fuel to the fire: the so-called 'liberal–communitarian debates' pitted conceptions of the good against one another. Liberal preferences for the 'rights' and 'liberties' of individual agents operating within 'neutral' political spaces (Locke, Rawls, Dworkin) were challenged by communitarian notions of 'moral identities' being constituted by the institutions, traditions and practices in which they are grounded (Hegel, MacIntyre, Taylor). At the same time, there was a growing sense of communal fragmentation, with church numbers in decline and shopping malls on the rise throughout the suburban sprawl of countless gated communities.

In North American theology in the 1980s, this context shaped the postliberal-revisionist debate, which found its own distinctive embodiment in a strange but temporary institutional rivalry between the divinity schools of Yale University and the University of Chicago. Like theological debates before it, and sociopolitical ones of the same period, there was the enduring problem of 'the one and the many', cast as either the 'insider–outsider' problem, or in terms of what constituted 'the public character of theology' when private–public distinctions break down. Both sides wanted to claim superiority in their approach to this important problem in religion and theology. Chicago tended to accuse Yale of a 'fideism' that was culturally isolated from discourse with other 'incommensurable' communities and traditions, and Yale tended to accuse Chicago of the foundationalist mistakes of an individualistic 'experiential-expressivism' that sought warrants for religion and theology that were available to any 'reasonable' person.[14]

The Yale–Chicago binary was a momentary instantiation of an enduring problem about particular and universal truth. The debates soon identified that theories of truth and meaning are contextually situated around concrete problems of communities but that this does not exclude the need for ontological reference that is external to the culture and language of a particular community. Chicago-like positions tended to concede the importance of the scriptural narrative for shaping ecclesial practices, and Yale-like positions tended to concede that mutually critical and mutually beneficial cultural-linguistic border crossings were possible on an *ad hoc* basis. However, once the polemics of the Yale–Chicago rivalry subsided, much of the debate appeared to subside with it. But the reality was that this debate simply became 'subtext' for a countless array of conversations in theology and religion. What has been left behind is a sense of where postliberalism is headed. What is the future of the postliberal programme? As I suggested in the Introduction, I believe the future of postliberalism is bound up with how postliberals interpret and extend Lindbeck's pragmatism and the issues related to it. Therefore, in the remainder of this chapter I return to examine the little book which has caused such a stir over the past 20 years.

## 1 Problems to which *The Nature of Doctrine* is a solution

*The Nature of Doctrine* not only claims a better model for the kind of world-description that the church practices but also claims to provide problem-solving tools that will enable 'story-shaped' religions to have greater coherence and fruitfulness.[15] Lindbeck's book specifically answers doctrinal problems he identified through his ecumenical work at Vatican II. However, one of the reasons the book has endured and sparked such intense debate is because it suggests that it actually solves problems which extend beyond its original context. It seeks to solve not only ecumenical problems but problems which extend throughout religion and theology (as Lindbeck's sub-title suggests).

Lindbeck's own life is itself instructive for understanding the problems that his work is intended to solve. Theoretical solutions are always already bound to historically situated people and the problems they face. So it is interesting to see just some of the ways in which the context and contingencies of a theologian's life contribute to the shape of his scholarly conversations. For example, the author of the phrase 'cultural-linguistic' even seems to imply in a rare self-reflexive article that he was aware of cultural and linguistic differences from an early age in China, where he spent the first 17 years of his life in remote Loyang (north central China), a town he describes as largely untouched by modern amenities or attitudes.[16]

Born in 1923 to American-Lutheran missionaries, Lindbeck lived for many years in a land that, in retrospect, seemed quite foreign to the modern world he would come to know as a young man. His early experiences in rural China of being 'set apart' from the habits of modernity must have provided an unusual contrast to his elite education in medieval philosophy and theology which followed. Lindbeck writes how his deep sense of being rooted in a tradition (Christian, Lutheran), yet in dialogue with other traditions, languages and cultures (Chinese, French, Roman Catholic), contributed to the overall shape of his later life and thought.[17]

After China, Lindbeck returned to the United States for his university education, earning his BA in 1943 from the premier Lutheran institution of higher education, Gustavus Adolphus College in Minnesota.[18] On graduation, he immediately prepared to go to New Haven, Connecticut and in 1946 he earned his BD from the Divinity School at Yale (where he first encountered H. Richard Niebuhr), followed by postgraduate work in medieval theology. His interest in Duns Scotus put him in regular conversation with some of the major figures in Roman Catholic scholarship. Studying with medievalists Etienne Gilson and Paul Vignaux, in Toronto and Paris, he deepened his interest in Lutheran–Roman Catholic dialogue that was to be such a hallmark of his later career as an ecumenist. Yale offered him a teaching job in 1952, and in 1955 he was awarded a PhD for his thesis, 'Is Duns Scotus an Essentialist?' The old guard of Yale was passing away (H.R. Niebuhr died in 1962) and Lindbeck was part of an exciting and influential new faculty, with Hans Frei, Paul Holmer, David Kelsey and Jaroslav Pelikan as just some of his young colleagues.

Lindbeck's growing reputation as a promising young medievalist at Yale University made him a natural choice for the Lutheran World Federation, who sent him to Rome as an observer at all four sessions of the Second Vatican Council (1962–65). It was this ecumenical context that raised many problems to the forefront of Lindbeck's concerns – problems he hoped could be solved for the sake of the unity (and diversity) of the church. Here he wrestled directly with the need for dialogue and the difficulties posed to this an ecumenical context dominated by Barthian neo-orthodoxy and Catholic neo-Thomism. He sought especially to solve what he saw as the problem of 'doctrinal reconciliation' in this new situation.

The puzzle was that ecumenical Christians were beginning to claim doctrinal reconciliation without making any apparent doctrinal capitulations – significant changes were being made but changes that vaguely claimed to be maintaining continuity with the unchanging truth of Christian faith.[19] Ancient issues of permanence and change were raised by these 'anomalies' of apparently sudden doctrinal agreement after centuries of genuine, long-standing disagreements. At the theological level, difficult questions about what true reconciliation entails were being asked. Lindbeck's book was, in part, trying to answer these very particular problems or 'anomalies' of the ecumenical movement.

In reflecting on this period of his life, Lindbeck noted that 'non-theological' influences in the 1960s were also formative, especially the linguistic pragmatism of the Wittgensteinians, the 'paradigm-shifting' work of Thomas Kuhn, the cultural and linguistically sensitive sociology of Peter Berger and Clifford Geertz, and the basic mood of 'non-foundationalism'.[20] All of this amounted to a deep awareness, emerging from reflection upon his own context, of the 'linguistic, social and cognitive construction of reality and experience.'[21]

Lindbeck published extensively on the Second Vatican Council and its significance for ecumenism, in Christian, non-Christian and Jewish terms.[22] Consistently in his writing, issues of unity and diversity, continuity and change, identity and difference, and reconciliation were foremost amongst his concerns. Whether he took up issues in Lutheran life, Roman Catholic theology, theological education or the nature of doctrine, he was always writing with the actual problems of his ecumenical context in mind. That context raised for him the question of the continuity of Christian identity and led him to solve the problems that he found burdensome to that identity, working towards 'orthodoxy', in what was increasingly being called 'the postmodern condition'.[23] The integrating concern that emerged from the very beginning of his life and came to a head in his mature theology is also a central concern in this book. The 'integrating centre' of his postliberal thought is ecumenically concerned with the central doctrinal rules for scripture reading.[24] Lindbeck writes as a Lutheran:

> I began to opt for a Reformation Christianity self-consciously opposed to modern Protestantism in both its conservative and liberal forms. Its starting point is neither biblicistic nor experientialist, and certainly not individualistic, but dogmatic: it commences with the historic Christian communal confession of faith in Christ. For the Reformers, as for the Orthodox and Catholic churches of East and West, that confession is the one expressed in the ancient *trinitarian and christological* creeds. The Reformers did not so much try to prove these creeds from Scripture (and certainly not from experience), but rather read scripture in their light, and then used the Bible thus construed *to mold experience and guide thought and action. God's word*, in their premodern hermeneutics, was *ever applicable*, and changed in import with the circumstances. It was not constrained to a single kind of meaning by inerrantist theories of inspiration or liberal ones of revelatory experience. My understanding of the implications of beginning with dogma has developed greatly (see *The Nature of Doctrine*), but not the creedal and confessional starting point. That has remained the integrating center of my later theological work.[25]

Lindbeck's opposition to 'modern Protestantism in both its conservative and liberal forms' reflects a dissatisfaction with modernism more generally. His earliest experience of remote 'premodern' China, his experience as a Vatican II delegate observer longing for the unity of a highly polarized church, his 'Barthian' reading of nineteenth-century 'liberalism', all contributed to his dissatisfaction with the prevailing categories modernity had offered. To heal theology and religion in modernity, he set out to solve what he saw as the absence of any real, unifying centre – *to discover some category beyond the binaries* of 'conservative and liberal'. From his statements about the integrating centre of his work, we can see the pragmatic importance Lindbeck wanted to give to the doctrinal rules (christological and trinitarian) required for the applicability and interpretive use of scripture: 'to mold experience and guide thought and action'. And yet the logic of that relationship is clear: the credal and confessional starting-point, that is, the incarnational and trinitarian shape of participation in the 'rule of faith' of a tradition is primary in the dynamic between doctrinal rules and scripture.[26] This hermeneutical starting-point is intended to guide the logic and action of the church. It is a starting-point which seems to further his concerns to solve problems or 'anomalies' by providing modern theology with a unifying centre (the 'rule of faith' or depth grammar of the creeds and confessions) that can help secure the continuity and 'truth' of Christian identity, yet also deal with contingency, change, and the reality of diverse contexts and communities.

It is important to understand the real and concrete situation Lindbeck faced, the particular problems his situation issued and the many factors which helped him formulate his response. Much more can be said about his life, but the point is more to show that there is a relationship between his life, the problems he was facing and the reparative logic he was following from early on in his career. What I intend to suggest is that this basic problem-solving approach displays pragmatic and theological tendencies, and that these tendencies are a significant but underappreciated resource for extending his thought to new situations. Next, we will examine these pragmatic tendencies, albeit in undeveloped form, in the plain sense of Lindbeck's major contribution to religion and theology.

## 2 Pragmatic tendencies in the plain sense of *The Nature of Doctrine*

Lindbeck's 'later theological work', as he recalls in the citation above, is indeed a reference to *The Nature of Doctrine: Religion and Theology in a Postliberal Age*.[27] As previously suggested, the book performs a problem-solving argument concerning the troubled practice of Christian doctrine, and religion more generally, in modernity. To ask how Lindbeck has solved the problems he faced is to ask about the book he wrote – and not necessarily the book critics read.[28] I argue that the kind of problem-solving he performs, or the *reparative* character of the book's argument, is itself an instance of a pragmatic tendency – but this claim needs to be tested.

In order to be sensitive to the book that Lindbeck wrote, I look at the 'plain sense' of the text and draw the reader's attention to the vaguely pragmatic tendencies there. To this end, I will draw the reader's attention to particular words (signs) which are indications of a pragmatic tendency. This is the main purpose of this chapter, simply to point to the tendencies. Most often, Lindbeck's pragmatic tendencies owe much to a Wittgensteinian 'linguistic pragmatism' in which language *works* or *functions*, or is *used* in a particular context *to solve a particular problem* or clarify a particular utterance. Pragmatic criteriology employs the language of 'fruitfulness' or 'usefulness' or considers 'effective consequences', and some forms of pragmatism presuppose the import of *teleological* ethics and the methodological need of thought *to direct action*. These are tendencies that are readily apparent in Lindbeck if the reader becomes aware of basic pragmatic categories. Such signs of a pragmatic tendency in Lindbeck can, however, be easily overlooked, as he leaves such pragmatic categories undeveloped. He does not draw our attention to the kind of pragmatism that would give his terms greater coherence, but I think this should not prevent readers today from doing so.[29] To this end, I find it helpful to my argument to renarrate Lindbeck's argument, in order to show why readers are right to notice Lindbeck's pragmatic tendencies and also to show these tendencies in their underdeveloped 'plain sense' before advancing to the next level of my argument.[30]

### The problem with doctrine

From the first sentence of the foreword to the book we can see the desire to move beyond existing categories: 'This book is the product of a quarter century of growing dissatisfaction with the usual ways of thinking about those norms of communal belief and action which are generally spoken of as the doctrines or dogmas of churches.'[31] Lindbeck locates the problem with 'the usual ways of thinking' about the nature of doctrine.[32] He writes that 'doctrines ... do not *behave* the way they should ...' and that 'we clearly need new and better ways of understanding their *nature* and *function*'.[33] The theory that Lindbeck proposes, his 'third' or 'postliberal way', is not, he says, 'specifically ecumenical, nor Christian, nor theological'.[34] The basis of his theory derives from 'non-theological' philosophical and social-scientific insights that were current at the time of his writing. He acknowledges this dependency, but places the originality of his argument elsewhere.

Lindbeck writes: 'what is new about the present work, in short, is not its theory of religion, but the *use* of this theory in the conceptualization of doctrine, and the contention that this conceptualization is *fruitful* for theology and ecumenism'.[35] What he thinks is most original about his argument is the functional aspect: his theory is *useful* for theology. Lindbeck promises that this functionalist approach provides a way of removing 'the anomalies that concern us', and these 'anomalies' have especially to do with 'doctrinal permanence and change' in the development of doctrines.[36] This is a problem-solving methodology that Lindbeck proposes and it is epistemological (though not 'foundationalist'); it is interested less in 'matters of fact' than in 'how to think' through problem-solving.[37] It claims, as a result, a certain measure of neutrality (though not universality) in construing this hypothesis about the nature and function of doctrine.[38]

Lindbeck's first chapter places the proposal in the ecumenical context where dealing with differences in the search for Christian unity is crucial. Though not constrained by this particular context, the ecumenical situation presents Lindbeck with a problem he wants to solve (concerning doctrinal permanence and change). He located the problem in doctrines because as an ecumenical dialogue participant he regularly experienced the tension between two competing views: those who thought that the dialogue was limited by irreconcilable doctrinal differences and those whose experience in the dialogue demonstrated that reconciliation was indeed possible on matters of doctrinal difference. The theory arises out of his own hope, grounded in his ecumenical experience at Vatican II, that *reconciliation* is possible. And he believes that a certain kind of conceptuality enables this possibility. His theory is aimed at ensuring this kind of possibility, and hopes that future theories (he does not claim his to be a completed theory) will seek more adequate conceptions.

### Three rival models?

Lindbeck identifies three ideal models, critiques the 'usual ways of thinking' about the first two models and argues for the superiority of a third option. The first model is what he calls the 'cognitive-propositional'. This is the (preliberal) view of religion and theology that understands propositional statements as truth-claims that correspond to objective realities, and believes that such statements (doctrines) are informative and assessable in cognitive terms. The second model is the 'experiential-expressive' and represents the Kantian 'turn to the subject' that sees religion as experiential, and doctrines as non-informative symbols of inner feelings. The first two models might be understood as the traditionally conservative and liberal positions – positions Lindbeck has found stifle ecumenical debate (recall his rejection of 'modern Protestantism' in both its conservative and liberal forms). They might also be understood as the 'objective' and 'subjective' alternatives. The problem, and this is the second stage of the argument, is that if doctrines are to be understood as *either* propositions about external objective realities *or* as symbols of inner subjective realities, then we arrive at a rigid dichotomy (or *dyad*) between the variable and the invariable, with no real dynamic between them. Lindbeck briefly entertains the possibility of a 'both/and' or 'hybrid' approach that could solve such a tension, which he thinks the Catholic theologians Karl Rahner and Bernard Lonergan offer. But despite some attraction here, Lindbeck thinks the 'hybrid' approach is actually a false synthesis, and suggests that another way is needed for his method of problem-solving that can move to a genuinely 'third' option beyond the stalemate.

A third model is needed to make 'the intertwining of variability and invariability in matters of faith easier to understand'.[39] This third model, which Lindbeck calls the 'cultural-linguistic', likens religions to languages, understood in Wittgensteinian terms, in their 'forms of life'. Religions, like languages, are what we use to identify and describe that which is most important in the universe, organizing forms of life. And if religions are like languages, then doctrine is the grammar of the language – or rather, doctrines are like the rules of a grammar: organizing, identifying and describing a particular language-game. This 'rule theory of doctrine' states that what is needed is not an understanding of doctrines as objectively or subjectively true but rather a way of using doctrines as 'communally authoritative rules of discourse, attitude, and action'.[40] This regulative view of doctrine shows that it is the way in which doctrines are 'used' or how they 'function' (in discourse, attitude and action) that is most important. That is, it is the way in which doctrines correspond to a lived reality, to good performance in a particular form of life. Or if we are identifying the pragmatic tendency, it is to attend to the practical, everyday effects of our concepts (doctrines).[41]

In this third stage of Lindbeck's argument, his 'cultural-linguistic' is judged to be superior to the more dyadic models because it locates the objective and subjective parts of doctrine within a larger whole. Doctrines are the communal beliefs (verified in practices) that emerge out of a communal reading of the biblical narratives (envisioning a 'story-shaped church').[42] In this sense, we might understand Lindbeck proposing not three rival models, but the 'absorption' of the propositional and expressive models into a 'cultural-linguistic' model, and so see postliberalism as itself a *repair and transformation* of the liberal tradition along rethought lines of textual mediation.[43]

## Kant and the liberal tradition

Lindbeck situates himself beyond the liberal tradition – but 'beyond' also suggests some relation to this tradition – so that his three basic categories are divided into '*preliberal* propositionalist, *liberal* experiential-expressivist, or *postliberal* cultural-linguistic'.[44] Lindbeck only briefly critiques the propositional model by appealing to Kant's 'reduction of God to a transcendental condition' and his 'revolutionary ... turn to the subject'.[45] His critique of the propositionalist tradition pales in comparison to a more extensive narration of the liberal tradition, which he traces from Kant to Schleiermacher through Rudolf Otto and Mircea Eliade. He writes: 'so weighty a heritage should not be jettisoned except for good reasons; but even if there are good reasons, it is difficult to abandon'.[46] Lindbeck shares with Kant a mediating tendency. For Kant, the mediation was between continental (Cartesian) rationalism and British (Humean) empiricism, and Kant sought a 'third' in his cognitive-ethical categories. For Lindbeck, however, the mediation is between experiential-expressivists and cognitive-propositionalists, and in this work we can see him reach for a 'third' in his *cultural-linguistic* (which also turns out to be, interestingly, a new kind of cognitive-ethical category). Though highly critical of it, and dispensing with some of its defining characteristics, Lindbeck shares with Peircean pragmatism specifically, an interest in *repairing liberalism* as a tradition, and uses a variety of tools to make this reparative argument. In this sense, one can see the 'liberal' transformed in Lindbeck's postliberalism.[47]

It is against this background that Lindbeck claims that he is offering a 'pre-theological' enquiry. He is aware that what he has proposed is 'a suspiciously secular-looking model of religion'.[48] But what he is more concerned about, after Wittgenstein, is whether or not it is a 'useful' model for religion and theology – indeed, his test is to ask whether it is useful for the ecumenical problems he is trying to solve. He thinks it is useful because it is a theory of religion that impacts the entirety of life and thought, shaping ethical practices, and communal descriptions of reality, beliefs, stories and doctrine. Lindbeck states succinctly the thesis of the book, and its relationship to liberalism, when he writes:

> a religion can be viewed as a kind of cultural and/or linguistic framework or medium that shapes the entirety of life and thought. It functions somewhat like a Kantian a priori, although in this case the a priori is a set of acquired skills that could be different. It is not primarily an array of beliefs about the true and the good (though it

may involve these), or a symbolism expressive of basic attitudes, feelings, or sentiments (though these will be generated). Rather, it is similar to an idiom that makes possible the description of realities, the formulation of beliefs, and the experiencing of inner attitudes, feelings, and sentiments. Like a culture or language, it is a communal phenomenon that shapes the subjectivities. It comprises a vocabulary of discursive and nondiscursive symbols together with a distinctive logic or grammar in terms of which the vocabulary can be meaningfully deployed. Lastly, just as a language (or 'language game', to use Wittgenstein's phrase) is correlated with a form of life, and just as a culture has both cognitive and behavioral dimensions, so it is also in the case of a religious tradition. Its doctrines, cosmic stories or myths, and ethical directives are integrally related to the rituals it practices, the sentiments or experiences it evokes, the actions it recommends, and the institutional forms it develops.[49]

Here we see the way in which Lindbeck himself identifies postliberalism as maintaining some relationship to the Kantian liberal tradition – while also extending well beyond it (so that 'postliberal' is appropriate). I will argue later that we might recognize the vaguely pragmatic criteria displayed above as inherited from Kant, who coined the term *pragmatisch*, as criteria which orient thought around human practice and purpose (not simply the crudely 'practical', but 'practical wisdom').[50] Peirce and Wittgenstein are best understood in relation to this tradition too.

For the postliberal, language and grammar are meaningful when they correspond to the purpose and form of life, in both its cognitive and behavioural dimensions. This can be identified as an instance of his Wittgensteinian 'linguistic pragmatism'[51] which extends liberalism in analytical, grammatical and pragmatic directions. This pragmatic-grammatical approach, however, is underdeveloped and tends, in the plain sense, to suggest an overly restrictive view of truth. This is a popular (and fairly undifferentiated) perception about pragmatism as well, but I will argue that it is a misconception about the theory of truth that Lindbeck's pragmatism would require, and to the degree that this restrictive view is true about Wittgenstein, Lindbeck is not wedded to it. In fact, he cannot be, as his overall view of truth is hardly restrictive and remains hospitable to ontological truth, even if that hospitality is framed within a dynamically conceived relationship between the Bible and the shape of lived reality.

### Truth as a 'living' proposition[52]

Truth for Lindbeck cannot adequately be expressed in either propositional or experiential terms. Lindbeck supposes that truth is best thought of analogically, as an organically 'lived' reality. He writes:

A religion thought of as comparable to a cultural system, as a set of language games correlated with a form of life, may as a whole correspond or not correspond to what a theist calls God's being and will. As actually lived, a religion may be pictured as a single gigantic proposition.[53]

The cultural-linguistic approach qualifies the propositional model by embodying it, in Wittgensteinian terms, in a 'form of life'. Truth or falsity, in these terms, depends on the success or failure of a community internalizing its religion (as a form of life). It is 'religion as actually lived' that may be understood as a 'single gigantic proposition' that corresponds to what is objectively and subjectively true (cf. God's being and will).

Earlier I noted how Lindbeck was dismissive of the propositional model, perhaps implicitly in favour of a genuine reconstruction, as he was primarily reaching beyond the experiential-expressive model to his cultural-linguistic approach. But he returns to the propositional, writing: 'we must not simply allow for the possibility that a religion may be categorially as well as symbolically or expressively true; we must also allow for its possible propositional truth'.[54] This notion of a 'lived' proposition is the way Lindbeck allows for this possibility – sharing in the pragmatic tendency to assess concepts in terms of their effects or consequences in life: a doctrine may be 'propositionally true' only as 'lived'.[55] It is a way of privileging performance, but it does not exclude modest claims to propositional truth (it only makes them interdependent upon a number of other factors).

In addition to the linguistic image of 'a single gigantic proposition' Lindbeck suggests a 'cartographic simile'. He writes:

a map, let us stipulate, becomes a proposition, an affirmation about how to travel from one place to another, only when actually *utilized* in the course of a journey. To the extent that the map is misread and misused, it is a part of a false proposition no matter how accurate it may be in itself. Conversely, even if it is in many ways in error in its distances, proportions, and topographic markings, it becomes constitutive of a true proposition when it guides the traveler rightly ... To draw the moral of the metaphor, the categorially and unsurpassably true religion is *capable of being rightly utilized*, of guiding thought, passions, and action in a way that corresponds to ultimate reality, and of thus being ontologically (and 'propositionally') true ...'[56]

Religion is like a map that corresponds to reality, but the correspondence (or lack of it) is determined by its *use* or *misuse*. This approach shares the Peircean pragmatic tendency to understand enquiry as an empirical process of constant revision according to the performative standards of the community of enquirers.

This might be understood as a kind of teleological attempt to retrieve some of the concerns of the cognitive-propositional model earlier discounted (that is, to locate their concerns for truth in future performance, which amounts to the 'postponement' of verification). It is a view of the cognitive dimension that is connected to his Wittgensteinian interest in language use, but also draws heavily from 'speech-act theory'. Lindbeck admits to his dependence upon 'J. L. Austin's notion of a "performatory" use of language', which maintains that 'a religious utterance ... acquires the propositional truth of ontological correspondence only insofar as it is a performance, an act or deed, which helps create that correspondence'.[57] Only in its actual performance *as* propositional truth can it possibly have that character. The 'performative' and the 'practical' become determinative for judging truthful correspondence (just as use determines meaning in Wittgensteinian terms) of propositions to reality.[58] We might also think of this as a kind of *practical soteriology of language*, where language is redeemed and made whole *through* the good performance of that discourse.[59]

Anticipating objections that his view does not make salvation 'ontologically real', Lindbeck suggests, reminiscent of Augustine's *Confessions*, 'the metaphor of a child learning a language'.[60] This '*process of learning*' entails making adherents 'better speakers of the languages they have'.[61] For the Christian this means becoming 'a new creature through hearing and interiorizing the language that speaks of Christ'.[62] This is bound up with a fallibilistic '*eschatologically futurist perspective*',[63] which becomes an increasingly important perspective for Lindbeck's implicitly pragmatic view of truth, which tacitly entails good performance, communal processes of enquiry and eschatological postponement, while securing the bases for continuity under conditions of constant flux.

## Continuity and change

One crucial question that arises frequently in Lindbeck's argument, arising especially out of his sensitivity to his ecumenical experience, is 'How is it possible for doctrines that once contradicted each other to be reconciled and yet retain their identity?'[64] How can the continuity of Christian identity be sustained in a situation that constantly changes how we conceive doctrines? Lindbeck wants to avoid the charge of 'relativism' even though his contextually sensitive argument seems, in the plain sense, to lean in this direction. He wants to find a way for theoreticians to speak about how doctrines are 'firm and flexible, both abiding and adaptable. To the extent that they [theoreticians] are unable to do so, their theories are theologically and pastorally *unfruitful*.'[65] In fact he seems to suggest that *doctrines that don't work, aren't doctrines at all* (they are merely an instance of 'language idling' to recall Wittgenstein again).

Lindbeck locates the continuity of Christian identity in the biblical narrative and its grammar. He writes: 'The novelty of rule theory … is that it does not locate the abiding and doctrinally significant aspect of religion in propositionally formulated truths, much less in inner experiences, but in the story it tells and in *the grammar that informs the way the story is told and used*.'[66] This is coherent with his 'integrating centre' which he found in the relation between scripture and doctrine, between scriptural narrative and the grammar that informs the way the scriptural narrative is described and used to serve particular and diverse purposes. Lindbeck extends this even further to distinguish between 'vocabulary and grammar'. Doctrines, like grammars, may change, as they organize a language – but to the extent that they arise out of the use of the scriptural narrative, there is 'relative stability' and continuity about their core regulative function (if not their expression). Lindbeck allows that some grammars may be deeper than others, but that perhaps the deeper the grammar, the more difficult it is to detect.[67] And perhaps this is to suggest, consonant with at least one kind of pragmatism, that there are grammars that are so deep they can only be discovered over an indefinitely long period of inquiry.[68] The implication, of course, is that doctrines that were hard won at Nicaea and Chalcedon, doctrines that have stood the test of time, may well display this kind of 'depth grammar' that corresponds to ontological truth. They are, at least, our best representations of an enduring 'depth grammar,' of rules that display the logic of scripture in Christian terms.

Lindbeck is sometimes worried, however, that the linguistic analogy could be taken too far, and occasionally turns to his favourite medieval semiotic analogy for more precise qualification ('it is at most the *significatum* not the *modus significandi* which remains the same').[69] The semiotic may well prove to be a better way of framing the issue Lindbeck wants to address (as Lindbeck's work entails the semiotic transformation of liberal theology). Nevertheless, Lindbeck believes the pragmatic-grammatical way of framing the issues offers the best explanatory model. Grammar, and its relative stability, provides the framework and medium for knowing and experiencing a language; likewise with doctrinal rules and scripture. He writes:

It may be more difficult to grasp the notion that it is the framework and the medium within which Christians know and experience, rather than what they experience or think they know, that retains continuity and unity down the centuries. Yet this seems to make more empirical, historical and doctrinal sense ... When put this way it seems almost self-evident that the permanence and unity of doctrines, despite changing and diverse formulation, is more easily accounted for if they are taken to resemble grammatical rules rather than propositions or expressive symbols.[70]

In this sense, there is always *an undetected, hidden, deeper grammar* that gives continuity to cultures and languages constantly in flux – and certainly in regard to Christian culture and Christian discourse. The deeper grammars are 'unconditionally permanent' statements (doctrines) of 'essential scriptural teaching'.[71] More surface grammars are 'conditional' or 'accidental', based partially on contextual demands, and may be either temporary or permanent, depending on what is best for the welfare of the community.

### Nicaea and Chalcedon

Lindbeck tests his rule theory on several doctrines, but I am interested primarily in how his rule theory tests with 'the unconditionality of classic Christological (and Trinitarian) affirmations'.[72] This is the point at which Lindbeck is most deeply indebted to Bernard Lonergan (the proponent of the hybrid model with whom he is in frequent conversation throughout the book) and Lonergan's reflections on the development of trinitarian doctrine.[73] It is the development of doctrine (an inherently ecumenical problem) that further stimulates and clarifies Lindbeck's questions about continuity and change, and stimulates the distinctions he makes about the creeds. Indeed, it is *the long-run* development of an inquiry that interests both Lindbeck and Lonergan. Lindbeck wants to know how we could test the rule theory of doctrine over time.

Lindbeck argues that we need to distinguish between doctrines (and their terminology) and the concepts of their contextual formation. But more is needed than simply a form/content distinction, which cannot be easily held. If doctrines are conceived of as rules, then 'the change in conceptuality need not change the truth claim or rule that is being enunciated'.[74] If the doctrines of Nicaea and Chalcedon were to be put in different terms, but followed the same rules as the original formulations, we would witness *'equivalent consequences'* if the rule was properly followed.[75] In the case of Nicaea, Lindbeck turns to Lonergan's thesis that Nicaea represented an instantiation of the

Athanasian rule 'that whatever is said of the Father is said of the Son, except that the Son is not the Father'.[76] This rule emerged out of a 'logical' or 'grammatical' analysis of 'the data of scripture and tradition' and was for Athanasius, according to Lindbeck, a rule about rules, it was a second-order rule of speech to the extent it functioned in this way (and guided how readers read the data of scripture and tradition).

Lindbeck sees three regulative principles or rules inscribed under the terms of Nicaea (again echoing Lonergan). The first is the 'monotheistic principle' (that there is only one God), the second is the principle of historical specificity (that Jesus was a real historical person) and the third is the principle of 'christological maximalism' (that ascribes every conceivable importance to Jesus without breaking the first two rules).[77] This final rule follows from the 'central Christian conviction that Jesus Christ is the highest possible clue ... to what is of maximal importance' and so leads to the inevitable development of the doctrine of the Trinity.[78] Nicaea, therefore, inscribes hard-won rules that emerged from communal thinking about the biblical narratives. These logical rules are what are permanent, not the terminology or concepts in which they are formulated at any given point in history. Lindbeck writes:

> the terminology and concepts ... may be absent, but if the same rules that guided the formation of the original paradigms are operative in the construction of the new formulations, they express one and the same doctrine ... There may, on this reading, be complete faithfulness to classical Trinitarianism and Christology even when the imagery and language of Nicea and Chalcedon have disappeared from the theology and ordinary worship, preaching, and devotion.[79]

Lindbeck says that this does not mean that the creeds should be rewritten for a new situation. Such creeds are 'rare and difficult achievements' and Nicaea in particular has taken on a liturgical importance that cannot be underestimated. But it is important to stress that it is not the doctrines of Nicaea and Chalcedon themselves which are authoritative, it is '*the rules they instantiate*'.[80] These are actually principles or maxims derived from a reading of scriptural narrative. They seek to inscribe the grammar, the rule, or the logic of scripture. Lindbeck then goes further, to say that since it is the rules which endure as normative and authoritative in Nicaea, then we have no further need either of the conceptuality that 'insists on an ontological reference'.[81] This is a careful point, and Lindbeck stresses that it does not 'prohibit speculations on the possible correspondence of the Trinitarian pattern of Christian language to the metaphysical structure of the Godhead, but simply says that these are not doctrinally necessary and cannot be binding'.[82] Lindbeck finds ontological questions about God's trinitarian life '*unanswerable this side of the eschaton*', and considers that 'ontological reference of the [trinitarian] theories may often be unimportant for theological evaluation'.[83] But it is vitally important here again to recognize that *Lindbeck does not exclude ontology*, but like Peircean pragmatism, locates ontological reference in the *eschaton*, in the future, and quite rightly notes that a regulative model moves towards more fruitful theological evaluations.[84]

### Faithfulness as intratextuality

What is more important than dogmatic propositions that claim adequate correspondence to ontological reality, however, is faithfulness to a 'text-constituted' idiom and world – that is, a faithfulness to the textual sources and norms of a tradition.[85] Faithfulness as 'intratextuality' is one of Lindbeck's key categories for judging different types of theology. 'Meaning' for propositionalists and expressivists alike is 'extratextual', that is, 'outside the text or semiotic system', whereas 'for cultural-linguists the meaning is immanent' inside the world and idiom of the text – meaning depends upon intratextuality (partly because sacred texts mediate reality).[86] Lindbeck, as the linguistic or *semiotic pragmatist*, says that in order properly to determine what the word 'God' signifies, examine 'how the word operates' within a semiotic system, and you will know how it shapes 'reality and experience'.[87] How the word actually 'operates' in the semiotic system provides the community with something like a rule. Faithfulness can be tested by judging how doctrinal descriptions '*correspond to the semiotic universe paradigmatically encoded in holy writ*'.[88] It is not simply a semiotic pragmatism at work here, but a semiotic interest in the scriptural narrative, what we might call a kind of 'scriptural pragmatism' which tests 'faithfulness' through a scriptural correspondence to a lived reality.

This insight leads Lindbeck to surmise that 'canonical texts are a condition, not only for the survival of a religion but for the very possibility of normative theological description'.[89] Scripture creates its own world of meaning, and claims that this meaning 'extends over the whole of reality'.[90] Christian doctrine, therefore, inhabits this 'scriptural world' absorbing the universe.[91] Lindbeck understands, for example, Augustine's entire theological enterprise as 'a progressive ... struggle to insert everything ... into the world of the Bible'.[92] It is scripture which defines reality, and therefore nonscriptural reality and experience obtain their meaning only inside the textual world, or in correspondence to it: 'Intratextual theology redescribes reality within the scriptural framework rather than translating scripture into extrascriptural categories. It is the text, so to speak, which absorbs the world, rather than the world the text.'[93] This requires, according to Lindbeck, a sensitivity to the *sensus literalis* of scripture. The literal meaning of scripture (the 'plain sense') is not a fundamentalist or historicist reading, but along literary lines it is the meaning of a text on its own terms. Or, 'what the text says in terms of the communal language of which the text is an instantiation'.[94] To read faithfully, i.e. intratextually, means 'to derive the interpretive framework that designates the theologically controlling sense from the literary structure of the text itself'.[95] This is to view scripture as a nonfictional novel, as realistic narrative ('history-like').[96] And it is the 'intratextual norm' of this realistic narrative which counts as faithfulness in matters of doctrinal (or metaphysical, etc.) dispute.

### Applicability as futurology

The second of Lindbeck's key categories for judging theology, in addition to faithfulness, is the category of 'applicability'. That is, different types of theology 'are judged by how relevant or *practical* they are in concrete situations'.[97] If faithfulness as intratextuality meant that the text determines the standards by which it is read, then applicability as futurology means that what is presently practical is determined by a concern for the future. 'In brief, a theological proposal is adjudged both faithful and applicable to the degree that it appears *practical* in terms of an eschatologically and empirically defensible scenario of what is to come.'[98]

Put differently, God's future judges human practices. In this sense, Lindbeck maintains the priority of the practical – or the priority of an ethics bound to eschatology – and assumes that inhabiting an intratextual form of life which orients itself around God's future will actually have a practical result (Lindbeck suggests 'democracy and science' were practical results of the church being itself in this way). One interesting comparison Lindbeck makes in this regard, cognizant of his hermeneutical starting-point and the attendant accusations of fideism, is to the Lutheran confession of 'justification by faith'. He writes 'as is true for individuals, so also a religious community's salvation is not by works, nor is its faith for the sake of practical efficacy, and yet good works of unforeseeable kinds flow from faithfulness'.[99] This amounts, not simply to a meditation on practice but to a meditation on God's future, and the practices or forms of life that faithfulness to that future would entail or elicit. This is also a sign of a renewed Christian pragmatism that avoids the banal reduction of Christian thought to 'what works' because it maintains its eschatological reference to truth, to ultimate reality described intratextually.

### Intelligibility as skill

Near the end of the book Lindbeck addresses two problems he anticipates critics will raise with concerns for the intelligibility, and therefore credibility, of religion and theology in a postliberal key.

> First, intratextuality seems wholly relativistic: it turns religions, so one can argue, into self-enclosed and incommensurable intellectual ghettos. Associated with this, in the second place, is the fideistic dilemma: it appears that choice between religions is purely arbitrary, a matter of blind faith.[100]

The antifoundationalism Lindbeck espouses in the plain sense, as he is well aware, makes his argument vulnerable to just such criticisms as relativism, sectarianism and fideism, *unless* he is able to show how the learning of one particular idiom and set of practices could actually 'be tested and argued about in various ways' and that *'in the long run'* these tests and arguments might 'make a difference'.[101] In this sense, Lindbeck's basic response to these charges is pragmatic and empirical in orientation (most akin, here again, to Peircean pragmatism). He writes:

> in this perspective, the reasonableness of a religion is largely a function of its assimilative powers, of its ability to provide an intelligible interpretation in its own terms ... it is subject ... to rational testing procedures not wholly unlike those which apply to general scientific theories or paradigms ... Confirmation or disconfirmation occurs through an accumulation of successes or failures in making practically and cognitively coherent sense of relevant data, and *the process does not conclude*, in the case of religions, until the disappearance of the last communities of believers or, if the faith survives, *until the end of history*.[102]

Lindbeck underlines the science-like reasonableness of religion and theology, in practical and cognitive terms, as a 'long-run' antidote to the relativistic and fideistic implications of his argument. He thinks this antifoundationalism accords well with Thomas Aquinas's premodern insistence on 'probable arguments' in favour of faith rather than any 'independent foundational enterprise'.[103] And what he proposes is the constant testing that comes in the process of critical learning over a long period of time.

Intelligibility, however, is concerned not only with critical learning but also with teaching. Rather than translating Christian faith into foreign languages, into foreign concepts, as the modern liberal foundationalist would do, Lindbeck proposes that the best way (the postliberal way) of exhibiting the 'intelligibility and possible truth' of the *kerygma* is in something like ancient catechesis – in the passing on of interpretive skills and practices.[104] Teaching the language and practices of a religion to adherents is to teach a form of life which is urgent and of the utmost importance.[105] It is this 'form of life' which will be credible or not, and therefore intelligibility is again a set of interpretive skills, or practices, in which different modes of behaviour are taught according to the 'the stories of Israel and their fulfillment in Christ'.[106] From this we can conclude that the testing of a religion's truth is bound up with the effect of scripture (or its logic) on the practices of communal life over the long-run of time (penultimately), and only verified (ultimately) at the end of history, at the *eschaton*.

Lest all of this sound too hopeful, Lindbeck characteristically sets this programme in a rather pessimistic mood (albeit a kind of Augustinian pessimism, ultimately with hope for the future). None of what he proposes, he thinks, is really possible in a progressively dechristianized 'Western culture'. He thinks that it will only become possible when the process of dechristianization is either completed or reversed (the latter he thinks less plausible). 'Disestablishment', Lindbeck thinks, is the way forward. Until that day comes, postliberals should 'prepare for a future when continuing dechristianization will make greater Christian authenticity communally possible'.[107]

The test of postliberalism, the test of the intelligibility and credibility of his proposal to heal modern theology and religion, is good *performance*.

> If a postliberal approach in its actual employment proves to be conceptually powerful and practically useful to the relevant communities, it will in time become standard. It was thus that the theological outlooks of Augustine, Aquinas, Luther, and Schleiermacher established themselves. There is no way of testing the merits and demerits of a theological method apart from performance.[108]

From these last lines of the book, we can see that Lindbeck even ends on a pragmatic note – stressing the fundamental importance of performative knowing that has always been central to all of the pragmatists.

In sum, these categories, which encapsulate Lindbeck's argument, perhaps also best encapsulate his own pragmatic tendencies. Beginning with 'the problem of assessment', his proposed three central categories for judgment – 'faithfulness as intratetxuality', 'applicability as futur-ology', and 'intelligibility as skill' – bear a marked resemblance to pragmatic categories. What sort of pragmatism will make coherent sense of these categories?

I have tried, as far as possible, gently and subtly to show the vaguely pragmatic tendencies in Lindbeck's argument, instead of placing a heavy interpretive grid of pragmatism over it. I have adopted as light a touch as possible because I think all of these implicitly pragmatic tendencies are signs that the 'plain sense' of Lindbeck's proposal is itself prepared to be developed in an explicitly pragmatic way – and in this final section I will argue, with Peter Ochs, that the semiotic pragmatism of Charles Peirce, and its theological roots in St Augustine, offer the best resources for making Lindbeck's Christian pragmatism explicit. In this sense, I have been *arguing inferentially*[109] towards a fruitful reading of Lindbeck that furthers his own project in Christian theology, and now I will argue more directly for my proposal not only to locate Lindbeck's pragmatism but to develop its potential.

### 3 Wittgenstein, pragmatism and Lindbeck

The pragmatic influence of Wittgenstein on Lindbeck bears further consideration. Lindbeck uses the later Wittgenstein to supplement philosophically his argument about the nature and function of God-talk, doctrines in particular. This dependency is not unique to Lindbeck, though much is owed to him for the use of Wittgenstein in theology and religion. Wittgenstein quickly became a philosopher who was thought to have much to say about God-talk in modern theology. Witness the success of books such as Fergus Kerr's *Theology after Wittgenstein*, and the efforts of many other theologians who have done their theology in the shadow of Wittgenstein.[110] Anglo-American theology is now permeated with all sorts of Wittgensteinian assumptions.[111] The assumptions entail the way in which the meaning of something (a word for example) is found only in its ordinary use, only in the way it works in a particular language and culture. This is to take Wittgenstein's grammatical view of theology, or, as he famously put it, to attend to 'theology as grammar'.[112] The nature and function of theology, according to Lindbeck's Wittgenstein, is to use God-talk in an 'intrasystematic' and coherent way – where doctrines are under-stood through their ordinary use, understood as a working grammar. This is what I call the pragmatic-grammatical view, and what Lindbeck calls cultural-linguistic, and it has become commonplace in modern theology today. In this sense, a new kind of pragmatism has been emerging in theology and religion, but without much critical attention.

When David Tracy commented in 1985 that Lindbeck was presenting theology and religion with a 'new linguistic version of one side of classical pragmatism', he had in mind the linguistic pragmatism of Wittgenstein as an extension of Jamesian pragmatism.[113] Though Tracy's comment went unexplored, his remarks anticipated Russell Goodman's recent argument that William James 'exerted a distinctive and pervasive positive influence on Wittgenstein's thought', displaying the coherence of Wittgenstein's claim that his own work represents 'something that sounds like pragmatism'.[114] What becomes clear, however, is that such a conversation between Wittgenstein and James refers us back to the founder of semiotic pragmatism, Charles Peirce.[115] Peirce does something that other pragmatists did not do: he maintains a commitment to scriptural realism in his pragmatism – largely due to his concrete reflection on the nature of signs – making his pragmatism better suited to Lindbeck's modest realism.

Though some have argued that Wittgenstein can be understood as a kind of realist, Wittgenstein himself did not make such claims, and is probably better understood for helping us to think contextually and functionally about the justification of beliefs. But Lindbeck wants to claim more than what Wittgenstein claimed.[116] If Lindbeck is a pragmatist – and it is my contention that he is – then he is not only a linguistic pragmatist after Wittgenstein. Indeed, an exclusive commitment to Wittgenstein, despite the heuristic help he gives to Lindbeck's argument, may be too reductionistic for Lindbeck's ultimately realistic claims.[117] His pragmatism has a realist texture to it that, however modestly, holds out (as Peirce did) for ultimate truth in the long-run. Peirce, and Lindbeck too, remind us that pragmatism and realism need not be at odds with each other. Though present at the philosophical origins of pragmatism in Charles Peirce, such realistic, non-relativistic forms of pragmatism have been neglected throughout its philosophical ascendency.[118] Whatever kind of pragmatism Lindbeck's work may suggest, it will be at a minimum modestly realist with respect to truth, and it will be contextualist (cultural-linguistic) with respect to doctrines and beliefs, and it will be pragmatic when it comes to use, practice and performance. This sets Lindbeck apart from some pragmatists in making him a realist. But the most important aspect of his pragmatism is that it is a 'scriptural pragmatism' that has theological concerns at heart. Such a hypothesis needs to be tested over time rather than simply be a claim to be asserted.[119]

Readers have thus far seen in Lindbeck a pragmatist who has stated his pragmatism vaguely enough to be open to interpretation but precisely enough to suggest particular directions coherent with his proposal. Readers are invited, by problems in the plain sense, to reinterpret Lindbeck. Those who interpret Lindbeck appreciatively, even when they engage his work in a way that seems to modify or clarify or extend his thought, seem to also transform him in a way that makes him more internally consistent, while simultaneously more open to that which is external, outside or other.

The major critiques of Lindbeck, the places where his argument has raised doubts for some readers, deal precisely with those issues of truth and change that Wittgenstein, I think, cannot readily bear. Other sources are needed to enrich the kind of pragmatism that Lindbeck is reaching towards. But where can readers turn? If they are to do justice to the pragmatism that Lindbeck reaches towards, then readers need to find those resources that can do justice both to Lindbeck's theological realism and his scripturally shaped pragmatism. As I suggested in the Introduction, I will turn to Augustine, who I argue stands at the origins of this tradition of Christian pragmatism, and to Peter Ochs, a contemporary pragmatic philosopher who has developed a realistic, scriptural pragmatism that complements what I think is implicit in George Lindbeck. I argue that Augustine stands at the origins of scriptural pragmatism, and Ochs has argued that Peircean pragmatism is an implicit development of this tradition. The cumulative effect of such a study promises to highlight a kind of pragmatism which can be a truly generative theological resource because it ultimately derives from a revealed logic, and in a way that complements and develops Lindbeck's dictum 'Scripture absorbing the world' in a distinctively pragmatic, dialogical and reparative direction.

# 2

# Augustine
## Theosemiotics and the Word of God

*'... to the semiotic universe paradigmatically encoded in holy writ.'*
(George Lindbeck)

At the heart of Lindbeck's textual pragmatism is a theory of signs that has some roots in the classical period, but discovers a profound beginning in the thought of St Augustine, and develops throughout the medieval and modern period, impacting Lindbeck's understanding of what it means to attend 'to the semiotic universe paradigmatically encoded in holy writ'.[120] Searching for the deepest resources available for the enrichment of Lindbeck's scriptural pragmatism, the chapter argues that Augustine is the prototypical semiotician for postliberalism, and that his semiotics are a kind of scriptural pragmatism that is theologically shaped by a trinitarian understanding of the incarnation of the Word of God. In the first and second part of the chapter I set forth these claims hypothetically, and in the third part I test them through a rereading of key Augustinian texts. In the fourth part I discuss the implications of this for readers of Lindbeck. I argue ultimately that Augustine's scriptural pragmatism is pre-eminently governed, in incarnational and trinitarian terms, by the *rule of charity*, which works to reconcile that which is opposed in interpretive disputes – a point that has a clear bearing upon what postliberalism means.

## 1 Why Augustine towards Lindbeck?

In examining the sources of Lindbeck's scriptural pragmatism we might be led in a number of different directions. We might turn to Wittgenstein's linguistic pragmatism as an explicit resource for this semiotic tendency in his thought, or we might think of the classical hermeneutic theory attended to by Hans Frei; or we might find cultural and linguistic understandings of sign theory in Peter Berger or Clifford Geertz. Karl Barth could lead us in still other directions. Looking further into the past, we might explore Thomas Aquinas, Duns Scotus and other medieval theologians as resources for his semiotic tendencies (and this might prove most fruitful of all, not least because Augustine stands behind much of medieval theology).[121] Much attention has been given to Lindbeck's stated dependence upon such thinkers. The work of Bruce Marshall has fruitfully explored resources in Aquinas, and in analytic philosophy.[122] Eugene Rogers has moved in a different direction through his work on Aquinas and Barth, working towards an implicit development of the postliberal approach to theology and religion through unexplored conversations.[123] Even though these excellent studies have looked to Lindbeck's explicitly stated sources and have taken us deeper into the meaning of postliberalism, they have not yet touched upon the scriptural pragmatism in Lindbeck. What would enrich our understanding of the nature of Lindbeck's scriptural pragmatism, and thus the semiotic theory implicit in his work? This chapter proposes Augustine as an apt, if neglected, resource for extending the meaning of postliberalism.

Lindbeck rarely cites Augustine. To be fair, seldom does he cite Barth (the original postliberal semiotician).[124] But Augustine is referred to in *The Nature of Doctrine* as a *paradigm* for the kind of theological method Lindbeck proposed. Lindbeck cites Augustine at critical junctures of the argument: on the interpretation of scripture,[125] on realism[126] and on practical performance.[127] Even in his famous opinion that 'a scriptural world is ... able to absorb the universe' he seems to have Augustine's own logical tendencies in mind, as it was Augustine who, in Lindbeck's words, best exemplified the 'struggle to insert everything ... into the world of the Bible'.[128] Lindbeck's common interest with Hans Frei to retrieve the 'classic hermeneutic' is striking when we consider that Lindbeck himself provides us with no rich description of the classic hermeneutic he envisions. In this he is happy to refer to Frei's work, and simply to point to paradigmatic exemplars such as Augustine. As a resource that reaches further back in time than all of the obvious theological sources for Lindbeck's work (Aquinas, Luther, Barth), Augustine's scriptural pragmatism points a way forward in our concern to extend the usefulness of Lindbeck for future generations.[129]

If my thesis is right, Augustine will help readers to move beyond merely contradictory ways of thinking through problems and towards thinking through the conditions that would make it possible to turn contradictory pairs into complementarities through a rule of charity. That is, Augustine might help readers of Lindbeck move towards more triadic ways of reasoning that, for the Christian at least, are firmly rooted in an incarnational, pneumatological and trinitarian understanding of God (what Lindbeck might call the rule of 'christological maximalism'). Augustine's trinitarian understanding of the triadic nature of the sign, and therefore of sign-interpretation, will hopefully enrich readers of Lindbeck with a scriptural pragmatism that is ruled by an embodied logic of mediation, reconciliation, redemption and love for the other – as we shall see in our redescription of Augustinian scriptural pragmatism – according to the rule of faith and its correlative, the rule of charity. Far from being a 'pre-theological' enterprise for Augustine, scriptural semiotics is a profound expression of a therapeutically and pragmatically sensitive hermeneutic, theologically shaped by an understanding of the incarnation of the Word of God. We might say that it is a semiotic grounded in the Word-of-God-made-flesh (the inner made outer) and that this theological tradition is inscribed in Lindbeck's 'cultural-linguistic approach' to theology and religion even if the theology is only expressed implicitly through his regulative theory of doctrine.

Throughout this chapter, Augustine may look postliberal to the extent that he sees scripture as the authoritative 'semiotic system' used within the community of its sign-users (who participate in reality through participation in that semiotic system) to shape beliefs and practices.[130] But Augustine may also transform what it means to be postliberal. This intervention is meant to affect our study of Lindbeck in several ways. It is meant to transform how readers interpret those burdens of the interpretive community we surveyed in the Introduction: questions about mediation, truth and change, and about signs, and the church–word–world relation. A turn towards Augustine will also enable those interpretive questions to be heard differently, clearing a space that enables new sets of critical questions to arise. On a broader but equally contemporary level, this chapter is meant to explain what happened theologically when the interpretive community understood 'Yale theology' as somehow set against 'Chicago theology', an assumption that became very deeply set in a short space of time, owing much to inherited traditions (viz. Barth and Schleiermacher) but also owing to fundamental issues in christology; and also to suggest a postliberal methodology that would enable such assumptions to be overcome. And, most importantly, because such theopolitical assumptions reinscribe just those habits of enlightenment reasoning that threaten to stifle all thought into those dyadic categories which characterize a divided church, the study is meant to insist upon the unifying and reforming nature of postliberalism (ecumenical catholicity) by seeking out the theological reasons for the triadic logic implicit in the postliberal argument.

Turning to Augustine to transform postliberal theology is a work of love. By the end of the chapter, it should also be clear that the rule of charity that governs Augustine's scriptural pragmatism might guide Lindbeck as well. More importantly, learning what the Augustinian paradigm of inserting the world into the Bible actually looks like in semiotic terms might teach us a genuinely theo-logical reasoning that can aid our reading practices today.

## 2 Augustine and theosemiotics

Semiotics (from the Greek *semeia*: 'sign') is the word that is used to describe the modern study of signs. It is sometimes understood as fundamental to the philosophy of language, even though it is broader than the study of linguistic signification, and true to its roots, is frequently identified with pragmatism. The history of semiotics as a modern discipline can be traced to its nineteenth-century Anglo-American origins in the thought of C.S. Peirce (1839–1914), or in the Continental structuralist tradition, through Ferdinand de Saussure (1857–1913). Divisions between Anglo-American and continental philosophy can be seen in semiotics as in other fields of study, and reflect the difference between Peirce and Saussure (which technically is the difference between a triadic and a dyadic understanding of sign theory).[131]

In this larger context, I am interested in relating George Lindbeck's cultural-linguistic turn, which borrowed much from Wittgenstein's linguistic pragmatism, to the Peircean-side of this history of modern semiotics. To this end it is important to recognize that this modern discipline finds, via Peirce, one significant strand of life in the ancient semiotics of Augustine. As we shall see in Chapter 3, Peter Ochs even argues that the very coherence of Peirce's thought points towards the critical importance of Augustinian theosemiotics. Indeed, my argument depends upon an account of the development of sign theory that is now well established by thinkers as diverse as Tzvetan Todorov, Umberto Eco, Robert Markus, B.D. Jackson and Brian Stock, all of whom acknowledge the seminal place of Augustine in semiotic theory.

Surprisingly, the relationship between Augustine and Peirce was entirely unexplored until Robert Markus wrote his seminal essay 'St Augustine on Signs' in 1957. This was the first work to show substantial links between Augustine's theory of signs and Peircean semiotics. Over the past 50 years, a small number of thinkers, Christian, Jewish and secular, have begun making regular references to Augustine's place in the history of semiotics. Tzvetan Todorov, the eminent French semiotician, opined that Augustine's *De doctrina christiana* could be considered 'the first semiotic work'.[132] Umberto Eco shows its influence on medieval semiotics, as well as both strands of modern semiotics (referring to the Peircean–Saussurean divide).[133] Most recently, Brian Stock called Augustine 'the first to have proposed a [triadic] relationship between the sender, the receiver, and the sign (normally a word), which subsequently becomes a standard feature of medieval and modern theories of language'.[134]

These returns to Augustine show that while most contemporary sign theory is based upon the Peircean definition of the sign ('something which stands to somebody for something in some respect or capacity'),[135] this definition derives from Augustine's definition in *De doctrina christiana*: a *sign* is some *thing* 'which besides the impression it conveys to the senses, also has the effect of making something else come to mind' for some *sign-reader*.[136] Both definitions stress the mediation involved in thinking about signs as things that stand in between something and somebody. As Peirce noted, the 'very word *means* signifies something which is in the middle between two others'.[137] In Peircean terms, semiotics might be understood as a whole 'science of mediation'. But in Augustinian terms, a 'science of mediation' takes on christological significance, as we shall see. The effect of neglecting the Augustinian origins of medieval and modern semiotics is akin to Alasdair MacIntyre's imaginary catastrophe of a world that has lost most of its scientific knowledge and now struggles to put the fragments together.[138] If Augustine does stand at the origins of modern semiotics, then we must recover the semiotic universe which gave birth to the semiotic theory. This inevitably returns semiotics to its scriptural and theological roots.

Many of the same thinkers who have seen Augustine at the roots of semiotics, have seen his theory of signs as a synthesis of ancient grammar and rhetoric. But a minority opinion is emerging that it is actually his reading of the scriptures that makes the difference and funds the semiotic moment. With inspiration from Robert Markus, Brian Stock and Peter Ochs, I claim that Augustinian semiotics is not primarily the result of a received classical rhetorical and grammatical tradition as some scholars have long argued. Though there are similarities with Aristotle[139] and subsequent thinkers (especially Stoic),[140] it is difficult to prove any direct dependencies.[141] What sets Augustine apart as a seminal figure in semiotics is that, extending the thought of his most admired church fathers, Augustine's theory of signs takes on much greater significance through his reading of scripture (especially Genesis, the Psalms, John and Paul)[142] because he is forced to appreciate the role of the reader. It is the *reading* of scripture (which he first learned from Ambrose and the Alexandrian tradition)[143] and the biblical principles of his hermeneutic that gave birth to the first semiotic work.

A vanguard of this view, Robert Markus has persuasively argued that the most powerful influence on Augustine's move to construct a theory of language as a system of signs came from his interest in scriptural 'signs', which could bring under one heading both the literal meaning of signs and the typological or figural sense of scripture.[144] Scriptural words are 'signs *par excellence*', and Augustine's 'theory of signs is meant to be, from the start, a theory of language [that is intrinsically theological] ... In this consists the originality of his reflection on meaning, and its ability to focus so many of his interests.'[145] It is from this concern with scriptural reading practice that he discovers theological meaning (mediation) in the triadic nature of the sign, and we might do better to think of him as a theosemiotician.[146]

As we shall see displayed in our reading of *Confessions* and *De doctrina christiana,* this insight into what I call 'the theosemiotic moment' is funded by an intense engagement with the scriptures and, paradigmatically, the prologue to John's gospel (in relation to the whole of the scriptures and the whole of linguistic capability). The theosemiotic moment – the point at which sign theory becomes more about the generation of meaning (signs having the indefinite and mediating 'effect of making something else come to mind') than simply the mechanics of inference (the deduction that this sign *is* that thing) – was born in Augustine's study of the scriptures (which dominated his thought from his *tolle lege* transformative reading of Romans to his deathbed where he read the penitential psalms).

For Augustine, reasoning consisted of those intellectual practices necessary to make sense of the sacred text because of the central place of Christ in his theology. Christ's incarnation as the Word of God, then, and not simply scripture, was 'the basis for the concept of the sacred sign'. Nevertheless, the scriptures mediate or 'textually replicate' the incarnate Word, providing an ongoing basis for Christian reasoning.[147] Augustine's discourse literally overflows with scriptural signs. Biblical allusions, imagery, paraphrase, metaphor and wordplay are the constant refrain. He thinks with and through the scriptures, which allows his thought a dynamism and flexibility that makes him attractive to this day. As Brian Stock notes, 'in his handling of the most complex signs, *sacramenta* (sacred signs) ...The major role is played by "scripture, which is ceaselessly meditated upon, and ever present in his thought".'[148] Scripture provides both the form and content, the medium and the message of his profound and enduring theology.

One of Augustine's most important semiotic innovations was to link signum with the sacramentum, which was to acknowledge the mediatorial role of the sign in the mysterious revelation of transcendent meaning. As we shall examine below, *tolle lege,* the command to read signs, was a defining experience in Augustine's life. It intensified his lifelong love of language in a way that 'baptized' signs for him – signs became sacraments, they mediated the transcendent in language. Language, because 'the Word became flesh and dwelt amongst us' (John 1.14), was inextricably bound up with the mysterious revelation of God in Christ.[149] It is therefore no surprise that his major book on how to teach Christianity, *De doctrina christiana*, would thus attend to the mediatorial nature of the sign and the logic of the scriptures.[150] Against the opinion of some classically oriented patristic scholars, I argue that Augustine's attentiveness to the Word of God was essential to his sign theory.[151] Michael Cameron, a specialist in Augustinian semiotics, agrees:

> The Word made flesh (John 1.14) discloses the capacity of the uncreated and supratemporal to 'dwell' in the created and temporal. Because of the symbiotic relationship between Christology and language (*doc. Chr.* 1.13.12), the incarnation constitutes the basis for a renewed sacramental understanding of signification whereby the sign not only represents but contains and mediates the reality it signifies ... [T]he bond of sign and reality is so close that the signifying thing takes the name of the thing signified ... [T]he sign incarnates meaning before it is understood to point the way to meaning. Functionally speaking, for temporal beings image is intrinsic to essence, and medium is elemental to message.[152]

It is out of this original and generative insight about the Word of God incarnate in language that Augustine's theory of signs develops – the logic of the incarnation guides his understanding of mediation, and thus the nature of the sign (and thus the nature of scripture). But to refer to 'the Word made flesh' is to refer not only to the incarnation of God in Christ but also to the semiotic universe in which such an incarnation occurs.

The shape of Augustinian semiotics is the shape of the biblical narrative. Augustine interprets Genesis allegorically 'to argue that Adam's sin led to the very institution of signs as a means of communication between God and human beings'.[153] Language before the Fall would have had isomorphic correspondence, knowledge of God would have been unmediated and direct. After the Fall, after Babel, knowledge is always mediated, always filtered through cultural-linguistic signs (to use Lindbeck's terms). But as David Dawson asks in Augustine's voice: *'how, then, will one be able to read Scripture in a way which makes its signs an antidote, rather than a catalyst, for sin?'*[154] If human signs are intrinsically sinful, how can they be read redemptively? What Augustine discovers is that an effective mediation is required, a new reparative relation, a 'third' to bridge (like Jacob's ladder) the linguistic gulf between God and human beings after the Fall – and it is the mediation of the Word which makes the scriptures legible as scripture. What is required is an effective mediation, a new reparative relation, a 'third' to bridge (like Jacob's ladder) the linguistic gulf between God and human beings after the Fall – the mediation of the Word makes the scriptures legible *as* scripture.

This answer that Augustine gives is found in a number of places, but is succinctly stated in *De doctrina christiana*, namely that God has given us the signs of sacred scripture to reveal his will, and in so doing, has provided

> treatment of so many diseases of the human will, starting out from language ... spreading far and wide through translation into a variety of other languages, and thus [coming] to the knowledge of the nations for their salvation. In reading it [the sacred scriptures] their one intention is to discover the thoughts and will of the authors it was written by, and through them [indirectly] to discover the will of God ...'[155]

Augustine believes that 'the Word made flesh' has enabled the signs of scripture to work as an antidote to sin in the reader.

Put differently, 'the semiotic universe paradigmatically encoded in holy writ' enables participation in the divine will – it inscribes and makes legible the reparative relation (the mediation of the Word) that can provide an antidote to the ruptures caused by the Fall. Augustine discovers that this mediation is found in the incarnate Word, and that scripture is but a 'textual replication'[156] of the Word made flesh (it instantiates God's will in sacred signs). But the textual mediation means that there remains a gap between what is given and what is received. By hearing[157] or reading[158] this Word publicly, a community of faithful readers may together be involved, may in fact participate in, this divine mediation which repairs and heals the semiotic ruptures both of the interpretive community and of the world they inhabit, not by glossing over the ruptures but by engaging them more deeply for the sake of our salvation.

Let us now examine the *Confessions*, where Augustine learns these hermeneutical skills, and then *De doctrina christiana*, where he seeks to teach them.

### Confessions and the rule of faith

Augustine recounts his time of instruction with Ambrose in Milan (which occurred 'sometime during the autumn of 384 and the first six months of 385'),[159] where he heard him preach 'the word of truth' every Sunday.[160] It was under the influence of this famous Bishop of Milan's *preaching* that Augustine became an inveterate *reader* of scripture.[161] Before this he says that he had 'resisted [God's] healing hands', by which he means those 'medicines of faith [Bible and sacraments]' applied 'to the sicknesses of the world' and given 'such power'.[162] Augustine begins to read scripture intensively during this period, sensitive to both literal and figurative meanings because of his admiration for Ambrose and the 'Alexandrian' tradition that had shaped his reading practices, yet also well aware of many interpretive disputes between Antioch and Alexandria.[163] It was also under Ambrose that he came to believe in the authority of scripture to shape the intellect and will of the community. Augustine writes:

> So since we were too weak to discover the truth by pure reasoning and therefore needed the authority of the sacred writings, I now began to believe that you would never have conferred such preeminent authority on the scripture, now diffused through all lands, unless you had willed that it would be a means of seeking to know you.[164]

This is a commitment to scripture as the basis for reasoning that he never wavers from, as we see especially in the closing remarks of the *Confessions*, where Augustine (*towards* Lindbeck) thinks of scripture as a kind of 'skin' that is 'stretched out over the peoples to the end of the age',[165] as itself a semiotic universe, or as he calls it, in contrast to the signs of astrology, 'the solid firmament of scripture'.[166]

Reasoning is acknowledged by Augustine as an activity that occurs under the 'solid firmament of authority over us in your divine scriptures'

– he writes that scripture is the 'work' of God's 'fingers', active in the world.[167] He believes that scripture itself, citing Isaiah 1.16–18, testifies to God's desire that *we reason in community through the scriptures for the sake of the world*: 'Come, says the Lord, let us reason together, so that light may be made in the firmament of heaven [the Bible as firmament] and give light over the earth.'[168] For Augustine, as much as for Lindbeck, scripture is a 'semiotic universe paradigmatically encoded in holy writ'; it is the light through which 'we shall see light'; it is epistemologically privileged in the interpretive community.[169] As Erich Przywara made clear in his synthetic reading, Augustine believes that authority 'opens the door' to reason, and the ultimate authority that opens the door to reason is the Word made flesh, which is also the Word made legible.[170] The scriptures are not simply 'an end to be perceived' but are 'a realm to live in', a road to travel along. Augustine expects Christians to be 'formed in mind by [God's] holy books'.[171]

Augustine confesses that 'for a long time past I have been burning to meditate in your law ['*meditari in lege tua*', i.e., scripture, recalling '*tolle lege*'] and confess to you what I know of it and what lies beyond my powers ... until weakness is swallowed up by strength ...'[172] This phrase 'weakness is swallowed up by strength' suggests the therapeutic aspect of scripture study that is linked to his conversion (as we shall see). The Word he meditates upon gives him access to a strength that swallows up weakness: the weakness of words, his own weakness, the weakness of the church, and the weaknesses of the broader community. Significantly, he sees the ethical importance of this when he writes: 'Lord my God, hear my prayer, may your mercy attend to my longing ['to meditate in your law'] which burns not for my personal advantage but *desires to be of use in love to the brethren* ...'[173] The scriptures swallow up, too, the weakness of a disordered self-love, and direct him towards broader horizons (i.e. the city of God). The *Confessions* themselves are constantly directed for the love of another.[174] Augustine's idea that 'the law must be lawfully used for the end of charity'[175] is a scriptural therapy of desire, aimed at reshaping the world for the sake of love. Augustine seeks to teach readers those reading practices that will have the desired salvific effect – that will perform a therapy of desire upon the reader. For that he turns to the Word made flesh.

In the seventh book of the *Confessions*, he compares what he reads in the scriptures (namely the Word made flesh in John 1.1–14) to what he had previously found in the Platonists. It is a foreshadowing of his 'conversion' in the eighth book. The passage is framed by a discussion of his enthusiasm for the *platonicorum libri* and the

Platonist understanding of the Logos [Verbum/Word]. The Platonist view that the Logos was an emanation of 'the One', sometimes even called 'the father, God',[176] seemed coherent with the Johannine doctrine of the Word as 'the true light which illuminates every man coming into the world'.[177] The first verses seem almost entirely Platonic to Augustine:

> There I read, not of course in these words, but with entirely the same sense and supported by numerous and varied reasons, 'In the beginning was the Word and the Word was with God and the Word was God. He was in the beginning with God. All things were made by him, and without him nothing was made. And the light shone in the darkness and the darkness did not comprehend it.'[178]

Augustine naturally reads the prologue to John's gospel in light of such Platonic teaching, but is surprised by an explicit difference: the incarnation of the Word.

Augustine discovered that the one thing missing from the Platonists – the difference of Christianity – was the most important of all, the historical, bodily indwelling of the Word of God: 'I read there [in the Platonist books] that the Word, God, is "born not of the flesh, nor of blood, nor of the will of man nor of the will of the flesh, but of God". But [the Johannine teaching] that "the word was made flesh and dwelt among us" (John 1.13–14), I did not read there.'[179] God was present not abstractly as 'emanation' of the One but concretely as the Word made flesh and dwelling (or 'tenting')[180] amongst us.

This reading of the Platonist tradition (the world), which places John 1.1–14 (the incarnate Word) at the centre of his thought, is also at the centre of the *Confessions* as a literary whole.[181] His meditation on John's prologue here is precisely in the middle of Book 7, and Book 7 is in the middle of the *Confessions* (with six books before and six books after). It is a turning-point, ultimately central to all of his life and thought, and it is important to see that the structural centrality matches the conceptual centrality of the incarnation of the Word for his thinking about signs.

The Johannine teaching about the Word of God made flesh and dwelling in us ['*verbum caro factum est et habitavit in nobis*'] was an interpretive 'rule of faith' for Augustine, where a particularly clear text functions as a rule guiding interpretive practice from within (again, a rule of 'intratextuality').[182] He thinks of this text as one of immense hermeneutical significance: a rule of faith through which everything else might be read in *relation* to it. In another place he will even proudly recount 'that a certain Platonist was in the habit of saying that this opening passage of the holy gospel, entitled "According to John", should be written in letters of gold, and hung up in all churches in the most conspicuous place.'[183] He believes that this text clearly distinguishes Platonism from Christianity, but also shows an intimate connection between the scriptural world and other conceivable worlds. The Johannine prologue functions as a rule for intratextual scripture study – that is, all obscure or problematic texts can be read in relation to this paradigmatic text, this rule of faith. But what also occurs to Augustine is that this text has universal significance, appealing to those 'outside' the faith as well as 'inside'; the incarnate Word is very much *public* truth.[184] It is truth for the church *and* for the world.[185] The prologue to John's gospel encapsulates for Augustine a particular hermeneutical tendency that redirects human desires towards participation in God's redeeming love for the whole world. It brings into profound relation both the Word made strange (divine) *and* the Word made familiar (human).

This discovery of the incarnate Word prepares us for the dramatic scene at the end of Book 8 where Augustine weeps in a garden, hears a child chant repeatedly the words '*tolle lege, tolle lege*', and interprets these words as a sign of a divine command to 'take up and read' the scriptures.[186] The divine 'inner' sense was semiotically embodied (encoded) in the 'outer' sense of human words. Augustine interprets the inner sense of these words as revelatory of the divine will, the divine Word. He responds in the faith that it is indeed God speaking to him directly in one sense, even if indirectly in a mediating other, through the words of a child. What he famously reads is a verse from St Paul's epistle to the Romans (we should recall that the whole of the eighth chapter of *Confessions* works through Romans, and this particular verse serves as a climactic sign, and a rule for his reading of Romans as a whole). Augustine is well acquainted with the scriptures by this point in his life and has even had several previous 'key reading moments' on the way to this pivotal Milanese garden scene (which alludes to other gardens such as Eden and Gethsemane). This particular experience becomes paradigmatic for him of 'good reading practice'. It is the catalyst not for sin but for his baptism, priesthood and service as bishop – a sign-reading experience which transforms his life in a remarkably short space of time. The text which he reads, Romans 13.13–14, commends him to 'put on the Lord Jesus Christ', not making any room for sinful ways of living (or reading). This scriptural 'light' *infuses* his heart ['*luce securitatis infusa cordi meo*'], relieves his anxieties and, making peace with God,[187] breaks all the doubt ['*dubitationis*'] and darkness of his tears. Augustine finds healing for suffering through this text (anxieties relieved, darkness broken), and also finds that he can stand 'in that rule of faith' ['*regula fidei*'], recalling (indeed fulfilling) at the end of Book 3 his mother's desperate hope and vision of his redemption.[188]

The text itself gives the impression that 'the rule of faith' is simply and profoundly the gift of faith in 'God made flesh' which comes by the hearing or reading of sacred signs. As his conversion text has it, 'put on the Lord Jesus Christ' means to put on this rule of faith, this embodied hermeneutic. It is an attempt to make explicit something that is implicit in good reading practice. Standing in that 'rule of faith' means participation in the Word of God through its textual replication in scripture.[189]

For Augustine, the 'rule of faith' is more frequently akin to the internal logic of the scriptures – quite literally the Logos of the scriptures – the 'inner' in Augustine's frequent inner/outer distinctions. This *regula fidei* guides the relationship between knowledge and wisdom, between letter and spirit, and between the outer and the inner 'sense' of a sign read in relation to other signs. John 1.1–14 'paradigmatically encodes' the 'rule of faith' required of good reading practice. The incarnational and trinitarian logic that this *regula fidei* inscribes teaches him a way of mediating the inner and the outer in a way that conjoins the two into a whole that does not obliterate its constituent parts.

This idea that a text can function like a rule first derives from the influence of Ambrose upon Augustine. Brian Stock describes the effect of Ambrose's *preaching* on Augustine as profound, 'the bishop proceeded deliberately from the literal to the spiritual sense of the text: it was not the one or the other that disarmed the wary Augustine, but *their combination into an effective unit*'.[190] And further, 'when he hears Ambrose commenting on 2 Corinthians 3.6, 'The letter kills, but the spirit gives life', what chiefly occurs to him is that *a text can be like a rule*, if literalism is abandoned and the spirit truly allowed to live in the hearer's mind.'[191] This particular insight, that a text can function as a rule, or a standard able to 'give life', instructs the way we should read Augustine as a skilled reader of the scriptures. What I claim is that his Word of God theology is at the heart of his *regula fidei* as well – and 'to stand in that rule' means a lived correspondence between a text and its effect upon real flesh and blood, the incarnational 'rule' of God's Word in the world. But in this sense it is also a rule about rules for reading ('faith comes from hearing') – all rules for reading (hearing) words must do what the Word made flesh does, namely *love*, and therefore save the world by indwelling it (it must textually replicate the Word). It is a scriptural pragmatism concerned to use the law lawfully, or use the scriptures according to the logic of scripture, for the love of God and neighbour (where the 'rule of faith' opens out into the 'rule of charity').

Partly because he had searched the scriptures in vain for so long (Manichaeans read the scriptures too), and partly because he learned particular theological insights through reading sacred signs in a way that transformed him, Augustine recognized the need to think seriously about how to teach Christians to read scripture well. He comes to believe that Christianity is a new redemptive society that is semiotically shaped by the Word of God for the sake of the world's salvation.[192]

## De doctrina christiana

Much of Augustine's thinking on signs was already in place by the time he wrote *Confessions*. Less than three years after his conversion in 386, in *De magistro* (389)[193] he was meditating on the nature of the sign, the relationship of *signs* (especially spoken words) to *things*, and most importantly, he was meditating on the use, purpose and meaning of language – especially through inner/outer distinctions shaped by his understanding of christology.[194] Augustine was then thrust into the priesthood (391) and not long after was made bishop of Hippo in the winter of 394/5.[195] As he rose to his responsibilities as bishop, in 396 he began work on *De doctrina christiana*, where he sought to transfer his scriptural reading skills to other Christians, and in the process gave us the origins of a distinctive sign theory. His earlier reflections on signs, in *De magistro*, are here transformed into a project of exegesis, with a 'Word made flesh' hermeneutical theology written into the heart of his semiotic pragmatism.

The prologue of *De doctrina christiana* charts a middle path[196] through various exegetical excesses of his day, and promises to help students 'make progress not only by reading others who have opened up the hidden secrets of the divine literature, but also by themselves opening them up [i.e. the scriptures] to yet others again'.[197] Augustine worries that teachers of the Bible are too 'eager to explain it to others, instead of referring them back to God, so that they too may come to understand it through his teaching them inwardly'.[198] He is not interested in the scripture being merely explained. He hopes that *De doctrina christiana* will teach students not only how to understand the scriptures inwardly, that is to understand the Word of God, 'but also for them to put into practice' what has been understood, to perform this Word.[199] As Roland Teske notes, for Augustine, 'the beginning and end of all exegesis is practical'.[200] Augustine wants to shape reading practices because he wants the Word of God to transform the way readers live and practise their faith – change the way people read, and you change the way they live. He sees scripture as 'a living salvific text'; it is not only for personal understanding, nor only for union with God but also – and this is the important claim – '*the source of solutions to the great issues of the day*'.[201]

In the prologue to *De doctrina christiana* Augustine refers to this passage in John where 'Thomas said to Jesus, "Lord, we do not know where you are going. How can we know the way?" Jesus said to him, "I am the way, and the truth, and the life. No one comes to the Father except *through me*"' (Jn 14.5–6). It is consonant with Augustine's whole approach in *De doctrina christiana* to think through the implications of this biblical reasoning about mediation, thinking hermeneutically about the '*through me*' of the incarnate Word. From the prologue to the end of Book 4, Augustine's incarnational theology is reflected in his constant insistence upon the non-dualistic *harmonia*[202] between letter and spirit, between outer and inner, between the temporal and the eternal, between the literal and figurative senses, between sign and thing, as indicative of the redemptive union of the human and divine in the Word made flesh.

Turning to Book 1, Augustine maintains that *De doctrina christiana* as a whole is therefore oriented around the *tractatio* of the scriptures, that is, the 'use' or 'treatment of the scriptures'.[203] Such *tractatio scripturarum* must rely upon and work towards or initiate a twofold movement on the way of discovery. Augustine's way of discovery, begins with *the unavoidable mediation of the sign*. 'All teaching is either about things or signs; but things are learned about *through* signs.'[204] The scriptures offer us a semiotic system that mediates 'something else' to us, they are 'signs used in order to signify something else', to effect something else.[205] Augustine writes, reasoning through Psalm 102, Romans 8 and John 1.14:

> For you will cure all my diseases through him who sits at your right hand and intercedes with you for us ... many and great are those diseases, many and great indeed. But your medicine [the scriptures and sacraments of the Church] is still more potent. We might have thought your Word was far removed from being united to mankind and have despaired of our lot unless he had become flesh and dwelt among us ...'[206]

The divine mediation of the Word in language is intimately bound up with his view of how scriptural signs both mediate and transfigure the shape of embodied reality.

By reasoning through the implications of the prologue to John's gospel, Augustine establishes in *De doctrina christiana* a relationship between the production of God's Word and the production of ordinary human language.

> How did [Wisdom] come [into the world], if not by the Word becoming flesh and dwelling amongst us? It is something like when we talk; in order for what we have in mind to reach the minds of our hearers through their ears of flesh, the word which we have in our thoughts becomes a sound, and is called speech. And yet this does not mean that our thought is turned into that sound, but while remaining undiminished in itself, it takes on the form of a spoken utterance by which to insert itself into their ears, without bearing the stigma of any change in itself. That is how the Word of God was not changed in the least, and yet became flesh, in order to dwell amongst us.[207]

The production of the Word of God is 'something like when we talk', Augustine writes. He thinks this movement from inner [Word] to outer [flesh] can also be seen (analogically) in the production of ordinary human language. The relational movement of something in our mind being transferred to the mind of another requires the mediation of language, outwardly embodied in the sound of words (which letters textually replicate) and having effects upon listeners. In this sense he is interested in reading the mediatorial nature of the sign theologically. Because all things were made through the Word (Jn 1.3), and because it is the Word made flesh that mediates God and humanity, he wants to imagine the closest possible link between his 'Word made flesh' christology and the production of cultural-linguistic signs in the semiotic exchange.[208] What governs his semiotics, then, he calls a 'rule of faith', which guides and directs his theory of mediation and his hermeneutic principles according to God's logic, which is incarnational and trinitarian, and therefore redemptive in its effects upon the community of interpretation.

The initial distinction that Augustine makes between 'things' (*res*) and 'signs' (*signum*) allows a highly original distinction between 'things used' and 'things enjoyed', sometimes simply called the use–enjoyment distinction.[209] Augustine writes, 'there are some things which are meant to be enjoyed, others which are meant to be used'.[210] This distinction is crucial, and has been variously interpreted, but the point Augustine makes is clear: signs are to be used and our use of signs should be for the enjoyment of the triune God, that is, for our salvation.[211] Since Augustine is concerned with what 'all treatment [*tractatio*] of the scriptures is aiming at', he stresses that any use of scriptural signs, any treatment of the Word, should bring readers into a practical, redemptive relation with the triune God.[212] This participationist and pragmatic interpretation of the use–enjoyment distinction fits nicely into the hermeneutical context of *De doctrina*. Augustine's use–enjoyment distinction in Book 1 outlines a kind of semiotic or scriptural pragmatism in which it is understood that the scriptures (as the textual replication of the Word) are meant for our healing, and any treatment of the Word of God should lead us to enjoy the triune God and therefore (reflexively) should have a therapeutic effect in the world (it should transform human desire and intellect). This interpretation of the use–enjoyment distinction has the advantage of holding together Augustine's hermeneutical emphasis upon the incarnate Word, discerning that Word in the signs of scripture (regulated by a 'rule of faith') and outlining an approach to scripture that is participatory and instrumental for the simultaneous yet ordinate love of God and neighbour (which Augustine calls a 'rule of charity').

We can see more clear evidence of Augustine's therapeutic emphasis when he writes about the 'treatment of scripture' in this way:

> Any treatment [*tractatio*], of course, is a way to health; so this treatment [*tractatio*] undertook to *restore sinners to complete health*. And just as when doctors bind up wounds, they do not do it untidily, but neatly, so that the bandage, as well as being useful, can also to some extent have its proper beauty, in the same sort of way Wisdom adapted her healing art to our wounds by taking on a human being ... the Wisdom of God treats the ills of humanity, presenting herself for our healing, herself the physician, herself the physic ...[213]

Once again, Augustine closely links the treatment of scripture with the salvific aims of God's Word and wisdom. This is a point not always appreciated in relation to the use–enjoyment distinction, primarily because the distinction is sometimes abstracted from its hermeneutical context in this *tractatio scripturarum* as a whole.[214] The meaning of scripture, for Augustine, can be found in its interpretive use for salvific ends. The use or treatment of scriptural signs is judged according to how effectively it moves the will and intellect of the reader into union with God's mind and will (that we love God and neighbour); and that effectiveness is reciprocally made visible in the love of neighbour. We shall know that such transformation has occurred by the fruit it produces, that is, by the correspondence between the use of scriptural signs and its effects upon lived reality.[215]

Augustine is concerned with God's capacity to use these 'scriptural signs to move readers to conversion',[216] to transform the reader from the inside through participation in the use of these signs, to move the (wounded) human will into union with the divine will, and then to redirect energy and action towards healing and restoration ('to complete health'). As Stock writes, Augustine believes that 'scripture offers the reader ... a privileged medium, through which God's will, framed in narrative, can be internalized and directed outwards as ethically informed action'.[217] This kind of scriptural reading after wisdom (after the Word) is precisely what Augustine hopes *De doctrina christiana* will teach, a Christian form of life shaped by this sapiential Word and directed outwards as ethically informed (restorative) action in the world.

In summarizing Book 1, Augustine provides readers with his rule of charity: 'So what all that has been said amounts to, while we have been dealing with things, is that the fufilment and the end of the law ... of all the divine scriptures is love (Rom. 13.8; 1 Tim. 1.5); love of the thing which is to be enjoyed',[218] namely, the triune God, and in evidence of that love, 'love of neighbour'. The signs of scripture should be used 'for our salvation' – used to carry the reader towards the goal of eschatological union with the triune God (from the words to the Word) with broad communal, even political, implications.[219] 'So if it seems to you that you have understood the divine scriptures, or any part of them, in such a way that by this understanding you do not build up this twin love of God and neighbour, then you have not yet understood them.'[220]

The scriptures are, for Augustine, like a scaffold intended to build up the structures of faith and hope and love.[221] But of course it is a scaffold that cannot be discarded save the eschaton – it is constantly necessary and useful.[222] Scripture, then, is not an end in itself for Augustine; it is a 'scaffold' to help us discover (through reading) the true inexhaustible meaning of what the scriptures signify for us. Augustine is interested in teaching the reader how to use the signs of scripture as God uses the signs of scripture, to restore 'the right order of love' in us, to do justice and restore sinners to 'complete health'.[223]

### Communities, problem-solving, and the triadic sign

In Book 2 of *De doctrina christiana* Augustine turns to a treatment of 'given signs' as inherently communal; we are taught that 'communities are constituted by how they understand the symbolic systems in use within them'.[224] As Augustine puts it: 'given signs ... are those which living creatures give one another'.[225] But all 'given signs' are ultimately 'given' by God and are inextricably bound up with God speaking creation and creativity in human community. God's own self-giving in the Word made flesh conditions the possibility that 'given signs' are meaningful for human community. Augustine certainly believes that 'the signs given by God, which are contained in the holy scriptures, have been indicated to us through the human beings who wrote them down', but he thinks that they are primarily useful for discovering the will of God indwelling in the human words.[226] The scriptures are a privileged site because they are the semiotic 'scaffold' through which God speaks his Word to heal humanity from the inside through our use of these *sacramenta*.

Augustine says, that because of Adam's Fall, human language became fractured and disordered.[227]

> It has not been possible for ... these signs to be common to all nations, as a result of a kind of sin of human dissension, where everyone grabbed at the first place for himself. A sign of this pride was the building of that tower to reach heaven, when humanity was rewarded for its impiety by discord in its speech ...[228]

The fallibility of 'given signs' affects the signs of scripture too, even though Scripture 'provides treatment for so many diseases of the human will' and (after Babel) is translated to all the nations 'for their salvation'.[229] But the healing comes precisely by participating in the will of God through reading the Word in the words. 'In reading [the scriptures] their one intention is to discover the thoughts and will of the authors it was written by, and through them to discover the will of God, which we believe directed what such human writers had to say.'[230] Therefore Augustine's interest is first and foremost with the 'intentional signs' of the scriptures that have been 'given' by the Holy Spirit to the community of readers *for their salvation*. He teaches readers the nature of the 'given signs' so that they may learn how God uses signs in order to heal us through our communal reading.

Establishing an account of the fallibility of language, and recognizing that the tremendous obstacles to interpretation are rooted in human sin, Augustine sets out a method of reading that ensures that sacred signs do not become a catalyst but an antidote to sin.[231] This he does, once again, through the Word made flesh. The scriptures make legible God speaking to us a Word that heals humanity from the inside – by being made flesh, that is, by indwelling humanity – when received by faith in human interpreters (the faith which comes by hearing, or reading, the scriptures). The mediating words of Scripture, then, can heal humanity (even the humanity of scripture itself) to the extent that they are read *as the incarnate Word is read* (the inner healing the outer), and when they are performed and made flesh 'in the community of readers which is the Church', they replicate liturgically, and through other forms of world engagement, the logic of the incarnation, which is the logic of scripture itself.[232]

Recall Augustine's definition that 'a sign ... is a thing, which besides the impression it conveys to the senses, also has the *effect* of making something else come to mind'.[233] The triadic structure implicit in Augustine's definition, that a *sign*[1] must *mean something*[2] to *someone*[3] as we have learned, is nearly the same definition that Charles Peirce gives to the sign in the nineteenth century, reminding us again of Augustine's influence on modern semiotics.[234] But what have modern semiotics lost in the transition from Augustine to Peirce? Markus writes: 'the triadic relation of signification is the key to Augustine's entire hermeneutic theory'.[235] What the triadicity of Augustinian semiotics suggests is that the meaningfulness of the sign is received within human community, and that such a community of sign-users will inevitably extend the meaningfulness of signs by discovering new relationships of signification. Why? For Augustine, it is because of this link between the Word and human language, between the divine self-giving of God in the Word made flesh and the ongoing communication of this God in scriptural signification. Augustine's triadic relation of signification took into fuller account (than protosemiotic thought allows) the role of the reading community and the effect signs have on readers precisely because it mattered that this divine Word was *for* the transformation of real reading communities. It is a Word that will not be returned void. And though it forgot its theological reasons, Peircean semiotics most emphasized the *effects* of this crucial third relationship of signification that extends meaningfulness through communities of interpretation, something we shall consider again in the next chapter (where Augustinian and Peircean semiotics might be seen as mutually complementary and enriching).

That 'pragmatic' (known by its effects upon a community) or 'triadic' notion of the sign relation is Augustine's most basic definition, and in it he stresses the importance of the community (namely the Church) in treating the signs of scripture, and it is not surprising that *De doctrina christiana* is read as a treatise on the formation of a Christian culture (which he will return to in *The City of God*).[236] He is concerned with 'given signs ... which living creatures give one another in order to show, as far as they can, their moods and feelings, or to indicate whatever it may be they have sensed or understood'.[237] Our only purpose in signifying, according to Augustine, is 'to bring out and transfer to someone else's mind what we, the givers of the sign, have in mind ourselves'.[238] It is an inescapably communal activity – which might be called the logic of relations, or simply triadicity.[239] There is a theological reasoning in this semiotic.

Just as we found the closest possible link between the Word and words, it is legitimate to see the same kind of link between Augustine's triadic understanding of signs and the triune name of God. The Father, Son and Holy Spirit suggest the triadicity (even the triunity) of the given sign (the incarnate rule of God's Word) and its meaning (its mediation) in relation to the reading community (where inspiration resides). The relationality of the 'third' is both the gift of the Holy Spirit (Pentecost having sign interpretation at its very heart), which is the bond of love between the Father and the Son, and simultaneously the gift of meaning to a community of readers. This informs his understanding of the inspiration of the scriptures, where Jesus Christ is read 'in the Spirit' as the Word made flesh.

Far from having a naïve view of inspiration, Augustine knows that the very humanity of the scriptures requires a human mediation to read these words 'in the Spirit' as God's words. He says, 'even the signs given by God, which are contained in the holy scriptures, have been indicated to us through the human beings who wrote them down'.[240] This human mediation, then, must be read as the mediation of the Word of God made flesh in the reading community who perform this Word (as Christ's body). Readers must become themselves a textual replication, a living salvific text made flesh for the healing of the nations. This is why the reading community plays such a central role, inspiring the embodiment or performance of the Word of God.

### Repairing semiotic problems in community

Much of Books 2 and 3 are oriented, not surprisingly then, around solving problems in the community of interpretation – a further development of 'scriptural pragmatism', repairing semiotic problems that arise in our reading. In order to discern the Word in the words, Augustine says we must be sensitive to the kind of semiotic problems we will face. He divides the kinds of problems that may arise into two main categories: signs that are unknown and signs that are ambiguous.[241]

For example, solving problems with literal signs that are 'unknown' involves increasing language skills necessary for knowing the sign–thing relation. If the problems seem related to 'ambiguous' literal signs, Augustine judges that linguistic and semiotic skills, history, context, reason and especially the *regula fidei* ('you should refer it to the rule of faith'), should all play key roles in solving the interpretive problem.[242] If the problem cannot be resolved by any of these means, Augustine says that as long as it does not contradict the historical context of the text, or the incarnational, trinitarian and charitable *regula fidei*, then the reader can interpret the text 'in any of the ways that are open'.[243] In principle, Augustine does not object to an infinite plurality of interpretations (including the extension of figural ones), granting that they do not contradict the 'rule of faith' (the law of love, which is now not only explicitly incarnational but also trinitarian in its stress upon the third, the Spirit in the reading community).

Similarly, when Augustine discusses problems with figural signs, he argues for bringing the literal-historical and the figurative-allegorical into a kind of triadic unity of letter and spirit. In other words, the truly triadic sign is the sign read or transfigured in the spirit to mean the (incarnational and trinitarian) transfiguration of the historical reality with the spiritual or allegorical reality. Figurative signs require the reader to unite the 'letter' and the 'spirit' of the sign–thing relation into some third effective understanding of reality, indwelling more deeply the fullness of meaning within the semiotic universe that the scriptures instantiate. Otherwise, Augustine says, we are 'enslaved under signs' rather than directed toward 'that reality to which all such things are to be referred'.[244] Literalism is enslavement, but if the spirit is truly allowed to animate the letter, and if this third thing can become a useful sign to the reader for salvation, then, Augustine says, there is 'spiritual freedom'.[245]

But what is important to notice here is that Augustine assumes that the problems of reading are to be fully engaged – they are, in a real sense, where all the action is. The wounds of the text, if you will, are like Christ's wounds, occasions to go deeper into the Word. The *aporias* of scripture are where his rules of faith and love are most needed, and his problem-solving semiotic is intended also to transform the reading community through such deep engagements with the reparative logic instantiated in such rules for reading difficult texts.

Good reading practices should guide present action, and seeking the good (i.e. 'the kingdom of charity'), also endeavour to remove that which obstructs the good. Augustine promotes a suprainstrumental view of scripture, in so far as scripture is not only to be charitably interpreted but charitably used for the sake of the kingdom, because, as he puts it, 'love reigns supreme', and he commends the reader to 'take pains to turn over and over in your mind what you read, until your interpretation of it is led right through to the kingdom of charity'.[246] For Augustine, 'love of God and neighbour' is the final arbiter in solving interpretive problems in community – but again, it is a dynamic orientation rather than a static one: the entire interpretive process is judged in terms of its ability to take you deeper into the logic of God's Word embodied in human flesh (this is what he means by using the law lawfully), and this can only be judged by its fruits in the reading community.

Scripture reading, then, is an inescapably communal activity – which might be called the logic of relations, or simply triadicity, the irreducible yet dynamic relation between a text and its meaning for a particular reading community.[247] Augustine's hermeneutic requires a bond of love to unite in a dramatic way these complex relations. No univocal or monographic interpretation will do. Here I find in Augustine something like a *vestigia trinitatis* in the logic of scripture itself, in a way that may even anticipate the relationship between the Trinity and revelation in Barth. For both Augustine and Barth, the Holy Spirit has a much more distributive place than the Father or the Son. This is probably just as it should be. In Augustine's *De trinitate,* the Holy Spirit is understood as the bond of love, that third which makes two into one without confusion, that third which co-inheres in both the Father and the Son, and in those who participate in this triune life through the scaffoldings of Word and sacraments. The semiotic third, likewise, reaches towards the real effects upon diverse communities participating in this Word.

In sum, Augustine transforms 'intratextuality' into an outward movement that aims at an embodied replication of God's work of repairing the world where it has been broken. The scriptural pragmatism he commends, then, is as ethical and sociopolitical as it is ecclesial and theological. The love of God must be embodied in communal practices of scriptural reading which bear effective sociopolitical witness to the religious and secular neighbour, that is, a programme of scriptural reasoning which follows a rule of love, a love that is known by its fruits.

I have argued that Augustine does indeed envision, in Niebuhr's words, 'Christ transforming culture', but he envisions it first as a kind of semiotic repair of the world, mediated through the scaffolding of scripture, or, to mix metaphors, guided by the light of this semiotic universe, paradigmatically encoded in holy writ. It is a mandate for making the sacramental reading of scripture a dynamic part of the church's world-engaging, sociopolitical life of loving God and neighbour. With Augustine we find the roots of a genuinely scriptural form of pragmatism aimed at healing the world through the Word.

# 3

# Ochs

## Peirce, pragmatism and the logic of scripture

Peter Ochs is a Jewish philosopher at the University of Virginia. His primary research has considered the inner consistency and development of the thought of the founder of pragmatism, Charles Sanders Peirce. Trained at Yale, Ochs's 1980 doctorate on 'metaphysical conviction' in the work of Peirce began a lifelong interest in the origins of pragmatic philosophy, and over time he developed a novel reading of Peirce that helped to explain the inconsistencies of his thought through a coherent understanding of his intellectual development. In 1998 the fruit of this extensive research appeared in *Peirce, Pragmatism and the Logic of Scripture*. The aim of this final chapter is to explore one aspect of that book about Peirce: it is a Jewish dialogical response to George Lindbeck. Ochs proposes a shared scriptural pragmatism between Jews and Christians, with implications for how Lindbeck might be read.

### 1 A rationale for turning to Peter Ochs

Like George Lindbeck, Peter Ochs offers an alternative to failed ways of reasoning in modernity, without being anti-modern. Ochs's alternative, however, involves a much more developed, if equally ambitious, reformative project involving the scriptures. With Anglo-American and continental postmodernists, Ochs identifies failures in the modern academy's paradigm of reasoning, but argues that while certain postmodern diagnoses about modernity may be correct, their rules for repair and strategies for imaginative reconstruction are lacking.[248] He suggests a postcritical return to the sources of classical pragmatism, especially in a return to the scriptures. And rather than give up on 'logic' altogether, as some postmodernists have done, Ochs suggests a return to logic too. His return to pragmatism, and his return to scripture, represent a return to rules of repair; that is, he attends to a reforming logic that responds to the intellectual suffering of the modern period and enables a constructive hermeneutic that can transform traditions of enquiry immanently and transcendently. His point of entry is in his sophisticated, non-relativistic, postmodern and pragmatic rereading of the philosophy of Charles Sanders Peirce, which rereads Peircean pragmatism as 'the logic of scripture'.[249]

Why does Ochs turn to Charles Peirce? Why do I turn to Peter Ochs as a complement to my Augustinian rereading of Lindbeck? One of Ochs's aims in his book is to display a triadic logic of relations within interpretive communities. This recalls the triadic structure of the sign we found in Augustine, and its significance in the light of his incarnational and trinitarian theology, and complements well my claim that Augustine stands at the origins of a Christian 'scriptural pragmatism' that I think adequately describes Lindbeck's postliberalism. The triadic logic that Ochs displays, however, gives explicitly corrective and constructive philosophical guidance to a programme of 'scriptural reasoning' between Jewish and Christian readers, and displays an openness to other religious and secular reading communities as well. Ochs turns to Peirce because he is the philosopher who offers a way of making these relations visible through a system of logical graphs that can diagram the incomplete signs or 'icons' of individuals by showing their mutual needs in relation. Peircean logic helps to correct and supplement the dyadic ('subject–predicate calculus') logic of Cartesian–Kantian thought through a triadic logic of relations that displays the interdependency of signs understood in semiotic and social terms. As one reviewer put the relational logic of the programme, 'People and words are both indefinite signs requiring other people/words to complete their identities/definitions.'[250] What this relational, triadic logic displays is the need for a 'third grade of clearness' which does not leave behind modern, that is, Cartesian 'clarity' or 'distinctness' but supplements it and asks with Peirce after the 'practical effects which the object of the conception would have'.[251] This chapter employs this relational logic in an effort to see how Jewish and Christian scriptural pragmatists display their mutual needs in relation to one another.

In an unpublished essay Ochs acknowledges that 'pragmatism' has sometimes been understood as belonging to the 'failed logic of modernity' but argues that the diagnosis that pragmatism fails only holds true when:

Peirce's followers – Dewey and James included – fail, out of sheer prejudice, to believe what Peirce claimed about pragmatism: that it is no more than a corollary to Jesus' words, 'that ye may know them by their fruit.' Peirce's pragmatism is the Gospel's law of love adopted as a rule of logic and tested by its fruit, that is, by its consequences for redeeming the indignities it was intended to redeem. Peirce's pragmatism is no more than a way of reading Scripture as a rule for reforming logic. Peirce devoted much of his work to articulating the details of the rule and very little of his work to disciplining and refining his very good instincts about Scripture.[252]

Such a statement, that 'Peirce's pragmatism is no more than a way of reading Scripture as a rule for reforming logic', is as true of Peirce as it is of Lindbeck, and before both of them it is true of Augustine too. Ochs's work is multifaceted, speaking to a number of critical audiences at once, but for each of his overlapping audiences his book does the 'disciplining and refining' of Charles Peirce as a scriptural pragmatist. This is where my interest begins because Ochs's non-relativistic, pluralist, postmodern approach to Peirce also disciplines and refines the scriptural pragmatism implicit in particular Jewish and Christian communal prototypes, the logic of which Ochs displays most practically in the final chapter of his book on Peirce. As a result, I claim that his work provides us with tools that can help postliberals continue the work of reform that George Lindbeck has begun. I also claim that placing both Lindbeck and Ochs in the Augustinian tradition helps readers to see the implicit theological claims that are being made in the work of these two contemporary thinkers.[253]

## 2 Peirce, pragmatism and the logic of scripture

First, and most generally, Peircean pragmatism is a philosophy of repair and reconstruction, fashioned after the American Civil War, fully aware both of the fragility of social life and of our capacity to repair, restore and reconstruct in the face of real problems involving the pain, suffering and errors of real people in communities.[254] According to Peter Ochs, Charles Peirce thought that his 'pragmatic maxim' was nothing more than a restatement of Jesus's identification of true knowledge with 'fruits', that is, with the actual effects of the knowledge: 'consider what effects, that might conceivably have practical bearings, we conceive the object of our conception to have. Then, our conception of these effects is the whole of our conception of the object.' This is specifically a philosophy aware of its real and present responsibility to the future and the past, and a philosophy especially aware of the importance of considering the practical effects of signs, people, words and conceptions in a suffering world. The radical claim that follows on from this is that Peircean pragmatism derives its logic from scripture.

Second, but more to the point for an Ochsian understanding of Peircean pragmatism, philosophy has the task, through writing, of diagramming the hidden, implicit rules 'through which modern society repairs itself'.[255] Peirce labelled this elemental writing 'enscribing' or 'scripture'. This is the occasion for Ochs to redescribe Peircean pragmatism – rightly I think – as 'the logic of scripture'. That is, he reads pragmatism as a philosophy of repair, suggesting that these repairs rely upon scripture, and therefore Ochs proposes that Christians and Jews reread pragmatism as a logic of scripture: 'that is, as a modern philosopher's way of diagramming the Bible's rules for repairing broken lives and healing societal sufferings'.[256] In this sense, Ochs has identified Peircean pragmatism as implicitly biblical, and has thus opened up new possibilities for understanding the truly theological resources available to the scriptural pragmatist because such pragmatism ultimately derives from a revealed logic (see Chapter 2).[257]

Third, Ochs's book on Peirce stands with communitarians such as MacIntyre and others who have long argued that all reasoning is 'tradition-constituted'.[258] In this sense, it is a kind of pragmatism keenly aware of philosophy's responsibility to the past of a particular tradition (spanning ancient, medieval and modern periods). Meaning is not generated out of nothing, but out of communities of interpretation, out of traditions of enquiry that endure over the long-run of time. As with our reading of Augustine's triadic semiotic, 'a sign means something to someone', all meaning is found in the logic of relations, and reasoning itself is a semiotic activity that happens over time in transgenerational communities, or 'traditions'. Reasoning has a social character, always already involving communal relations with the past, present and future. As a result, tradition and community are woven into the heart of Ochs's work, and this is why real, concrete communities of enquiry (as we shall see) are the focus of his conclusions and the focus of this chapter.

Fourth, being concerned with 'traditions' of enquiry also means that he is interested in the ability of traditional reasoners to self-reflect on the deepest resources in their tradition of enquiry for their rules of self-correction. This is why Ochs might describe his work as a kind of 'radical traditionalism' because he wants to reason within traditions by going back to the generative 'source' (the *radix*) of the tradition, in the case of Jews and Christians through a study of the Bible's rules for self-correction in tradition.[259] But the intratextual reasoning that happens within traditions also requires for Ochs a dialogical reasoning with other intratextual traditions (e.g. dialogues that are Jewish and Christian, medieval and modern, religious and secular). In this sense, dialogue is understood as a kind of intertextual reasoning between such 'radical traditions' whose particularity and difference is understood as essential to understanding the complementary nature of their relationship.

This kind of 'radical traditionalism' can be seen in the broadest terms when Ochs writes that the original mission of Peircean pragmatism was 'to place the modern project of philosophy back in the pre-modern tradition of practice from which it has sought to divorce itself'.[260] The Peircean repair of modernity is understood as a 'return' to sources in the sense that he sees the modern project as inextricably bound to the medieval one; it is 'an attempt to repair the repair'.[261] That is, to see the differences of medieval and modern thought as an indication that they are complementary ventures, with pragmatism offering the analytical tools of repair that could enable us to see the continuity between them, and better deal with the real doubts (discontinuities) that prompted an entire 'secular' tradition of thought to arise and flourish out of another 'religious' one. It is an attempt to see backwards and forwards at once the broad scope of the Western intellectual tradition, with a return to scripture at the hermeneutical centre. Ochs would have us think of Charles Peirce not as a modern foundationalist, nor as a premodern one, but as the first postmodern and post-foundationalist thinker: Peirce attempted to move beyond the failures of modernity (viz. the failed Cartesian repair of scholasticism) through immanent rules for repair. Likewise, Ochs would have us think of Judaism and Christianity as a complementary venture, with pragmatism offering the analytical tools of repair that could enable us to see the continuity between them, and better deal with the real doubts (discontinuities) that prompted an entire scriptural tradition of life and thought to arise and flourish out of another scriptural tradition.

## The structure of the argument

It is instructive to note features of the whole structure of the book. The first six chapters of *Peirce, Pragmatism and the Logic of Scripture*, describe Peirce in a way that accounts for his intellectual development and inscribes principles of self-reflection and self-correction which Ochs uses to show that the problems with Peircean pragmatism are actually able to be repaired from within. These six tightly argued chapters make up the first part of the book and introduce 'pragmatic methods of reading' that interpret or reread the problems of Peirce's pragmatism. Such methods instruct the reader as Ochs proceeds to diagram as well as correct problems in reading Peirce's early critique of modernity (or what Peirce called 'Cartesianism'), as well as problems in his early and 'normative' theories of pragmatism, displaying the pragmatic methods of reading he has set forth along the way, culminating in a sixth chapter, 'a pragmatic reading of Peirce's lectures on pragmatism'.

The early Peirce, according to Ochs, has many errant tendencies (foundationalism, conceptualism, nominalism), but none of these problems are intrinsic to his pragmatism, and in fact a postmodern and pragmatic reading of pragmatism itself insists on an internal correction of these problems within his thought. The second half of the book, though it consists of only two chapters, significantly extends Peirce. In the seventh chapter he applies this 'pragmatic method of reading' to Peirce's mature pragmati*cist* writing, and in the crucial eighth and final chapter, he seeks to 'prove' the truth of his hypotheses by displaying their effective significance ('practical effects') for particular communities of interpretation. Though much of the book shows its significance for pragmatic philosophers, his final chapter highlights the effective significance of his work for Jewish and Christian communities.

Ochs's final chapter is my primary concern, but not at the expense of the argument that Ochs makes about Charles Peirce in the preceding chapters of the book, for this is methodologically integral.[262] Ochs embarks on a threefold process of (1) drawing our attention to problems in Peirce; then (2) compassionately using Peirce to heal Peirce (repairing problems through internal modes of correction); before (3) displaying the practical effects of such a rereading of Peircean pragmatism for scriptural reading communities. Ochs offers Peircean scholars the grounds for an internal correction and a clarification that provides the best explanatory model of Peirce's mature pragmatism; but on a level more immediately practical for 'scriptural pragmatism', Ochs offers scriptural theologians and philosophers of religion a reading of Peirce that impinges directly upon their work, promising a 'non-reductive' hermeneutical approach that enables religious 'communities of interpretation' similarly to resolve difficult problems, and so release new possibilities as well as deeper levels of understanding and consequence.

The book is self-consciously aware of such a reader, a reader who reads within a real community of interpretation. Ochs displays a method of reading that might repair what has failed in the reading of potentially any given system of signs (if read in its 'concrete reasonableness') for a particular community. One of the strengths of the book is to show that it is not just the failures at reading Peirce in community that Ochs thinks can be corrected, but failures of reading scripture in community as well. He argues that this philosophy of repair is at the heart of Peircean pragmatism, which was aimed not at recreating the norms of modernity but at repairing the failure of modern attempts to replace medieval systems of philosophical and theological reasoning. He argues that modernity itself was a project of repair that had forgotten its true aim: repairing the failures of scholasticism.[263]

## The reception of the book

The book as a whole represents a many-layered theory of how Peircean pragmatism not only developed over time but also intentionally set in motion self-correcting strategies to ensure its continual development as a reparative practice. *Peirce, Pragmatism and the Logic of Scripture* has yet to be fully received by Peirce scholars,[264] but signs of its eventual reception are beginning to show as the book receives a serious hearing amongst contemporary Jewish philosophers and Christian theologians (who see the practical significance for their communities).[265] Their response has been prompted partly because at the heart of Professor Ochs's theory of Peircean development is the hypothesis that 'the logic of scripture' is the key to understanding the coherence of Peirce's thought as a philosophy of repair; but mostly because Ochs directly addresses particular Jewish and Christian thinkers, asking them to rethink pragmatism *as* 'the logic of scripture', as a kind of scriptural pragmatism at the heart of their semiotic universe.[266] Their response has also been prompted by the fact that the way Ochs reads Peirce has the greatest implications for scriptural readers.

Ochs has not reinvented Peirce as 'scriptural pragmatist', for as we have seen, Peirce himself wrote 'that his pragmatic maxim was recommended by Jesus' words, "Ye may know them by their fruits."'[267] But by taking Peirce's biblical claim seriously (something no other Peircean scholar known to me has done), Ochs offers a coherent (if highly complex) understanding of Peirce, one that enriches both Peirce studies and what might be meant by 'scriptural pragmatism' to any given community of readers. The rest of this chapter attends to what is meant by 'scriptural pragmatism' for particular reading communities that Ochs identifies.

## The logic of the argument

Readers learn that Ochs understands Peircean pragmatism as a philosophy of repair, and that pragmatic 'definition', 'reasoning', and 'reading' consists in 'the performance of correcting other, inadequate definitions of imprecise things', and that our interest (as readers) should be in 'how Peirce would correct himself'.[268] Correcting 'inadequate definitions of imprecise things' relates directly, then, to the twin problems of modernity that Ochs identifies as the tendency towards over-precision, which is 'rationalism', or the tendency towards under-precision, which is 'irrationalism' (terms which function in a way similar to Lindbeck's 'cognitive-propositional' and 'experiential-expressive'). Ochs argues that Peirce discovered a way of avoiding the horns of this modern dilemma by appreciating that as a discourse becomes more and more abstracted, it becomes vague and imprecise. When there are signs of vagueness, such signs 'may be defined only with respect to particular contexts of interpretation'.[269] A vague, imprecise text therefore only takes shape through what Ochs calls 'corrective reading', which always must have meaning 'for some community of readers'.[270] His thesis resides, therefore, not in a correction of Peirce *per se*, any more than this thesis aims at a correction of Lindbeck *per se*, but Ochs aims specifically 'to correct problems in the way Peirce would be read by a given community'.[271]

As with the scriptural pragmatism of Augustine, Ochs similarly discovers a scriptural rule of compassion (or, as Ochs also puts it, 'the more indefinite rule of love') and discerns that this scriptural rule contributed to the corrective character of Peircean semiotics. To Ochs, this means that the 'rule of charity' can be understood triadically as 'a strictly corrective semiotics: something is a sign (an index) to someone (an agent–interpretant) of a need to respond in a caring or loving way'.[272] Peircean philosophy can be understood to enrich what Ochs calls the 'diagrammatic form' of scriptural reading (something akin to the 'plain sense'), but also argues that the scriptural rule of compassionate love enriches the corrective nature of Peircean semiotics (something akin to the 'interpreted sense'). This has a natural affinity, according to Ochs, to certain Jewish practices of textual reasoning.

Much of his work is an attempt to think critically about this natural affinity between Peircean pragmatism and the Jewish textual reasoning that he calls 'rabbinic pragmatism'.

Ochs likens the Peircean method of corrective reading, or rereading, to the rabbinic practice of scriptural interpretation, consisting of a plain-sense reading (*peshat*) of an explicit text and a deeper level of reading (*derash*) of the implicit text. The rabbinic scriptural pragmatist is a semiotician, a reader of signs who is always 'discovering an implicit text within the explicit text'.[273] Such a reading, however, of the implicit in the explicit, is only stimulated 'when something burdensome in the plain sense' calls for an interpretive reading.[274] As Ochs puts it in a discussion of textual and conversational implicature in Eco and Grice, 'we mean more than we say', and therefore texts mean more than what is plainly and explicitly stated.[275] We might say that the meaning of a text is always stated in the explicit text, yet only partially so, because the meaning is also deferred 'to some other occasion' when the implicit text is read in response to some contradiction or textual difficulty occasioned by the community's reading of them for a particular purpose.[276] As Ochs puts it,

> because the plain sense in question is the plain sense of Scripture (*torah*) as God's revealed word, the rabbis assume that the textual burden is merely apparent and that the non-burdensome meaning of a given passage will be disclosed through further 'searching out' (*derasha*: 'interpreted meaning', or the result of 'searching out').[277]

This preserves the truth and intention of the text without obliterating its constantly changing relation to particular communities of interpretation. It shows that truth and meaning are to be found in the quality of the relation of a text to a community of readers.

For the Peircean scholar, such an approach provides a fresh interpretation that is faithful to the plain sense of Peirce and yet encourages us to rethink the way pragmatic philosophers have understood Peirce. The rabbinic or exegetical paradigm is especially apt, not only because Peirce describes pragmatism in scriptural and hermeneutical terms, but because it helps to show that such a pragmatism would encourage us to interpret 'a philosopher's thought according to a critically refined principle of his or her own thinking'.[278] Ochs imagines Peirce not as the great modern system-builder but as 'the philosophic healer' compassionately employing 'the tools of mathematical imagination and logical rigor to repair, or at least respond to, the various species of intellectual suffering that complement what Peirce called Cartesianism and others, more recently, call "modernism".'[279] When these same tools are turned back upon Peirce's own thought, the effect is not only a coherent view of his intellectual development but also a compelling hermeneutical theory that has practical implications for how we read a given system of signs (Ochs calls it a 'Method of Interpretation and Repair').

Professor Ochs goes into great technical detail to display Peirce's arguments and his pragmatic reading of them. These details are beyond the scope of this study. However, his comments on Peirce's understanding of communal forms of argumentation are important to observe because they establish a particular standard and method that Ochs himself follows. According to Ochs, Peirce recommended a realist method of 'multiform argumentation' along the model of the sciences, but in the spirit of scholasticism.[280] 'Multiform argumentation' means something like Lindbeck's 'rule theory', in that it entails following 'the laws of logic' that have been 'recommended to us by the *suppositio communis*'.[281] It entails an 'inherited wisdom and shared habits of reasoning' within a 'community of respected inquirers'.[282] In this sense, Ochs understands Peirce as philosophically preceding thinkers in the twentieth century who argued, against Cartesian 'foundationalism', that all our forms of reasoning are 'tradition-constituted.[283] This 'post-foundationalism', however, is non-relativistic. Unlike some forms of 'traditionalism', it looks towards the future, to the long-run of enquiry (understood teleologically and eschatologically) when the truth will be verified by a kind of consensus (that is, a patient, trusting, dialogical, non-reductive kind of communal verification over an indefinitely long-run of time). This 'model of the sciences' invites a kind of communitarian thesis to emerge, against the so-called modern tendency towards individualism, and enables Ochs to be genuinely concerned with truth-seeking, unlike some of his postmodern counterparts.

The overall thrust of his complicated and detailed discussion about multiform argumentation is to show that Peirce eschewed the individualistic implications of modern logic and called for a 'social principle' in logic. This calls for a shift in intellectual virtues. 'Postmodern' enquirers

> must replace the desire for individual certainty with the sentiments of 'charity' (care for the indefinite community and for its rules of inquiry), 'faith' (supreme trust in these rules) and 'hope' (expectation that the community will enact these rules indefinitely and, therefore, achieve its goal).[284]

To the Christian reader, Peirce's invocation of the theological virtues in a discussion of logic can hardly seem a casual affair, and Ochs makes it clear why we might read Peirce as a logician who at least has an implicit conversation with scripture and the Christian tradition running throughout his work. Theological virtues are also apt because what Peirce offers is a deeply ethical form of logic, even if he has sublimated its theological sources.

Ochs says (in a sentence that could have appeared in *The Nature of Doctrine*) that 'the logic of belief is a logic of action, while the logic of propositions serves only as a formal logic'.[285] Peirce is interested in the logic of belief, in 'a readiness to act in a certain way', because as he puts it, 'the logically good is simply a species of the morally good'.[286] If we are to attend to the 'pragmatic meaning of a conception', we will look to 'the sum total of its practical consequences for the long run of experience'.[287] This is true for other pragmatists too, but Peirce especially turns it in a logical, linguistic, semiotic direction, claiming that all thinking is in signs, and he understood that the meaning of human beliefs (concepts or doctrines) could be found in the rules or habits of action that such signs effect. For Peirce, valid hypotheses are those that propose logical ends of action.[288] The highest good for Peirce was in the 'concrete reasonableness' of mediating signs for actual behaviour.[289] Doctrines, Peirce might say to Lindbeck, are 'nothing but the deliberate preparedness to act according to the formula believed'.[290]

But if all thinking is done in signs, where do ideas come from? This is the very interesting question that helps turn phenomenological questions into theological ones. In Peirce's 'Neglected Argument for the Reality of God', and in numerous other places, he writes that '[abduction] is the source of all of our ideas'.[291] Abductive reasoning is where 'insights' into the 'the general elements of nature' come from, and they come through 'musement', through the imagination, through dialogue and a kind of meditative play (it is an abstract form of prayer). Logical ends can be evaluated inductively and explicated deductively, but they can only be proposed abductively.[292] This is why he can say that 'abduction is "the only logical operation which introduces any new ideas"'.[293] Another word for this is 'revelation', and this gets to the heart of what Ochs believes is 'the logic of Scripture'. Essential to understanding how this logic 'works', however, is an appreciation of a central feature of Peircean logic: the relationship between A-Reasonings and B-Reasonings. Whatever else may be said about the book, understanding this aspect of the logic is crucial for understanding the dialogue he hosts between rabbinic and Christian scriptural pragmatists.

The most felicitous way of displaying the 'logic' that informs the whole of the book, and especially the dialogue his work engenders between Jewish and Christian scriptural pragmatists, is to redescribe a dialogue between a 'textualist' and a 'philosopher' that Ochs hosts in an essay that was written '*for* George Lindbeck'. Observing this dialogue will help us to understand the logical dynamics of A- and B-Reasoning involved in his treatment of rabbinic and Christian forms of scriptural pragmatism.

### 3 A- and B-Reasonings: Peter Ochs and George Lindbeck in dialogue

In December 1993 Peter Ochs presented a paper, 'The Logic of Scripture, Philosophy's Role in Rabbinic Inquiry', at the Yale Jewish Studies Tribute to George Lindbeck. The essay appeared the next year in *Modern Theology*, the journal that had hosted some of the most intense debates over Lindbeck's work in the previous decade. The essay, with a new title 'Scriptural Logic: Diagrams for a Postcritical Metaphysics', was dedicated to Lindbeck, whom Ochs describes (building upon his earlier stress on the shared tendencies of Lindbeck and Jewish after-modern philosophers) as a postcritical 'textualist'. Ochs suggests that 'there is a mode of philosophic inquiry proper to the postcritical orientation', and implies that on the Christian side this philosophic tendency has not been as strong as the textualist tendency that Lindbeck has represented.[294] Further, Ochs suggests that the postcritical textualist (Lindbeck) and postcritical philosopher (Ochs) need each other, and that their exchanges can be 'diagrammed as a rule of reasoning'.[295] Ochs hosts such a dialogue, again using Charles Peirce as his philosophical muse and scripture as his text. In doing so, we get to the heart of issues that have concerned readers of Lindbeck.

Ostensibly this dialogue that Ochs shapes is between a 'textualist' and a 'philosopher', which we can take to mean a dialogue between Lindbeck and Ochs by considering the original context in which the paper was given (in tribute to Lindbeck) and the terminology used to describe the position of the textualist (shown below).

The 'textualist' questions the very notion of 'the possibility of dialogue' as 'putting the idea before the actuality' (which is suspected as some 'onto-theological' endeavour). The textualist worries that the philosopher wants to reduce the 'reading of Scripture to terms brought in from outside Scripture', and this is precisely what the textualist wants to avoid: extralinguistic models of scriptural theology.[296] We can assume that these are terms that describe George Lindbeck's position.

The 'philosopher' responds that *reading scripture, if it is to be a theologically significant activity, must be transformative* 'and transformative reading means reading by one for whom the scriptural word is not yet known in the way it will be known'.[297] That is, readers are themselves external to the text, and the scriptural word of that text has the power to transform them through a genuine engagement that is ripe with possibility. And further to the logic of this engagement: 'Scriptural inquiry finds its purpose in transformational consequences; to transform one's practice is to change according to some rule or standard of practice; and to display a rule of practice is to *diagram* it.'[298] And these diagrams 'always introduce terms from outside the practices they diagram'.[299] They inscribe 'revelation'. We can assume that these are terms that describe the position held by Peter Ochs.

The textualist might find the philosopher's argument acceptable at first glance because the practice is informed by the text, and so is therefore not truly 'external'. The textualist invokes the Wittgensteinian insight that the scriptures are like a language game capable of 'absorbing the world'.[300] But the philosopher replies,

> I do not ... believe that learning the Bible is just like learning a language ... that claim has heuristic value [in the context of Lindbeck's critique of extra-linguistic models of scriptural theology] ... [But] once, however, we have situated scriptural theology within the activity of reading scriptural language, *then* we need finer distinctions.[301]

The philosopher claims that skills of language learning and literacy are important but insufficient: 'It does not account for the *transformational* dimension of Bible learning [in which the Bible comes to the reader as much as the reader comes to the text] ...'[302] The particularity of the reader is located somewhere *outside* the text, and therefore the relationship between the Bible and the reader is a complex, mediated, dialogical and performative relationship, and this dialogical performance, this transformative 'dimension of Biblical language' is not reducible 'to the terms of a given grammar, because it brings some particular grammar into question'.[303]

In Ochs's imagined dialogue, the textualist replies that, just as this dimension of biblical language cannot be reduced to a given grammar, so it cannot be reduced to a given diagram. The textualist accuses the philosopher of wanting to be both a postmodernist and a modern foundationalist. The philosopher is accused of being 'postmodern' because he wants to 'interrupt scriptural reading on behalf of a reader outside the text' and 'modern foundationalist' because the philosopher 'intimates that the diagramming may offer us something *more* than grammar'.[304] This seems paradoxical to the textualist. The philosopher responds: 'You have found me out, indeed. I want to call the diagram a logic of scriptural reading.'[305] The 'incredulous' textualist thinks he understands the philosopher as agreeing to a return to 'foundational and onto-theological practices: to substitute some finite set of icons for the complex customs of a community of reading!'[306] At this point it seems the dialogue has turned into a metaphysical argument.

But the philosopher (let us now simply recognize him as 'Ochs') finally clarifies that this is not the case. Ochs insists that his project as a Jewish Peircean philosopher entails a non-foundationalist attention to a logic of repair:

> No, I am envisioning *a postcritical and thus non-foundationalist logic.* To do this, I begin with Charles Peirce's pragmatic and neo-scholastic understanding of 'logic' as, on one level, the *context-specific* standard of reasoning that is implicit in any activity of reasoning and, on a second level, the explicit standard of reasoning one adopts in order *to correct faulty reasoning* on the first level.[307]

These two (dialogical) levels of 'logic' Ochs labels *A-Reasoning and B-Reasoning* in his Peircean alternative to foundationalism. Ochs cites Peirce, who writes, '*You may recognize that your habits of reasoning are of two distinct kinds, producing two kinds of reasoning which we may call A-Reasonings and B-Reasonings.*'[308] The first level of reasoning is called a 'B-Reasoning' (in scriptural interpretation, Ochs will call it 'the plain sense'). B-Reasonings are as a rule very useful, teaching us a great deal, but they are frequently in error. When a person realizes that this reasoning is bad, a new standard for correction is needed – but for Peirce, this new standard does not exclude the old standard of reasoning, the new *redeems* the old. When a B-Reasoning is faulty, it means that it conflicts with our A-Reasonings, and A-Reasonings represent that second level of reasoning, reasonings which are rarely in error but which are inherently vague and hidden throughout our B-Reasonings and seem to do little to advance knowledge. Though our B-Reasonings are almost always in error, the 'A-Reasonings remain intact, as reliable if imperceptible standards for correcting B-Reasonings'.[309] A-Reasonings, in this sense, are a deeper logic which are only perceptible through the process of correcting the faulty logic of B-Reasonings.

All our B-Reasonings must be fallible. This faces squarely the reality that our reasoning does fail, without sacrificing our genuine need of a standard for how to go about correcting our failed reasonings. But here the textualist wonders how the philosopher can avoid the foundationalist reduction implicit in his appeal to A-Reasoning. Ochs the philosopher provides a critical answer derived from the same resource that Lindbeck the textualist insists must 'absorb the world'. His answer, in brief here and later at book-length, amounts to his rereading of Charles Peirce on the logic of scripture:

> I believe the answer is that [Peirce] *understood his process of diagramming itself – rather than any other depiction – to be a diagram of A-reasoning*. That is, he took the mathematician's activity as a paradigmatic moment of what the inquirer does when, in order to correct some faulty B-reasoning, she appeals to the A-reasoning that 'underlies it', so to speak ... in this way, otherwise hidden, indubitable rules of reasoning could be diagrammed.[310]

Ochs uses Peirce actually to repair rather than abandon modernist modes of reasoning, and thinks that *scriptural reading* is to serve *as* the A-Reasoning to repair modernist reasoning.[311] Therefore, Ochs argues that scriptural reading must be rediscovered as underlying modernist modes of reasoning and, as a result of this implicitly internal influence has the power and authority to correct it. This means bringing scripture to the world in order to repair the world; it is the claim that scriptural reading (or divine revelation itself) can actually alleviate the burdens of modernity.[312]

For Ochs, and Peirce, it is the 'interpreter' or the 'reader' who transforms what the 'scribe' of scripture has inscribed.[313] This Peircean convention diagrams 'the activity through which a revealer-God discloses ("scribes") words ("original graphs") to a prophet ("interpreter"), as well as the activity through which the prophet's words (as Scripture) discloses meanings to a community of interpreters'.[314] A further Peircean convention reads this 'graphed Scripture as a symbol of "*The Truth*, that is, of the widest Universe of Reality"'.[315] Scripture itself holds out for a non-foundationalism that does not give up on truth – that is to say, a dialogical, corrective and transformative reading of scripture which diagrams a reasoning of the widest possible significance ('universe of reality').

Such readings would disclose possible alternatives to failed B-Reasonings, and because the alternatives are informed by an ultimate truth, an A-Reasoning, the process itself would be understood as revelatory. This A-Reasoning could not be exhibited in any particular graph but is diagrammed by the activity of graphing itself. The failures of B-Reasonings stimulate other 'corrective' B-Reasonings. But there must be a limit case ('The Truth'), and the limit of any indefinite series of such failures stimulates what is no longer B-Reasoning but an ultimate or A-Reasoning. For Ochs, A-Reasoning would have a visible diagram in scripture, but the logic of A-Reasoning would be the logic of scripture. In other words, God's presence is revealed to us through 'processes of *corrective reasoning*' – that is to say that God's presence is '*made visible only in the B-Reasonings that* [a process of A-Reasoning] *generates*'.[316] That is to say that God's presence is revealed through the practice of scriptural interpretation that happens in-between A- and B-Reasonings.

This process of A-Reasoning, which Ochs calls the logic of scripture, Peirce called the process of musement (meditation, pure play). 'In sum, the process of musement brings the logician to a direct *perception* of the reality of God, and it is this perception that gives the logician reason, in the short run, to trust in the reliability of inquiries that will be tested only in the long run of experience.'[317] This logic which guides all scientific enquiry (according to Peirce), is really a scriptural logic according to Ochs. The actual process of logical reasoning points to a direct experience of God's reality. The reasoning process is itself a trace, or a sign or a *vestigium* of God's presence (and thus actually present in some sense).[318] Needed, however, is a third mediating reasoning, according to Ochs, which would link 'A-reasonings to particular B-reasonings'.[319] Ochs cannot say what this third reasoning is, but he can say what it does. It reveals, it is 'the art of revealing', and what it reveals is 'scripture'. It is, literally, a *'theo-logic'*:

> God would be revealed to the postcritical philosopher by way of an activity of diagramming, and the logic of this activity would be the logic of vagueness, the logic of dialogue, [and] the logic of pragmatism ... would appear as the logic of problem-solving – the logic of 'science', but with an expansive understanding of 'science'. This means that the logic of problem-solving would be a theo-logic: a rule for reasoning that emerges from a direct perception of the reality of God.[320]

For Peter Ochs, the postcritical philosopher, theology matters. That is to say that God matters, and matters to the way we reason, the way we think, the way we read and reread, make mistakes and correct them. God is intimately bound up with all the processes of reasoning that might be easily taken as having nothing to do with God. The link that Peter Ochs makes here is that our processes of reasoning can find the source of their redemption in the communal reading of scripture.

My brief summary of this essay only displays some of the conversation between what may well have been a real conversation between Lindbeck and Ochs. But it should be apparent, even given the limits of my redescription, that the conversation is also intended to point out that the postcritical philosopher is seeking to give the postcritical textualist a transcendent standard of correction that enables a fuller engagement between scripture and the world it might 'absorb'. It deals with the real implications of a God who reveals, and reveals himself, through the mediating logic of scripture.

The dialogue highlights Lindbeck's need to relate his pragmatic theory of truth to the logic of scripture. Ochs's understanding of A- and B-Reasonings puts corrective pressure on Lindbeck to develop his scriptural pragmatism in precisely this direction. For example, in an Ochsian understanding, the scriptural pragmatist would test first the general plausibility of a corrective supposition, assessing whether or not it respects the plain sense of a problematic reasoning and whether 'some finite community of plain-sense readers' can confirm this respect for the plain sense.[321] Second, general plausibility would give way to particular validity: 'the supposition is not only plausible but also valid for some representative member of such a finite community ... it is pragmatically warranted by the community if it is plausible and valid for one of its members'.[322] Third, and finally, the proof of the supposition is shown in whether or not 'it actually works by stimulating changes in practice that remove a given problem'.[323] The third proof cannot, of course, be conclusive proof; it can only claim degrees of success (relative strength) 'within and among certain communities'.[324] In this sense, then, the proofs of pragmatism 'complement a pluralistic but non-relativistic notion of truth'.[325] This is the kind of theory of truth appropriate to Lindbeck's scriptural pragmatism, for it is a theory of truth that is capable of transforming practices through faithfulness to the logic of scripture.

This A-Reasoning and B-Reasoning relates to the two interpretive tendencies of Peircean thought, pragmaticism and pragmatism, and the two interpretive tendencies of rabbinic thought, the *derash* and *peshat*, or what in Christian communities might be called the 'rule of love' and 'rule of faith' (these two tendencies are ordered but are also co-inherent in trinitarian terms). What these tendencies indicate is a concern for a standard of correction, for repair, that is grounded in God. In Peirce's 'Neglected Argument for the Reality of God', his reference to God is shaped 'by way of some history- and story-shaped vocabularies', and those communities which are shaped by both scriptural and pragmatic vocabularies will be able to display a dialogue that Peirce himself did not achieve.[326] Therefore Peircean philosophers may not follow Peirce as far as such theological claims, but 'scriptural pragmatists' will do so. Such 'scriptural pragmatists' are theosemioticians who are communally gathered and 'envision inter-communal dialogue across linguistic borders, but not independently of them'.[327]

## *Rule of faith and rule of love (compassion)*

Ochs is guided by a number of hypotheses about Peirce, but at this point in his argument he turns directly to consider that concrete communities of such 'scriptural pragmatists' will be an exposition of what he calls 'Peirce's pragmatic rule'. In an important exposition of one of these hypotheses, Ochs writes that

> Peirce's pragmatic rule diagrams both a Scriptural rule of compassion and a Scriptural rule of faith. The rule of faith is that, for the sufferer who is also a member of the community of scriptural readers, suffering is itself a vague sign that one's redeemer is at hand: a human care-giver for finite sufferings, and a divine Redeemer for infinite ones ... The rule of compassion is that, for the scriptural reader who observes suffering, this suffering is a determinate sign that the reader must become redeemer and help the sufferer.[328]

We are interested, then, in how specific 'communities of scriptural philosophers' actually follow these scriptural rules of faith and compassion. The two groups of scriptural pragmatists that Ochs turns to are Jewish and Christian sources for this exposition of his argument as a whole. The interest of this thesis is to enquire as to the degree that they can help enrich our study of Lindbeck.

In the remainder of this chapter I will explore the relationship between these concrete communities that Ochs identifies as 'rabbinic pragmatism' and 'Christian pragmatism' in his conclusion to *Peirce, Pragmatism and the Logic of Scripture*. I describe each in turn, before describing how Ochs believes Jews and Christians need each other. But again, the purpose is to show how Lindbeck needs Ochs and, more implicitly, how both thinkers need Augustine.

### 4 Rabbinic pragmatism

Ochs identifies four moments in twentieth-century 'rabbinic pragmatism'. The first three of these moments are well represented by '[t]he German-Jewish philosophers Hermann Cohen, Martin Buber and Franz Rosenzweig [who] introduced a critique and extension of Kant's transcendental philosophy that appears, in the context of this book, like the foundations of a rabbinic semiotics'.[329] Ochs calls these 'the pragmatic moment', 'the phenomenological moment' and 'the dialogic moment'. These three moments, all represented by German-Jewish thinkers, collectively display a theory of redemptive knowledge. The fourth moment is represented by Peter Ochs's former teacher

Max Kadushin. Ochs labels this 'the pragmaticist moment', and it complements a theory of redemptive knowledge with a text-based, semiotic approach to reasoning.

### The pragmatic moment in rabbinic semiotics

The first of these figures, Hermann Cohen (1842–1918), advocated a 'prophetic Kantianism' according to Ochs and initiates 'the pragmatic moment' in rabbinic semiotics. Founder of the Marburg school of Kantian philosophy, Cohen declared that 'philosophy understands itself to be ethics'.[330] He claimed that while Platonic thought provides philosophy with epistemology, the Hebrew prophets provide philosophy with its *raison d'être*, to encounter humanity in its suffering and end this suffering. Here compassion is the rule, the force that guides and directs an entire world-view. Cohen believed that 'rabbinic semiotics' could enrich and extend the Cartesianism and Kantianism to its biblical and prophetic roots. Cohen responds to Cartesianism, for example, on semiotic grounds:

> a sign of real problems is a call for help, which is, first, a call for someone to hear that someone is suffering. It is, second, a call for someone to examine the context of the call and figure out what is really the matter. It is, third, a call for someone to do something to resolve the matter and alleviate suffering.[331]

This signifies for Ochs the first formal moment of rabbinic semiotics as the pragmatic (and prophetic) moment, which 'reads the claims of Cartesian inquiry as a sign of as yet unidentified, real problems'.[332] This means that another reader (or community of readers) is required besides the one who 'calls for help' and the one who 'hears' and 'examines' that suffering.

### The phenomenological moment in rabbinic semiotics

Ochs interprets Martin Buber's 'transcendental biblicism' as 'a loving critique' of Cohen. Buber agreed with Cohen in his compassionate response to suffering, but saw that Cohen had failed to note the relation 'between a tradition and the one who suffers'.[333] In his famous work, *I and Thou*, Buber worried that Cohen had wrongly followed Kant in his tendency to construct 'the last home for the God of the philosophers'.[334] By 'identifying God with an idea of reason' Buber worried that Cohen's system lacked the 'love of God' he thought was central to personal relation with God. Buber's solution was in this priority of the divine relation. He did not ask Cohen to abandon reason but to take up much more thoroughly and systematically 'the *a priori* of relation'. That is, 'to discover that reasoning about ethics is reasoning about relations and that we reason, in the first place, *from* concrete relations'.[335] These concrete relations are 'engendered by language', that is they can be diagrammed with words, with symbols or signs (semiotics). Furthermore, there are 'elemental relations' which 'give meaning to reasoning' – what Buber calls 'the primary words', the elemental relations of 'I–Thou' and 'I–It.' This second phenomenological moment of rabbinic semiotics, which transforms 'definite' symbols into 'indefinite' ones, is precisely what the prophets did, paradigmatically recorded in the scriptures. It opens up the ability to hear suffering at a deeper, more particular level. To make the correlation to the Cartesian–Kantian project this would mean 'transforming propositions of a Cartesian–Kantian ethics into the particular propositions of a prophetic transcendentalism'.[336] As Ochs puts it: 'the Cartesian–Kantian logician would have to conjoin a determinate and a universal proposition: "This person is suffering", and "I feel moved to (or I ought to) care for people who suffer."'[337] In Buber's terms, there are clearly two involved, yet no way of accounting for their relationship. Buber would want the logic, as in Peirce's logic of relations, to involve a third, vague symbol that 'joins event and response: "This is an occasion that 'moves-me-to-care-for-the-suffering-I-see'."'[338] This triunity shows in itself 'the mystery of how the virtue of compassion may be learned'.[339] Ochs's point is to show that both the logic of relations we find in Peirce and the logic we find in Buber's turn to the biblical prophets is a biblical logic. Ochs takes this as an opportunity to ask a critical question: 'If Buber answers that the virtue is already available in biblical discourse, we are left with the question: how does biblical discourse enter into the practice of individual members of the tradition of western philosophic discourse?'[340] Ochs finds the answer to this question displayed in the complementary work of Franz Rosenzweig and Max Kadushin.

## The dialogical moment in rabbinic semiotics

In this turn from Cohen to Buber and now Rosenzweig, Ochs is calling attention to the twentieth-century Jewish 'return to scripture'. But it is Rosenzweig who 'serves for many Jewish thinkers today as a paradigm of *teshuvah*, or of "return"'.[341] A student of Cohen and friend of Buber's, Rosenzweig offered a 'transcendental rabbinicism'

in his book *The Star of Redemption*, which attempts a Jewish transformation of Hegelian thought in conversation with the whole Western
tradition (ancient, medieval and modern). Idealism had sought to
redescribe the world in such a way as to 'repair suffering on the spot',
but instead it denied the 'fear of death', the fear of what is singular, of
the philosopher's own death. For Rosenzweig, philosophy denies these
fears and so is not able to deal with real suffering. Citing the Song of
Songs, Rosenzweig proposed in *The Star* that 'love is as strong as
death'; rather than denying the 'singularity of suffering', it actually
redeems it on the terms 'that suffering itself delivers', and delivers
through the revelation of love. As Ochs puts it:

> God's love ... is an act, not an idea. It is an act of reawakening a relationship that
> was concealed by suffering, rather than of predicating something new of the sufferer.
> The primary act of the lover is simply to call for love itself, to say 'Love me!' and,
> through the imperative voice of this call, to elicit a reciprocal act by the beloved: an
> admission of love.[342]

Following Robert Gibbs, Ochs calls this Rosenzweigian admission of
love a 'confession' that is both 'liberating and painful'. This confession
of love 'is itself the process of atonement', overcoming the 'illusion of
completeness without love, in the presence of my lover's demand to
love'.[343] Ochs sees this confession of love as itself the pragmatic transformation of Cartesian–Kantian philosophy. He writes that this
confession alone 'replaces Cartesian anxiety with the expectation of
help and thus with a demand for change'.[344] The Cartesian 'I', the *ego
cogito*, gives way to the discovery of a 'new' I. This new 'I' is not alone,
but stands unhappily within a community, a tradition of reasoning
which is burdened by particular, finite problems. The solitary thinking
self is no longer understood as solitary but as dialogical in response to
the suffering of the 'other'.

The Rosenzweigian point, in Peircean terms, is that

> the other's love ... is such a symbol, whose intrusion of the I may, if it is received (and
> this receptivity is as contingent as grace) stimulate a process of redemptive inter-
> pretation, a reparative semiosis. The engine of this semiosis is a dialogue between
> the other's love (as symbol) and the I (as interpretant). As the I is transformed
> through this dialogue, so is the meaning of love transformed with respect to it.[345]

This means that the tradition, the community of interpretation in
which one suffers, becomes both the source of the complaint and the
resource for repair. Ochs writes 'to repair tradition is "the common
labor" of such an assembly, and dialogue is the engine of repair ... for

the individual in community, love is a symbol of reparative work'.[346] Everyday Jewish life, according to Rosenzweig, is 'infused with [this] law of love', which calls for a return to the community, and to 'works of love' that repair the world (*tikkun olam*).

For Ochs, Rosenzweig represents a 'third formal moment' in rabbinic semiotics. 'In Rosenzweig's terms, the logical thinking of the community of western philosophers is thereby transformed into "speech thinking" (*Sprachdenken*), whose rules are displayed in the "grammar" of reparative dialogue, rather than in the a priori categories of a universal canon.'[347] This is the grammar of a dialogue between 'a philosophic sufferer' and 'a rabbinic redeemer'. The redemption comes from within the tradition because, as Rosenzweig shows, the philosophical idealists are 'Jews or Christians who have forgotten that the tradition they are reforming is not "philosophy" (which is not a tradition but an event within tradition), but Judaism or Christianity'.[348] The philosophic sufferer and the rabbinic redeemer are, however, interdependent. The rabbinic redeemer serves to remind the philosopher of her place in the communal tradition, and the philosopher reminds the rabbinic redeemer that there is suffering in the community. This third moment, which 'appears like the foundation of rabbinic semiotics', is crucial for Ochs's project. It establishes one of his most basic hypotheses that the resources for repairing modernity are accessible to us in the logic of scripture, and it shows that this logic is dialogical. But while the German-Jewish aspect (Cohen, Buber, Rosenzweig) of rabbinic semiotics provides crucial categories, Ochs claims that they are incomplete in themselves.

### The pragmaticist moment in rabbinic semiotics

Max Kadushin, Ochs's teacher at the Jewish Theological Seminary in New York, was searching for a way beyond Orthodox Judaism's resistance to reform. Well aware of Rosenzweig's rules for reform in 'speech thinking', Kadushin studied the logic of rabbinic discourse, and called this rabbinic logic 'organic thinking'. Kadushin believed that midrashic discourse (rabbinic literature of the Talmudic period) inscribes everyday judgments about Jewish communal life and conduct that are 'performative implications of Scriptural discourse for life in some Jewish community ... the Scriptural texts function as vague symbols that acquire definition only in their performative interpretations'.[349] Every textual interpretation is, then, 'occasioned by some failing' in the Jewish communal life and conduct, and recommends repairing those failures by reforming an interpretive aspect of the tradition. Ochs argues, as I do in relation to Lindbeck, that Kadushin's work would be better served if it were restated in the terms of Peircean scriptural pragmaticism. And while, like Lindbeck, Kadushin 'eschewed semiotic and pragmatic vocabularies', it is worth citing Ochs's redescription of Kadushin's method of repair in full:

> [Kadushin's] method of repair is, in its first moment, to reassert the authority of Scripture – Torah – as the source of all rules of repair. The second moment is to reassert the privileged function of rabbinic literature (the Mishnah, Talmuds and midrash) as a prototypical interpretation of Scripture. The Third and definitive moment is to identify the specific rules of repair that are displayed in the rabbinic literature *and* that will contribute successfully to repairing the present failing. These rules are usually diagrammed by a collection of rabbinic value terms, each of which refers to a particular rabbinic 'value-concept' or virtue. The fourth moment is to substitute the rabbinic value-concepts for whatever existing value-concepts have, in the interpreter's opinion, inadequately served the contemporary community.[350]

In this sense, Kadushin was looking for a logic of repair that was indigenous to rabbinic rationality, and discovered it in the prototypical interpretations of scripture. But Ochs seeks to correct and diagram Kadushin's work, and in doing so provides readers with, when taken together with the German-Jewish philosophers, a new account of rabbinic semiotics, or what Ochs calls 'rabbinic pragmatism' that both informs and is informed by his work on Peirce.

As the rabbinic pragmatist most akin to Lindbeck, Kadushin sought to uncover the 'grammar' of rabbinic theology, and to do so through concrete occasions of scriptural exegesis. Through these exegetical studies he diagrammed the 'value concepts', those cognitive concepts that function as rabbinic norms (e.g. God's justice, mercy, loving kindness, spoken word). For Ochs, the grammatical nature of rabbinic theology means, in Kadushin's organicist terms, that 'the logic of rabbinic thinking is displayed in the ways these concepts relate to one another and in the way each one of them exhibits its "drive to concretization": what we would call its pragmatic force'.[351] Kadushin, however, erred in his foundationalist tendency to interpret these findings 'ahistorically', treating the value-concepts as if they were context-free 'essences'. What Ochs proposes is that this errant tendency, which he likens to errant tendencies of Peirce's early pragmatism, can be helped by the pragmaticist corrective to which Peirce subjected his own pragmatism. This pragmaticist corrective would clarify 'the mediating, pragmatic rule that remains vague in his work', and in turn could then be reapplied 'as norm for correcting his writings'.[352] This leads Ochs to suggest that the fourth, formal moment in rabbinic semiotics should be understood as the pragmaticist moment. And this is where Peircean A- and B-Reasonings highlighted above are particularly instructive. Here, the pragmaticist rabbinic semiotician, in response to suffering, 'reconceives the community's practices as two-tiered pairs of rules'.[353] On one tier are the problematic B-Reasonings, which are those failed responses to particular needs. On the second tier are paradigmatic instances, or diagrams of A-Reasonings, which are pragmatically redemptive rules for reforming problematic B-Reasonings by bringing them into dialogic relation with the sufferer in question. As Ochs describes this, 'the redemptive rules are symbolized by words of Scripture, interpreted, by way of rabbinic midrash, as "I–Thou" words or indefinite symbols. To reform current practices according to these rules is also, in some finite way, to reform traditional readings of Scripture'.[354] This Kadushin-inspired moment is clearly the culminating point of Ochs's analysis of the way Peircean and rabbinic pragmatism correlate and complement one another.

### Rabbinic semiotics and the rule of love

The four moments of rabbinic semiotics – the pragmatic, the phenomenological, the dialogical and the pragmaticist – work towards a method of repair and renewal that unites a number of influential Jewish thinkers in the late nineteenth and twentieth centuries in a complementary project. Ochs wants to see the German-Jewish tendencies and the American-Jewish tendency of Kadushin as mutual complements that produce a genuinely 'rabbinic pragmatism', bringing a text-based semiotic approach to reasoning together with the German-Jewish philosophers' theory of redemptive knowledge. In search of redemptive norms that could guide their responses to philosophical suffering, Ochs understands that the German-Jewish philosophers and the American-Jewish textualists need each other. He reads these two, informed by his study of Peirce, as two complementary aspects of 'the community's pragmatic rule: a dialogue of "diagrammatic" Jewish philosophy and "corrective" rabbinic pragmatism'.[355]

But rather than leave his synthesis prone to abstraction, he identifies 'the Society for Textual Reasoning' as a real, present-day, 'flesh-and-blood community' of both Jewish philosophy and rabbinic studies whose practices actually exemplify this third kind of complementary option. For this contemporary community of Jewish (and some Christian) scholars, pragmatic reasonings are rooted 'in a relationship with God, whose attributes of mercy and justice are graphed in

Scripture, as interpreted in the classic rabbinic literature'.[356] These two attributes of God, mercy and justice, complement the two rules of pragmatic reasoning (the rule of pragmatism and the rule of pragmaticism). The first rule 'guides compassionate responses to suffering', where God's justice serves as a 'divine No!' to problematic vocabularies, and God's mercy serves as a 'divine Yes!' that reshapes vocabularies to respond more adequately to the real sufferer. The second rule, the pragmaticist one, serves only to correct 'any inadequate responses to suffering by explicating the Rule of Pragmatism that should guide them'.[357] Citing rabbinic midrash on Exodus 2.23–25, where the Israelites cry for help, God hears their cry, remembers his covenant with Abraham and is moved to respond to their suffering, Ochs suggests that there is a triadic semiotic of divine love in this context and mode of God's compassion for Israel:

> In semiotic terms, divine compassion appears as the *interpretant* for which Israel's suffering is a *sign* whose redemptive *meaning* is God's-being-moved-to-care-for-this-suffering ... If the biblical reader comes to expect that cries like this will elicit divine responses like this, then the reader's expectations will display three irreducible elements: an indicative utterance, a response, and the rule of compassion that relates the one to the other.[358]

Ochs sees in particular places, such as in the case of widows and orphans (Ex. 22.21–22), or in the case of strangers (Ex. 23.9), or in the imperative to love your neighbour as yourself (Lev. 19.18), that this indefinite 'rule of love' issues signs to 'those who would imitate' the semiotics of divine compassion, entailing the need to be-moved-to-care-for-the suffering-of-another.[359] Therefore he suggests that the rule of love can be diagrammed indefinitely as 'being-moved-to-readiness-to-care-in-whatever-way-might-be-indicated', whereas the rule of compassion 'appears to specify the context and mode of care'.[360]

The indefinite rule of love and its more context-specific 'token', the rule of compassion', illustrates a corrective, triadic semiotics: 'something is a sign (an index) to someone (an agent-interpretant) of a need to respond in a caring or loving way'.[361] But this is a dialogue between Jewish philosophy and Peircean semiotics, and the implications of Ochs's findings move in both directions at once. Some reviewers have accused him of misusing Peirce to authorize rabbinic semiotics, or worse, to have forced rabbinic semiotics into a Peircean mould.[362] But such criticisms miss the dialogical dynamic between the two. It is true that 'Peirce's semiotics contribute a diagrammatic form to this scriptural reading', but it is equally true that 'the scriptural rule of compassion contributes' to the corrective character of Peircean semiotics. Peirce helps rabbinic semiotics to be more self-reflexive about the logic of scripture, but the scriptural logic of love helps Peircean corrective semiotics become a rule of compassion in which a sign elicits 'a caring response from the agent-interpreter'.[363]

### David Weiss Halivni and the Ezra-story

A concrete example of how the logic works in relation to the Society of Textual Reasoning can be displayed in Peter Ochs's comments on David Weiss Halivni, a well-known Talmud scholar whose work supports an Ochsian account of rabbinic pragmatism. In *Revelation Restored*, Halivni argues that the school of Ezra and his scribes received a maculate Torah that had been compiled, redacted and woven into a canonical fabric (in the fifth century BCE). The work of Ezra and his scribes involved the restoration of this revelation to the repentant nation of Israel who longed, after the Babylonian exile, 'to return to the Torah of Moses'.[364] But Ezra and company did not do this by changing the written words of this Torah. They preserved what they received (written Torah), even where passages conflicted or seemed suspect, because the Pentateuchal text was for them inviolable, it reflected the holiness of this revelation to Moses at Sinai. Ezra instituted uniform and coherent practices in the tradition which enabled exegetical work on the Pentateuchal text to be an unending restoration of what was revealed at Sinai (Torah). As Halivni concludes:

> the covenant of Sinai was realized by means of Ezra's canonical Torah; thus Ezra's canon received retroactively a Sinaitic imprimatur. The destiny of the nation began in earnest, and our canonical Torah was born, etched in inviolable holiness – not by fire on tablets of stone, but by faith upon human hearts.[365]

Israel received a maculate Torah, replete with all the difficulties critical scholarship points out today – 'nevertheless, this text, with all its problems, is evidently the selfsame Torah that was placed before the people of Israel upon their return from exile ... the written word served as the concrete symbol of revelation – perfect, awe-inspiring, and beyond reproach'.[366]

Ochs comments explicitly on Rabbi Halivni's method, which he calls 'pragmatic historiography', in the book *Textual Reasonings: Jewish Philosophy and Text Study at the End of the Twentieth Century*.[367] Halivni is responding to modern, historical-critical hermeneutics and offers Talmudic scholarship another, deeper level of historiography that can do justice to the role that the historian plays in the writing of history. On Ochs's description of Halivni, his work promotes 'two levels of historiographic research'.[368] The first is the 'plain-sense historiography' while the second is 'what we may call "pragmatic historiography"'.[369] As with Ochs's own Peircean concerns about A- and B-Reasonings, as well as his rabbinic textual concerns about the *peshat* and the *derash*, and his theory of redemptive knowledge, these two levels of historiography belong together in a co-inherent way.[370] 'Pragmatic historiography' can never contradict the plain sense (following the rabbinic dictum 'the text must not be led outside the bounds of its plain sense').[371] Pragmatic historiography may respond to the suffering or burden of the plain sense, but the pragmatic repair it performs must not contradict the plain sense. Halivni provides readers with not only a sense of how the plain sense and the interpreted sense are interrelated, but also how this respect for the plain sense always already entails respect for the needs of a concrete community. Put differently, there is simultaneity between the demands that the texts make upon readers (*peshat*, 'plain-sense historiography') and the questions that readers bring to the texts (*derash*, 'pragmatic historiography').[372]

In reflecting on what the oral Torah means (in relation to the written Torah), Ochs highlights the debates between rabbinic scholars that it is either a 'second revelation from Sinai that complements the written Torah, or the rabbis' strictly human activity of interpreting the written Torah and transmitting that interpretation to subsequent generations'.[373] Or, Ochs adds a third option: it might be 'something in-between' these two options. If it were something 'in-between', then this 'would refer to there being both a divine or revealed and a human and fallible dimension of the non-written Torah'.[374] This third way is clearly how Ochs understands Halivni's position, and in Christian terms it begins to sound logically similar to the sacramental or incarnational understanding of scripture that I argued was central to an Augustinian scriptural pragmatism in the previous chapter. The Augustinian lines implicit in Peircean semiotics might already inscribe a theological understanding of redemptive mediation, and so here it may not be surprising that Ochs believes that Jewish and Christian understandings of scripture can be seen as complementary in Peircean logic.

## 5 Christian scriptural pragmatism

Ochs has shown his own interest in the complementarity of diverse Jewish thinkers as parts of a whole family resemblance to the scriptural logic of divine compassion (rule of love) that complements the Peircean rule of pragmatism. But as suggested above, this interest in family resemblances extends, according to such a rule of compassion, to Christian thinkers as well. Ochs believes that particular Christian pragmatists further complement the rabbinic pragmatists he has identified. He calls these Christian pragmatists 'postcritical theologians', but they are known better by Lindbeck's term 'postliberal'. Principally, Ochs names George Lindbeck and Hans Frei as his Christian pragmatists.

After acknowledging some of the impetus for postliberalism in Barthian theology, Wittgensteinian philosophy of language use and anthropological linguistics, Ochs offers the thesis that helped to generate this present study: postliberalism, like rabbinic semiotics, displays the rule of pragmatism. Ochs offers an excellent analysis of Frei's seminal work, *The Eclipse of Biblical Narrative*, and its critique of 'mediating theology' (which, in effect, does not mediate between orthodoxy and naturalism in the way it hopes because it merely reinscribes the semiotics of Cartesian binaries, lacking the postcritical, triadic semiotics of scriptural pragmatism); however we will forgo attending to Frei despite the dividends it would pay. Our central concern is with Ochs's response to Lindbeck and to Lindbeck's readers. Ochs describes the 'postcritical theology' of George Lindbeck as a recommendation for certain changes to be made in Christian theology today. He writes that when students of postcritical theologians such as Lindbeck 'recommend and evaluate such changes, these students make use of some logic of theology (or, more generally, some Christian philosophic theology)'.[375] Ochs sees Lindbeck providing theologians with logical tools for repair and reformation:

> When placed in the service of particular Christian beliefs and applied to the problem of Christian religious practice today, these changes may stimulate certain ministers-*cum*-postcritical theoreticians to repair their ministries in certain concrete ways. When they legislate and evaluate such repairs, these practitioner-theorists make use of some pragmatic logic of applied theology (or, more generally, some philosophy of Christian practice).[376]

Lindbeck introduced 'a method for transforming the contrary poles of mediating theology into the complementary aspects of postcritical scriptural interpretation'.[377] And from the outset of Ochs's description of the book, we are already rereading Lindbeck in triadic terms, in a way which does justice to the book Lindbeck wrote but casts new light on the ways Lindbeck has been read. In this reading, Lindbeck's cognitive-propositionalists and experiential-expressivists are not the contrary poles of mediating theology; they are transformed into 'complementary aspects' of his third, 'cultural-linguistic' whole that can better respond to the suffering of a divided church. The traditionalists (propositionalists), who read 'church doctrines as "truth claims about objective realities" and Scriptures as referential signs of those claims', and the liberals (experiential-expressivists), 'for whom religious knowledge gives expression to "common core experiences" that are available to all humans at all times', actually complement one another through mutual, corrective semiotics (they need each other if they want to respond to the particular ecumenical imperative that Lindbeck's work issues). This is a clarification of Lindbeck's argument, one that already begins to displace a number of the problems that emerged in the interpretive tendencies of his readers (see Introduction). The traditionalists are unable to account for doctrinal change as effectively as the liberals, but liberals are unable to account for the 'power of doctrines to authorize and sustain communal discourse' as effectively as the traditionalists.[378] As Ochs understands the logic of Lindbeck's argument, these issues of truth and change are the ones at stake, and they are precisely the issues that emerged in many responses to the book.

Ochs understands that the cultural-linguistic 'third' Lindbeck issued understood religion in semiotic terms. It understood religion as a 'common sense', 'at once ... a determinate code in which beliefs, ritual and behavior patterns, ethos as well as narrative, come together as a common semiotic system, and also as the community which is that system in use'.[379] Ochs highlights the inherent assumptions here, 'that a religion may be understood as a system of signs ... [and] that such signs display their meaning in the way they inform behavior in the community of sign users'.[380] He takes Lindbeck's emphasis upon the 'semiotic universe paradigmatically encoded in holy writ' seriously. In this postliberal pragmatism, scripture is the 'paradigmatic graph' or the 'semiotic code' which is

> defined only through indefinite series of conditional resolutions to act. For the Christian community, the Bible is thus not a sign of some external reality, but a reality itself whose meanings display the doubly dialogic relationships between a particular text and its context within the Bible as a whole, and between the Bible as a whole and the conduct of the community of interpreters.[381]

The triadic semiotics of scriptural pragmatism, 'the narrative meaning is the meaning *of* the text *for* its community of readers', is consistent with Lindbeck's postliberal approach to religion and theology, and helps deal more adequately with the central issues of truth and change already identified.[382]

Ochs understands that the Christian pragmatist will need to have recourse to the whole 'continuum of beliefs' that links theory and practice both within and without the social order of Christian common sense. And while Lindbeck is first committed to the 'within' of the Christian community, he is also committed by extension to conversations between members of various religions who could make 'grammatical remarks to each other about living, believing, and ritually enacting what their religion is about'.[383] The postcritical theologian will, then, use any type of belief that is apropos the 'type of problem that the practice must repair'.[384] That is, in Peircean terms, there is a corresponding 'A-Reasoning' that has the appropriate 'depth' to correct a particular series of failed 'B-Reasonings'. Ochs has redescribed Lindbeck as a Christian pragmatist who seeks to repair Christian theology and wishes to enrich Lindbeck's logic of repair by placing him in conversation with both rabbinic and Peircean pragmatists (and thus enacting a feature inherent in Lindbeck's own argument). It is not because Ochs wants unnaturally to turn Lindbeck into a pragmatist (either rabbinic or Peircean) that he hosts this conversation, but it is because Ochs sees pragmatism (with Peirce) as simply a logical explication of Jesus's words 'ye may know them by their fruit', and therefore as a grammatical remark that makes sense within the social order of Christian common sense. What Ochs sees at work in Lindbeck, analogues aside, is a Christian scriptural pragmatism that is aimed at the reformation and repair of Christian theology, enabling modern theologians to reclaim their proper function as biblical reasoners and practitioners of a faith that is theoretically and practically redemptive in the church and the world.

Lindbeck's rule-theory of doctrine, Ochs concludes, is thus 'served by a pragmatic theory of truth'.[385] Doctrines are understood as rules because they have pragmatic force 'beyond any specific context' and yet 'display their meaning propositionally with respect to specific contexts of practice, which are specific ways of describing the world and how to act in it'.[386] Traditionalists might understand that the truth of a proposition (such as 'the dead are raised') 'corresponds to some objective order of things', whereas liberals would either deny the helpfulness of making expressions an issue of truth or falsity, or would stress the 'identifiable quality or feeling' of such expressions. According to Ochs, Lindbeck's rule-theory requires a pragmatic theory of truth that is capable of 'distinguishing among three categories of truth-terms'.[387]

As stated above (in section 3), there are three levels of pragmatic truth that Ochs identifies: (1) *plausibility*; (2) *validity*; and (3) *strength*. A scriptural pragmatist such as Lindbeck would test first the general plausibility of a corrective supposition (say, some doctrinal reconciliation), assessing whether or not it respects the plain sense of a problematic reasoning, and whether 'some finite community of plain-sense readers' can confirm this respect for the plain sense (no doctrinal change in the plain sense).[388] Second, general plausibility would give way to particular validity: 'the supposition is not only plausible but also *valid* for *some* representative member of such a finite community … it is pragmatically warranted by the community if it is plausible and valid for one of its members'.[389] Third, and finally, the proof of the supposition is shown in whether or not 'it actually *works* by stimulating changes in practice that remove a given problem'.[390] The third proof cannot, of course, be conclusive proof, but can only claim degrees of success (relative strength) 'within and among certain communities'.[391]

This is precisely how Ochs thinks that the logic of Lindbeck's ecumenical and interreligious argument works, and therefore he seeks to show how well it is served by this pragmatic theory of truth. For example, in Lindbeck's 'third' way:

> … A specific *reading* of the rule [doctrine], 'the dead are raised', is *plausible* (has truth$_1$) if it respects the plain sense of Scripture and is *valid* for some finite Church community. This reading is *valid* (has truth$_2$) if it diagrams a community's indubitable beliefs in a way that would correct any problems in [the] plain sense of a given set of scriptural texts and, thus, in the communal behaviors appropriate to the plain sense. It is *strong* (has truth$_3$) if it in fact significantly transforms a community's plain-sense readings and its corresponding behaviors.[392]

In this sense, then, the community provides pragmatic 'proof' for both the plain sense of its doctrines and its ability to correct problems that arise in the communal behaviors that are appropriate to the plain sense (and this significantly helps to explain the phenomena that Lindbeck observed at Vatican II: doctrinal reconciliation without doctrinal change). Ochs believes that this approach complements 'a pluralistic but non-relativistic notion of truth'.[393] Such a proof involves precisely the pragmatic notion of truth that Ochs finds in Lindbeck's thought. Ochs helps us enrich Lindbeck's terms in such a way as to remove the obstacle of relativism that has encouraged at least one set of problematic readings of Lindbeck to arise in the interpretive community. It is non-relativistic because there are general standards for plain-sense reading, and especially so in the case of 'theosemioticians' because the community links these 'elemental rules' for reading to the creator God. For the theosemiotician, 'pragmatic logic ultimately serves some set of indubitable beliefs' because the inquiry is based on faith in God.[394] It is pragmatic because 'the strength of our corrections will be measured by their capacity to predict how this community actually solves these problems'.[395] Indeed, 'ye may know them by their fruit' is paradigmatic of this rule of corrective reading.

This is theologically significant. In Augustine we saw that 'the elemental rules of a social order' that Ochs identifies as linked to the activity of a creator God[396] are specifically guided, in Christian terms, by the incarnational activity of a triune God. Bringing Augustine and Lindbeck into conversation with Ochs helps us to see that linking the everyday practices to the elemental rules of scriptural reading is another way of speaking about the integration of theory and practice, and such a linkage provides the validation for context-specific performances of Christian communities reading the rule, 'the Word became flesh and lived among us' (Jn 1.14). It places the economy of salvation in semiotic terms and allows for a dynamic of transformation to emerge out of scriptural reading.[397]

It is crucial to pay close attention to the way Ochs has described the logic that readers of Lindbeck might follow. As Ochs describes it, readers of Lindbeck might repair real problems in Christian doctrine and religious practice using a pragmatic logic derived from the reading of scripture and the elemental rules of a social order semiotically encoded there. This is the logic we found implicit in Lindbeck, but not always in his readers. It is the logic we identified in the classic hermeneutic of Augustine. And it is the logic we find at the heart of Jewish reasoning as well. In fact, we can see the lines of this hermeneutical continuity between Judaism and Christianity, and, within Christianity, between ancient and modern instantiations of it.

### 6 Why rabbinic and Christian pragmatists need each other

The penultimate hypothesis of Ochs's book is then that Christian and rabbinic pragmatisms share a number of complementary features. He argues that though different in content they share certain family resemblances that are worth our attention. Both share a post-foundationalist critique of modern, dyadic Cartesian enquiry and suggest that the communal performance of scriptural interpretation provides elemental rules for a triadic, scriptural corrective to modern Cartesian enquiry, which opens out into a third common feature in that both pragmatisms intend 'a reformational reading of Scripture'.[398] Their common critique of modernity, and their common tendency to 'locate rules for correcting modernist inquiry in performative interpretations of Scripture', means that for both pragmatisms, these interpretations reread scriptural texts as vague symbols of rules of conduct that are defined only in specific contexts of action within respective communities of readers. From the perspective of any particular, historical inquiry, the meanings of these rules will appear to change from community to community and from context to context.[399]

There is no explicit rule for why this is the case. That is, what we can find common to rabbinic and Christian pragmatism is a vague scriptural pragmatism that can best be clarified through diagramming the incompleteness of each, and their need for mutual correction. In the twelfth and final stated hypothesis of the book, Ochs suggests that pragmatic reading, rather than being stimulated by errors or conflicts in the plain sense, will be stimulated by vaguenesses. For example, in rabbinic pragmatism, Kadushin's corrective textual approach appeared to complement Rosenzweig's diagrammatic philosophical approach, yet the plain sense of their writings does not always authorize readers to read them as complementary. Neither explicitly acknowledges the need of the other, and both tend to be self-enclosed (rabbinic texts are self-disclosing, speech-thinking is self-correcting, and both assume that God is immanent in the Jewish community's reading practices). In this sense, Ochs believes that rabbinic pragmatism is inexplicit in both its corrective and diagrammatic modes. Rabbinic pragmatists tend to reinforce the apophatic tendencies of their tradition, and is only 'selectively attentive to the errant conceptualism of modern theology', without explicating the role of 'theological diagramming', or 'theosemiotics'. This vagueness stimulates the need for a complement in Christian pragmatism. However, the problem is that Christian pragmatism is also vague and provides an incomplete rule for the correction of modernist enquiry. This is because, while Lindbeck does explicitly acknowledge the import of rabbinic studies for the postliberal,[400] 'the indigenous rabbinic rules of interpretation would not be meaningful' to postliberal readers on any terms other than those defined by the conditions of postliberal enquiry.[401] Ochs judges that such a redefinition is not currently available within the explicit parameters of postliberal theology, and this illustrates the incompleteness of the postliberal 'rule for correcting the conceptualist tendencies of classical and modern theology'.[402]

These respective sets of vaguenesses in the plain-sense reading of these texts cannot be alleviated on their own. They require a dialogical and complementary engagement with one another. The commonalities of scriptural pragmatism can only be validated by the procedure of rereading, and thus clarifying, the vaguenesses of rabbinic and Christian pragmatism as: the 'corrective and diagrammatic complements of a procedure for repairing modern theology'.[403] This process of scriptural pragmatism, in turn, has implications for how to reread vaguenesses in the plain sense of Peirce's theosemiotics, but we can only allude to this dimension of his argument. The crucial aspect for this study is how this helps us to read Lindbeck.

Ochs writes that postfoundationalist, postliberal theologians such as Frei and Lindbeck have come to see that 'Christian scriptural interpretation may be more similar to *rabbinic* scriptural interpretation than previously assumed.'[404] Lindbeck has written explicitly on the similarities between Martin Luther's treatment of scripture and Max Kadushin's rabbinic pragmatism. Such an invitation to Jewish–Christian dialogue through the scriptures is tremendously significant. It has not been the dominant mode of Jewish–Christian dialogue, but Ochs believes that it might become so if the dialogue is guided by the rule of pragmatism. When Ochs looks at the way this dialogue has been carried out in his present study, between his rabbinic and Christian pragmatists, he sees a number of methodological tendencies common to both. Rabbinic and Christian pragmatists

(a) 'inquire about God's attributes', not in relation to phenomenological experience but through their reading of scriptural texts and the traditions of interpretation those texts generate;

(b) their reading of texts is in response to human suffering;

(c) this suffering that stimulates their reading is 'already a sign of the response to suffering', and that 'scriptural readings bring redemption by bringing sufferers and healers into dialogue in the company of God';

(d) and therefore, reading with a community of such dialogical readers is done 'for the sake of changing the practical and communal conditions of suffering';

(e) but in order for the communal reading to be truly dialogic, and therefore curative, it is necessary 'to read with others within the community who read differently';

(f) this assumes that all readings will not be the same, and that redemption will require a dialogue of difference;

(g) such dialogical reading practices will strengthen each particular community's reading practices by mutually complementing and clarifying them;

(h) Peircean 'theosemiotics' provides tools for showing the rule of pragmatism that guides this particular dialogue that Ochs has hosted.[405]

Therefore both rabbinic and Christian pragmatists share the scriptural rule of love, even as this rule is 'transmitted' differently through church doctrines in the Christian tradition, and through the words and concepts of rabbinic midrash in the Jewish tradition. But here we see that the method of interpretation must 'transmit' the scriptural rule of love, as much as the doctrines or midrashic words do. Ochs is Lindbeckian, then, when he writes that 'the scriptural rule ultimately teaches by way of its own performance'.[406] That is, the 'diagram' or the writing (the transmission) of the scriptural rule of love is always incomplete, and this incompleteness or 'lack' will ultimately 'stimulate the new reader ... to reread the incomplete diagram as a sign that its completion is at hand'.[407] With reference to the common methodological aspects above (a–h), the reader reads the sign of incompleteness (suffering) as 'itself a sign of what the reader lacks' and responds dialogically in compassion for the other. Identifying 'what the diagram lacks' is also a way of 'uncovering his or her own ignorance' and enables the reader to '*participate in* – rather than merely observe – the interpretive rule that has been diagrammed. And it is this participation, rather than the diagram that merely stimulated it, that symbolizes the rule [of scriptural love or compassion].'[408]

The whole purpose of writing about the scriptural rule (through doctrine or midrash) is 'fulfilled only when readers are stimulated to search beyond the diagram – *and thus beyond the terms of their present knowledge and discourse* – to participate in the scriptural rule by transforming their own way of knowing'.[409] This is the method of reading that Ochs thinks can only be learned by careful attention to 'what does not work' in the way the reader enacts the scriptural rule of love. For 'what does not work' is an opportunity to reread the 'diagram' or the writing as 'a stimulus to change', that is, to respond compassionately to the suffering because the suffering itself is a sign of the redemption to come. Ochs writes: 'By learning anew and modifying their habits of reading, readers acquire the capacity to receive reparative care from those who teach the scriptural rule. This is what it means to read the rule of pragmatism as a token of the scriptural rule of love.'[410] As Ochs sees it, this is deeply Peircean, because Peirce not only read the gospels, and likened his pragmatism to the 'older logical rule' of scripture, 'By their fruits ye shall know them', but also said that the gospel of Christ is this scriptural rule of love.[411] This is the basis for Ochs's claim that both rabbinic and Christian pragmatisms are well complemented and clarified by Peirce's rule of pragmatism (as a token of the scriptural rule of love.)

## Conclusion

If my thesis is right, that George Lindbeck is best read as a Christian scriptural pragmatist, what difference does Ochs's account of scriptural pragmatism make for postliberal theology? The difference that Augustine made was to show how very deep scriptural pragmatism goes within the Christian tradition, and to help us in our task of rereading Lindbeck with new eyes. Peter Ochs responds to Lindbeck in a way that also enables a new reading of his work. Together, Augustine and Ochs help us work towards a programme of scriptural reasoning both within traditions and across cultural-linguistic boundaries. What Ochs sees at work in Lindbeck is a Christian pragmatism that is aimed at the reformation and repair of Christian theology, enabling modern theologians to reclaim their proper function as biblical reasoners and practitioners of a faith that is compassionate and responsive to the suffering of the 'other' in the world. This is to read Lindbeck as a scriptural pragmatist who believes that reading the scriptures will repair our worlds.

But Lindbeck and Ochs have different reasons for this repair. For Ochs, this repair has an intratraditional justification in the Ezra story. But will the Ezra story that Halivni tells and Ochs depends upon suffice for Christian pragmatists? Will Christian postliberals be able to say, in the way that Halivni and Ochs do, that at the heart of the orthodox faith there is a vision of the 'maculate text' and also claim that the elect community can 'repair' that text, and in doing so 'repair the world'?

Perhaps these questions are partly answered for Christian scriptural pragmatists by turning to Augustine's crucial question: *How can the reading of signs become the antidote rather that the catalyst for sin?* If we take Augustine's references to the Word of God made flesh to signify both the person of Jesus Christ and scripture simultaneously, then we may begin to see the christological reasoning that such a pragmatism entails. Consider a passage from the heart of the *Confessions*, where Augustine writes in Book 7:

> I sought a way to obtain strength enough to enjoy you; but I did not find it until I embraced 'the mediator between God and man, the man Christ Jesus' (1 Tim. 2.5), 'who is above all things , God blessed for ever' (Rom. 9.5). He called and said 'I am the way and the truth and the life' (Jn 14.6). The food which I was too weak to accept he mingled with flesh, in that 'The Word was made flesh' (Jn 1.14), so that our infant condition might come to suck milk from your wisdom by which you created all things. To possess my God, the humble Jesus, I was not yet humble enough. I did not know what his weakness was meant to teach.

Your Word, eternal truth, higher than the superior parts of your creation, raises those submissive to him to himself. In the inferior parts he built for himself a humble house of our clay. By this he detaches from themselves those who are willing to be made his subjects and carries them across to himself, healing their swelling and nourishing their love. They are no longer to place confidence in themselves, but rather to become weak. They see at their feet divinity become weak by his sharing in our 'coat of skin' (Gen. 3.21). In their weariness they fall prostrate before this divine weakness which raises and lifts them up.[412]

If we take this passage about the mediation of the Word (eternal truth) made flesh to also be about scripture, then we immediately can recognize Augustine delineating the way in which we might understand the 'inferior parts' or wounds of scripture as part of Christ's own redemptive weakness. Indwelling the problems and aporias of the text thus becomes the very avenue by which healing and nourishing are possible for the reading community. This may help us to consider what the Ezra story might entail in Christian terms.

For Christians, the Ezra story must be christological in some significant way. The wounds of the 'maculate text' can be read as Christ's wounds, and the 'repair of the world' might be read as requiring the agency of Jesus Christ, who is 'world-repair' made flesh, the immaculate Word of God made maculate in being made human ('For our sake he made him to be sin who knew no sin'). Augustine's Word of God theology provides the basis in the orthodox Christian tradition for displaying this christology within the semiotic structures of communal scripture reading. The cultural-linguistic turn that Lindbeck's work signals is thus better framed within this broader Augustinian tradition of a cultural-semiotic turn towards the Word of God. The cultural-linguistic signs encoded in holy writ become the 'Word of God' to readers only when reading or hearing the Word leads to the performance of the very thing it mediates, or in Augustine's terms, only when it leads readers right into 'the kingdom of charity', only when it transforms reading communities into a different kind of order – an order of love.

This requires certain reading skills that I argue are christological (the interpretive replication of the Word made flesh). The skills involve faith, hope and love, and as they did for Augustine, require readers to perform the logic of the incarnation in their reading. In Ochsian terms, this means a recognition that the scriptures are in some sense both 'wounded', indefinite, incomplete, maculate, and simultaneously the very source of repair the world so desperately needs. In Christian terms, one strong biblical image for this is that of St Thomas, who came to believe in the risen Christ only when he put his fingers into Jesus's transformed wounds. Placing his fingers in the wounds of the Word made flesh, he finds healing through a revelation of such intensity that it could not help but be made public ('My Lord and my God!'). So too in the reading of scripture. It is in the wounds of the text – the gaps, the aporias, those caverns of humanity – where readers will discover the revelation of God's Word, especially if they learn to read as God reads, learn to reason as God reasons, in the world-repair that is Jesus Christ.

# Conclusion

## Transforming postliberal theology

This book has been headed towards a theologically informed scriptural pragmatism that makes Christian communities simultaneously more engaged with their own deepest sources, more engaged with the Jewish other and more publicly responsible for the flourishing of the whole world through an attentiveness to the incarnational logic of scripture. In this conclusion I will highlight some of the important themes for this reading of George Lindbeck and stress the theological hermeneutics that direct readers towards scriptural pragmatism. The book concludes with a brief *enchiridion* for reading Lindbeck.

### Towards scriptural pragmatism

How far has postliberal theology come through the course of this book? There is certainly no easy way of synthesizing all of the complex descriptions that we have encountered. A whole community of readers would be required for such a task. Each of the three chapters have very different textures, and can be read independently of one another; and yet these three are also interrelated in some generative ways that I hope will provoke further thinking about the relationship between postliberalism, pragmatism and scripture. This conclusion, then, is not intended to provide neat answers to all of the questions that the book has posed. It can, however, recall what the argument has been, and make some tentative observations about the practical ways in which postliberal theology is being transformed.

Looking back, we can see at least four things displayed for readers of Lindbeck. First, we learned that *The Nature of Doctrine* does have vaguely pragmatic tendencies, largely associated with the linguistic pragmatism of Ludwig Wittgenstein. I challenged the assumption of many of Lindbeck's earliest readers that this pragmatism was a deficit to his proposal, bringing with it theological problems concerning truth, relativism, the text–world relationship and sectarianism. Rather than seeing pragmatism as a 'secular-looking' deficit in Lindbeck's postliberalism, I argued that his pragmatism was of a 'theosemiotic' (rather than simply linguistic) kind, and that his interests were best served by linking pragmatism and revelation in a dynamic way. This I called 'scriptural pragmatism', and acknowledged that it was under-developed in Lindbeck. I then proposed to develop Lindbeck's 'scriptural pragmatism' by going deeper into the Christian tradition for resources that could aid this development. I described how Augustine stands at the roots of such a theosemiotic pragmatism, and enabled readers of Lindbeck to see the ways in which pragmatism might be linked to the revelation of God's Word. Finally, there was my proposal to read Lindbeck's 'scriptural pragmatism' through a Jewish engagement with his work that both carried forward the Augustinian scriptural pragmatism and showed how Lindbeck's work is complemented by twentieth-century Jewish models of 'rabbinic pragmatism'.

Put more simply, my argument has thus far suggested that (1) Lindbeck is a pragmatist; (2) his pragmatism needs to be developed to display its theosemiotic and scriptural dimensions; (3) such a development of scriptural pragmatism can be resourced by its theological roots within the Christian tradition in St Augustine; and (4) such a scriptural pragmatism is complemented by Jewish scriptural pragmatists in the twentieth century. With these main features in mind, I can now draw some practical implications for how readers of Lindbeck might proceed.

## 1 Trinity, truth and texts

The earliest readers of Lindbeck believed that his pragmatism entailed problems with his theory of truth and its corollary: relativism. Relativism is an ancient philosophical problem. There seems to be no easy answer to the observation that human experience is always subject to the pressures of differing contexts, cultures and sign systems. But the postliberal tendency, which can be seen quite early in the work of H. Richard Niebuhr and is certainly present in Lindbeck too, has been to relativize 'relativism' with the revelation of God as the ultimate reality.[413] This revelational or theocentric *realism* is apparent in Lindbeck through his semiotic attentiveness to revelation and in his christological and trinitarian commitments implicit in his regulative view of doctrine. This admits to fallibilism and a humble view of the penultimacy of human knowledge, but it does not admit that penultimate knowledge has no real relationship to the ultimate reality of God. Implicit in Lindbeck's postliberalism is a christological and trinitarian understanding of mediation that ensures the relativity of relativity by a faith in the reality of God that seeks to understand how all human experience relates to the logic of relations that is God's triune life. Another way of expressing this realistic response to relativism has been the turn towards pragmatism.

In this book, this has been a turn towards Peter Ochs and the work of Charles Peirce. Suggesting Peirce as a supplement to Wittgenstein helps with truth, texts and transformation. But what it is not intended to be is a dominant theory which displaces all other philosophical aids. In an unpublished work, Nicholas Adams has discussed the necessity of 'seminars' which can aid our houses of worship in tradition-constituted reasoning. There are many different 'seminars' that can aid postliberals in their task of faithfulness to the scriptures. Peircean pragmatism is simply one philosophical 'seminar' among others that may converse with the scriptural reasons of the tradition, but it is one seminar that works naturally with the issues that postliberal theology has been faced with – and it is also a seminar that has been unduly neglected by theologians.

More generally, all forms of pragmatism, including scriptural-semiotic or cultural-linguistic forms, focus on the particular, the practical and the contextual – and in this sense always admit to the reality of relativism that postliberals squarely face. Additionally, most early forms of pragmatism share a certain priority of the ethical. This is only eroded in those forms of pragmatism that disconnect ethical questions from an attentiveness to truth and meaning. However, scriptural pragmatism differs from most other forms of pragmatism in that it follows the basic postliberal tendency to avoid this erosion by grounding ethics in the revelation of God. At least in Ochsian terms, Peircean pragmatism aids the move to ground ethics in the revelation and reality of God. One can speak of a 'moral ontology' or of moral realism in this regard, but the preference of postliberals has been with a more concrete and particular concern with 'theosemiotics', with God's role in sign-production and sign-reception in communities of faith.

The questions that critics have had with Lindbeck's pragmatism are typically linked to these problems of relativism that are supposed to be part and parcel of a 'pragmatic theory of truth'. What both

Augustine and Ochs suggest is that there is no singular 'pragmatic theory of truth', but that attentiveness to truth matters (e.g. A- and B-Reasoning), and matters for scriptural pragmatism especially because it proceeds on the hypothesis that God is real, and generates all that is real ('faith seeking understanding' is an expression of this theocentric realism). Truth-seeking for both Augustine and Ochs is also theosemiotic. Both thinkers understand God to be the generative source and fulfilment of all meaning and truth and, with Lindbeck, both thinkers perform truth-seeking through the 'semiotic universe encoded in holy writ', for this is where the logic of scripture is understood to be God's logic. The postliberal debate about truth is one that will continue for some time, but critics should not say that postliberals have not been working hard at thinking through the implications of their realism.

Bruce Marshall has most recently argued in his book *Trinity and Truth* that Christians have good analytic reasons for identifying the Christian God as 'the truth'.[414] In this book he furthers the postliberal debates about truth by arguing that the triune God is the centre of Christian belief, and he proceeds to show precisely how such a claim is justified in what amounts to a theological engagement with analytic theories of truth and epistemic justification. I am not in a position to judge Marshall's analytic argument, but it shows the seriousness with which postliberals are willing to take a long-term view of working through difficult questions in conversation with complex philosophical traditions of enquiry.

Rather than making absolute claims about 'the truth', I suggest that the structure of revelation itself is trinitarian, that there might also be a trinitarian shape to semiotics and, more specifically, that there may be a trinitarian shape to the theory of mediation implicit in the meaning of signs. This is not to diminish Marshall's theological treatment of an analytical understanding of truth; it is simply to say that hermeneutical and semiotic approaches might prove to be another accessible way to think about the interdependent issues of meaning and truth that postliberalism has raised, because they help scriptural readers in a practical and performative way that analytic treatments of truth alone seem not to.[415] Marshall's main objection to the hermeneutical turn is that it does not forward a truth-dependent account of meaning.[416] But the semiotic reflections from Lindbeck to Augustine to Ochs do point towards the interrelationship of truth and meaning in a trinitarian and scriptural way, and may alleviate Marshall's worries that the hermeneutical turn gives up on truth in a way that Christians simply cannot do. The centrality of texts and reading communities, and their relationship to the world, have become key to the way postliberals have tended to respond to concerns about truth.

This is especially preferred because the central concern of postliberalism has not been (despite Lindbeck's brief 'excursus on truth') *about* 'theories of truth' or 'epistemic justification' so much as it has been about a hermeneutics of the Word of God – about the nature of texts and how the communities that read them relate to the world. The mediation of truth inheres in all the questions we can put to postliberals, but the everyday practical issue is hermeneutical-pragmatic. In this sense, postliberalism is about 'how to read well', or what Lindbeck might call 'practical wisdom' with regard to scriptural reading.[417] The disclosure of truth is not dependent on arriving at the right theory of truth – but the disclosure of truth does depend on God's Word, on biblical language and on the communal interpretation of such scriptural signs that is open to ongoing communication with the God who reveals.[418]

Christian postliberals who argue for such a scriptural-semiotic and community-based conception of meaning and truth will not be errantly relativistic to the extent that they take their 'thick' communal descriptions of God to be public truth – that is, made publicly accountable, *open to the judgment of the other*, over the long-run of time. It will be realistically hoped that the truth-claims will correspond to ontological reality, but access to this reality is always already mediated through signs, and as such, correspondence can only be tested (and thus proven) through performance. This privileges performance (embodiment as the doing of the Word), but in a way that is inseparable from the reading of sacred texts that richly describe the relationship between divine and human action.

In this sense, Lindbeck's realism is not interested in 'closure' but in remaining open to judgment. Lindbeck did not endeavour to provide a complete account – either of meaning, or truth, or justification. His proposal offers a scriptural pragmatism that does not seek doctrinal or narratival closure but invites participation in a particular, tradition-constituted form of a religious and ethical life that cannot be confined by any formalistic system determined by a single theory of truth – even if claims to a 'modest cognitivism' do inevitably signal an enduring Christian interest in ontological realism. The need for an open-ended, improvisational form which gives shape and structure to the kind of conversation Lindbeck advocates requires a 'scaffolding' like scripture, which offers us the rich descriptions needed to think and converse with others *through*. Conversation with the scriptural 'other' (whether the 'other' is ecumenical, religious and/or secular) requires similarly rich descriptions, but also requires a hermeneutic of compassion, charity, or a rule of love that guides interpretation to postpone judgments about the rational deficiency of the other until all situational particulars have been appreciated (which may be an indefinite amount of time).[419] The love of truth requires patient conversation with those who read differently.

In sum, one of the strengths of Lindbeck's book, in response to his critics, is that he does not offer a *definition* of truth. His interest in the truth is always practically guided by that which is accessible within the mediating semiotic system in use. This does not mean that there is no truth 'beyond' that semiotic system, only that truth is identified with God in such a way as to prevent the mind from grasping it as such without the mediation of signs. This is why Lindbeck is happier with likening Christianity to a whole gigantic proposition (a whole semiotic universe), rather than reducing it to a set of propositions.[420] Communal engagement with the scriptures is itself a journey into truth for Lindbeck, but a journey of intensification, of searching out the truth of the scriptures, discovering and performing the faith that is inscribed there.

## 2 Word, world and sectarianism

The earliest readers of Lindbeck worried much more, however, about his conception of the text–world relation, and its corollary: sectarianism. A number of responses can be made to this concern, but the primary answer is theological.

An appreciation of the theological character of Lindbeck's pragmatism has important consequences for interpreting his work. One instance of the interpretive clarification hoped for is in my claim, implicit throughout, that *Lindbeck does not so much 'reverse' the experiential-expressive but performs its semiotic transformation.* He discovered – with anthropological and philosophical support – that the liberal theological concern with 'experience' lacked the unavoidable mediation of signs, of cultural-linguistic signs; it especially lacked theosemiotic mediation. I pointed to theological support for Lindbeck's view in Augustine. Lindbeck has thus inscribed an inherent christology (basically Chalcedonian) throughout his cultural-linguistic or semiotic theory of mediation. Augustine offered us an occasion to interpret

Lindbeck's semiotic universe in terms of the Word made flesh, thus enriching a christological understanding of his semiotic theory of mediation and enabling a theological interpretation of Lindbeck's anthropology.[421] From this theological interpretation may flow a number of responses that mitigate worries about postliberal tendencies towards 'sectarianism'.

### The problem with 'scripture absorbing the world'

To read Lindbeck theologically is to not be restricted by the plain sense of his text but to read *The Nature of Doctrine* in the light of the more indefinite rule of love and its concrete concern to be compassionate to the other. For example, Lindbeck is famous for his absorption metaphor to describe the relationship between scripture and the world.[422] However, maintaining the metaphor of 'absorption' does not do justice to Lindbeck's overall project if read solely in the plain sense. While it is rhetorically skilful and polemically clever to think of the Bible absorbing the world rather than allowing the worldly categories to overwhelm the biblical ones, it can be a misleading thought. It misleads readers to think that Lindbeck means simply to reverse the experiential-expressivist understanding of the text–world relationship when his argument does not demand this at all, and I advocate that he not be read in this way.

In this sense, scriptural pragmatism only seeks *a new verb* for Lindbeck's slogan that scripture might absorb the universe. Insisting on a literal interpretation of this slogan runs counter to the way the text–world relationship has worked throughout history. Has it not been the case in history that communal Bible reading has been more likely to change the world than to absorb it? Or more precisely, can we imagine with Augustine, Lindbeck and Ochs that the scriptures provide us with resources for not only forming a culture but also solving the problems that inevitably arise within it? Might we be better off envisioning scripture conversing with the world and the world conversing with scripture in a way that transforms everyone involved in such a conversation? And who will initiate such conversations but those for whom the scriptures are culture-forming and world-transforming?

Without clarification, 'absorbing' is simply an inadequate verb for the text–world relation, and readers should not take the metaphor literally.[423] It needs to be supplemented with more dynamic metaphors of 'conversation' without losing Lindbeck's sense of the Bible being culture-forming and world-transforming. Needed is a different kind of attentiveness to the Word and its relation to the world. But for this kind of attentiveness help is needed both from within the tradition and without.

## Hegemony, orthodoxy and the rule of love

The 'orthodoxy' that Lindbeck envisions has never been accused of hegemonic relations towards the non-Christian other. This totalitarian critique is the flip-side of sectarianism, and it is an accusation sometimes aimed at orthodox theologians. But for Lindbeck, 'orthodoxy' is ruled by faith in the Word and in the scriptures that textually replicate this Word. It is also steeped in the belief that such faith enables good performance and the development of those skills that inscribe the incarnational logic of scripture in the church and in the world. This, I have argued, places Lindbeck in the Augustinian tradition and suggests a certain affinity between Augustinians and postliberals.

John Milbank has also brought a version of postliberalism (admittedly a version which is more French than Anglo-American) into conversation with Saint Augustine, but to very different effect.[424] Milbank's postliberal Augustine is a 'metanarrative realist'.[425] This is a way of saying, by way of Augustine, that Lindbeck's postliberalism entails a realism (an entire practice which refers to reality, a 'giant proposition') that seemed limited by the argument Lindbeck made in *The Nature of Doctrine*. Milbank's 'postcritical' Augustinian proposal argues that 'more place must be given to propositions, and so to ontology, than Lindbeck appears to allow'.[426] But is this what a reading of Augustine brings to Lindbeck? Augustine clearly cares about 'reference to reality'. But 'metanarrative realist' does not seem well suited to the Augustine we encountered in Chapter 2. The phrase may not quite do descriptive service to either Augustine or Lindbeck, though perhaps the term correctly describes John Milbank.[427] The evidence here suggests that Augustine's realism (and his idealism) is of a scriptural kind. So, if Augustine and Lindbeck hold in common a theocentric, revelational or 'scriptural realism', then the 'ontology' that Lindbeck allows is precisely a scriptural performance of life. It does not dismiss metaphysics; it listens to, converses with, 'absorbs' and transforms the categories of metaphysics into scriptural categories.[428] To say that 'more place must be given to propositions' is to misread Lindbeck (and Augustine) who does not seek a greater or lesser place for 'propositions' but a more modest, and more integrated place for them – a place for them within a much wider 'semiotic universe paradigmatically encoded in holy writ' which can be indwelled.

Milbank likewise insists on the centrality of the incarnation, but misses the force of Lindbeck's 'christological maximalism', which actually inscribes the incarnational and trinitarian *regula fidei*, the scriptural standard or 'measure' of all Christian interpretations of reality. If it is true that Lindbeck has ignored 'the structural complexity of narrative', and that he therefore is 'dangerously ahistorical', as Milbank charges, then Lindbeck has not met his own criteria, and therefore can be corrected on the basis of his own christological maximalism as a rule for reading the scriptures (which are read as historically realistic). But quite to the contrary, Lindbeck's 'semiotic universe' does suggest a structural complexity, and one that has been underexplored in contemporary theology. If Milbank asks Lindbeck to be more 'ontological', then Lindbeck might well ask Milbank to be more 'semiotic', that is, more attentive to the 'semiotic universe encoded in holy writ'.[429] Perhaps, far from providing readers with a 'narratological foundationalism' that 'fails to arrive at a postmodern theology', Lindbeck has opened the door for a non-totalitarian, theological and semiotically sophisticated scriptural pragmatism that has been seen protologically inscribed in Augustine and developed through the work of Peter Ochs. Rather than reading Lindbeck, as Milbank does, as not Augustinian enough, I have proposed that the better way forward is to suggest how Augustinian he might be.

Reading Lindbeck as an Augustinian guards orthodoxy against hegemony by restoring the ancient rule of charity as the guide for those reading communities who seek to participate in and perform the Word made flesh. No claim to orthodoxy (to the rule of faith) rings true without this rule of love, which is more concretely a rule of compassion, a rule which guides practitioners of faith to repair suffering in the world. Needed again are 'doctors of the church' like Augustine who are hermeneutical healers, people in community who can solve semiotic problems that have ethical and political significance in the social body.

Jeffrey Stout has recently hoped that postliberals would guide the church to engage in an exchange of reasoning across cultural-linguistic borders and in a process of 'holding one another responsible'.[430] Stout worries that postliberals are giving up their mandate and responsibility to repair the world. He worries that they are becoming resentful, whether totalitarian or insular in their relation to the non-Christian other. These are legitimate worries that postliberals should not dismiss. Stout helpfully observes that 'surgeons are not praised for the depth of their rage against disease but for their contribution to a patient's survival and well-being. We want their incisions to be wisely chosen and supple in execution, not as deep as can be.'[431] Some theologians today are not enough like the wisest of surgeons, and such a concern applies equally to some readers of Lindbeck who tend to cut deeper into the patient than a more practical wisdom would require.

Churchly theologians, if they are also wise surgeons, will want to restore their patients to full health, not leave them dismembered on the operating table. When even the most pacifist theologians in America or Britain employ violent rhetorical strategies to cut deeper into their patient than is warranted, everyone loses. The world loses because it simply stops listening to churchly theologians whose incisions seem unwise. The church loses because it fails to act redemptively in the world, and thus actually fails to 'be the church'. I expect that what Hans Frei meant by 'generous orthodoxy', and what Lindbeck's scriptural pragmatism entails, counsels against such tendencies. For generosity and charity have the quality of tempering the self-defeating orthodox tendency to rage against this present order.

The rule of love supplies this constant corrective to those thinkers whose good concern for orthodoxy gets consistently displaced by their rage and intractability in the face of the world's sin and suffering. An orthodoxy which fails to follow the rule of love will not ultimately provide the kind of fruitfulness that flows from the deepest resources in the tradition. Through following a rule of compassion, theologians may begin to make wise, supple incisions into the wounds of the church and the world. If this were to happen, then Lindbeck's vision would be more faithfully enacted, and orthodoxy would be not only generous but also reparative in both the church and the world.

### Resolving the problem with sectarianism: conversing with the scriptural other

Postliberalism is a programme for repairing religion itself – but not for the sake of the religions alone. The ambition of postliberalism should be seen as calling for nothing less than another reformation – one that puts a premium on rethinking fractured relationships from the inside-out, both within the church and beyond its gates. Lindbeck's dialogical movements towards conversing with Jews signals that his own Christian understanding of the peoplehood of God is coherent with a Jewish one that seeks *tikkun olam*, the repair of the world.[432] Whether the problem is sectarianism or the logical inverse, totalitarianism, Lindbeck's work suggests a different way which avoids both tendencies.

In Lindbeck's latest collection of essays, *The Church in a Postliberal Age*, he looks back on *The Nature of Doctrine*, aware of both its intentions and its impact. Lindbeck recalls that the book was intended as a prolegomena for an abandoned ecumenical project in 'comparative dogmatics'.[433] It is easy to see signs of this project in the book, especially in his penultimate chapter dealing with issues that divide Catholics and Protestants, such as the Marian dogmas and 'infallibility'. I have largely left such issues untreated in this book. I would like to return, however, to a methodological concern with his forgotten yet still embedded ecumenical project in 'comparative dogmatics'. How would this have proceeded? How would his treatment of 'the interrelationships of the religions' have contributed to such a comparison? Lindbeck's own concern for the 'comparative' has increasingly turned towards the 'dialogical' and the 'scriptural', and especially towards rethinking the relation between the church and Israel. He writes:

> [A] comparative dogmatics needs to take a different form than I originally envisioned. It should start with ecclesiology and, included in that, with what might be called 'Israel-ology'. The two cannot be separated in a scriptural narrative approach: Israel and the Church are one elect people, and rethinking their relation is fundamental to ecumenism. This rethinking must be theological, i.e. based on Scripture as it functions in communities for which the scriptural witness to the God of Israel and Jesus is authoritative.[434]

Lindbeck has been working at his dialogical and scriptural dogmatics over time. The shape of this dogmatics seems simultaneously intratraditional and extratraditional, both for the church and for the Jewish 'other' who is an integral part of the Christian story. Lindbeck understands that the ability to rethink the church's relationship to Israel in a way that is faithful to the gospel is crucial for his ecumenical project. Not only does this ecclesial dialogue with Israel put corrective pressure on ecumenism, but it also highlights how politically and ethically significant his project is for the world. This feature alone should overcome accusations of 'sectarianism' in the pejorative sense. Not only are Lindbeck's own uses of the word misleading, but when critics charge him with 'sectarianism' they inevitably miss the heart of the project.[435] Lindbeck does not argue for the Christian equivalent of 'gated communities', but something much more like a 'journey of intensification' that should simultaneously lead to encountering the concrete 'other' through the mediating signs of their particular identities.[436]

There is no systematic way of envisioning this conversation, but that should not mean that the conversation does not happen at all. The '*ad hoc* apologetics' hoped for in Lindbeck's proposal entails a real commitment to the public exchange of reasoning, and in that public exchange Christians have a responsibility to represent their tradition faithfully, making explicit their scriptural reasons in conversational response to the 'public'. Over the course of this book we have seen some of this exchange of reasoning between Christians and Jews. With Lindbeck and Ochs, we can see 'signs' of the church and Israel engaged in a kind of dialogue that has a different timbre than past approaches to Jewish–Christian relations. Both thinkers can see that the church and Israel need each other, and for deeply scriptural reasons: the church and Israel belong together in some significant way. And both thinkers are calling for 'another reformation' of the church and of Israel.[437] Since Lindbeck and Ochs are fairly understood as 'traditionalists', such 'radical' thinking about reformation may seem paradoxical. On the traditional side of things, it may seem that adherence to the tradition will mean that nothing changes. On the radical side it may seem that the constitution of a Judaeo-Christian tradition is being proposed. However, our study of Peter Ochs has shown that complementarity does not entail the dissolution of difference. 'Rethinking the relation' does not mean a mathematical reduction of turning two into one but rather discovering the thirdness that characterizes the relation of the two. What it means is that both traditions may be radically faithful and share a number of significant practices, including scripture study.

In a footnote in *The Nature of Doctrine*, Lindbeck gives readers a seed of his later trajectory on the church–Israel relationship:

> … the logic of the biblical narratives leads to the conclusion (usually denied in Christian history) that Israel and Gentile Christianity are parts of the one people of God and will retain their respective identities (though, it may be hoped, not their past or present relations) until the end (Rom. 9–11). The task of the Gentile church is 'to stir Israel to emulation' (Rom. 11.11), and it can be inferred that the Jews may at times have a similar role *vis-à-vis* Gentile Christians (Rom. 11.19–24). While analogues of this relation could also obtain with other non-Christian religions, they would, within most theological frameworks, be rather distant ones.[438]

It is simply worth underlining that the complementary nature of scriptural pragmatism in both Jewish and Christian forms, set forth so well by Peter Ochs, was also hinted at by Lindbeck in *The Nature of Doctrine*, over 20 years ago. In some places, Lindbeck is even interested in the shared reasoning of all the 'biblical religions', sometimes referring specifically to Islam in relation to the church and Israel. But he clearly gives priority to the church–Israel relationship, and this is an instance where 'faithfulness as intratextuality' drives him to embrace the religious 'other' through his postliberal interest in the particularity of Israel and Jesus. As early as 1984, Lindbeck is envisioning a 'common good', a shared practice of scriptural reasoning between Jews and Christians. And Lindbeck's 'journey of intensification' might mean further extensions to the religious and secular other through the scriptural, narrative approach he takes.[439]

The original anxieties and hopes of postliberal theology are now becoming tempered and matured by a theosemiotic, pragmatic realism that is not simply able to 'get outside the world of the Bible', nor simply interested in 'the Bible absorbing the world', but is able to bring the Bible into conversation with worlds that are always both inside and outside its terms of reference. For Jewish and Christian postliberals, this not only means conversing with one another as theopolitical Abrahamic allies (though it increasingly has meant at least this) but also means facing other readers, both secular and religious ones, who care not only about 'exchanging reasons' but about conversing with the other in ways that deepen participation in one's own tradition, and so enable that tradition a greater faithfulness, applicability and intelligibility through the transforming presence of God's Word in the communal reading of Scripture.[440]

Most communities, religious and secular alike, seem woefully disconnected from the past, and thus from those sources of wisdom that might provide reparative insight into the fissures that threaten further fragmentation. The whole complex of associations of biblical and liturgical allusions that give coherence to Western culture needs to be remembered. Postliberals are the ones who remember, and also discover anew, the wisdom and logic of the scriptures as they face the material problems of the day in conversation with their religious and secular neighbours. It may be said that there is a conservative tendency here; but it is matched with a fearless commitment to develop, to change and grow, to transform and be transformed, to bring together in incarnational ways the wisdom of the past with the reality of the present. Scriptural pragmatism means making the signposts of scripture the cultural standard for guiding the transformation and transfiguration of ecclesial life. In Christian terms, that transformation and transfiguration will only occur, however, through utter faithfulness to the Word made flesh in Jesus Christ. In this, Hans Frei was right to see in Lindbeck a type of orthodox Christian humanist.

In practical terms, this transformative vision of postliberal theology bringing the Bible into conversations with the world will require Christians to become more highly skilled readers of scripture. This means that much more intensive practices of scripture reading in Christian communities are needed: Christians need to take text-study as seriously as the Jews have done. And at the same time, this will mean a concerted effort on the part of Christians to bring the reasoning and logic of these scriptures *unapologetically* and charitably into conversation with others who are not Christian.

### 3 A brief enchiridion on faith, hope and love

In sum, this book commends a transformation, a different way of reading Lindbeck as a scriptural pragmatist. His own three 'rules' for assessing postliberal theology – faithfulness, applicability and intelligibility – are recast in terms of the theological virtues. Lindbeck's central rules for assessing postliberal theologies correlate with the traditional catechetical concern about faith, hope and love.[441] These virtues were central to both Augustine and Ochs, and they are implicit in Lindbeck's catechetical and Thomist tendencies too, picking up the proximity of his thought to 'virtue ethics'.[442] To close this book with theological virtues is to commend and honour Lindbeck for his own faithfulness, applicability and intelligibility as a Christian theologian.

#### *'Faithfulness as intratextuality': rule of faith*

Lindbeck's postliberal rule about 'faithfulness as intratextuality' correlates to the theological virtue of faith itself. He puts a premium on the Pauline phrase, 'faith comes from hearing', and the implication is that faith comes 'from hearing God's Word'. This means that the theological virtue of faith also means being hermeneutically skilled in semiotics because faith is always already mediated to us through signs. Faith is thus a kind of apprenticeship in sign-reading. To read the signs well, Augustine teaches in *De doctrina christiana*, means the enjoyment of the triune God. The order of love is implicit in his theological hermeneutic. However, Augustine teaches that the use–enjoyment distinction, like the faith–works distinction, means that the 'for God's sake' *means* 'for neighbour's sake' too (see Chapter 2). Augustine writes:

> I have written a book about this question, with the title *Faith and Works*, where I have demonstrated as best as I might with God's help how according to the holy

scriptures the faith that saves is the one the apostle Paul described plainly enough when he said 'For in Christ Jesus neither circumcision nor uncircumcision counts for anything; the only thing that counts is faith working through love' (Gal. 5.6). But if faith works evil rather than good, without doubt, as the apostle James says, it 'is dead in itself' (Jas 2.17), and he also says, if a person says he has faith, but does not have works, will faith be able to save him? (Jas 2.14).[443]

It is difficult to conceptualize that something can be *ordinate and simultaneous* – this difficulty has meant much struggle over Augustine's teaching here.[444] But as I have suggested, theological doctrines such as the incarnation and Trinity help us to conceive of the relationship properly, guarding readers from christological errors in what otherwise seems to be 'pretheological' in Lindbeck's method.

When Lindbeck claims that intratextual theology 'redescribes reality within the scriptural framework rather than translating Scripture into extrascriptural categories' he undoes the 'church–world' division that liberal models of theology have tended to practise. Lindbeck calls us to move beyond the twofold strategy of liberal theology, which keeps the text bound to a notion of objective historical evidence, and then insists on a kind of crosscultural translation of the text into categories the 'world' would understand and find relevant (which, at a minimum, is pedantic towards the world). Like Barth in the previous generation, Lindbeck methodologically opened up a postliberal path for recovering more ancient ways of reading the scriptures that enable full engagement in the problems and possibilities of a postmodern world. Intratextual theology is not about becoming more concerned about the church than about the world. It is about changing the nature of the relationship to better reflect the rule of faith: a rule whose theological content was made more explicit in my treatment of Augustine. It rests on the basically Pauline but also Augustinian assumption about the relationship between faith and works, which actually inscribes, once again, an incarnational and trinitarian rule of faith.[445] It makes 'faith-fulness as intratextuality' the *sine qua non* of the church because it is only from this primary faithfulness that good works will come, including the work of engaging the 'other' and seeking the peace of the earthly city.

### 'Applicability as futurology': rule of hope

Lindbeck's rule of 'applicability as futurology' correlates to the theological virtue of hope. This is an eschatological concern for both dogmatics and ethics, which is namely 'to shape present action to fit the anticipated and hoped-for future'.[446] An eschatological vision of the kingdom of God mediated through scriptural signs guides the moral good sought for this present moment. What Lindbeck suggests he is after in following such a rule of hope is 'communally responsible action in the public world', through attentiveness to the biblical vision of the kingdom of God.[447] The vision here is eschatologically expansive, and culturally ambitious – it is hopeful that such an attentiveness to the biblical vision of the kingdom of God will itself be generative and 'responsible for the wider society'.[448]

Lindbeck's vision thus comports well with Augustine's use–enjoyment and classic faith–works distinctions. Lindbeck writes, reminiscent of Augustine:

> a religious community's salvation is not by works, nor is its faith for the sake of practical efficacy, *and yet* good works of unforeseeable kinds flow from faithfulness. It was thus, rather than by intentional effort, that biblical religion helped to produce democracy and science, as well as other values Westerners treasure; and it is in similarly unimaginable and unplanned ways, if at all, that biblical religion will help *save the world*.[449]

The highly significant 'and yet' in the sentence above indicates how Lindbeck's faith–works might be read. Lindbeck is as convinced as Augustine that the ordering of these relationships is significant. But just as it is easy to misread Augustine on this point, it is easy to misread Lindbeck too as advocating withdrawal and isolationism. It is a method for shaping (and judging) present action in the world in accordance with the scriptures. It is in this sense that 'scriptural pragmatism' reasons about 'practical efficacy' through a heightened pitch of attention to God's logic revealed in communal scriptural reading which is as responsible to future generations as it is faithful to past ones.

### *'Intelligibility as skill': rule of love (or compassion)*

The rule of 'intelligibility as skill' correlates, somewhat surprisingly, to the theological virtue of love. As St Paul writes, 'the only thing that counts is faith working through love' (Gal. 5.6). But the occasion for reading Lindbeck's concern with 'intelligibility as skill' *as* a concern with the 'rule of love' comes through reading him through the lens of Augustine and Ochs. For both thinkers, knowing cannot be separated from loving. So what does this have to do with 'intelligibility as skill'?

I argue that 'intelligibility as skill' must involve a responsiveness to the suffering of the other. This requires hermeneutical healers and apprenticeships in the redemptive reading of signs. Lindbeck is quick to point to catechesis as his primary example of how one can learn the intelligibility of the Christian form of life. But surely the whole shape of that life is formed around the love of God and neighbour – fundamentally directed as love towards the other. The Augustinian note of realism that Lindbeck characteristically ends on is that for this catechesis to become effective, a whole process of dismantling christendom may need to occur. What Lindbeck hopes is that the radical reduction of the church will mean a purification of it (guarding against assimilation) and in this sense, repair and recover an integrity that now seems all but lost. But is this the whole story?

Lindbeck is mainly concerned here with the 'attractiveness' of the 'Christian community and form of life', and this attractiveness is bound to practising 'new modes of behavior' that are learned through 'the stories of Israel and their fulfillment in Christ'.[450] By stressing 'intelligibility as skill', I understand Lindbeck to be moving beyond (without entirely leaving behind) both cognitivist and experientialist appeals to what is 'immediately intelligible' and towards his own charitable concern that 'the vitality of Western societies may well depend in the long run on the culture-forming power of the biblical outlook in its intratextual, untranslatable specificity'.[451] At the most basic level, this means teaching hermeneutical skills – apprenticeships in the reading of signs (e.g. *De doctrina christiana*). But such semiotic competency is intended to form a culture that acts in a particular way in the world: a redemptive and responsible way.

For Lindbeck, as for Augustine and Ochs, the rule of faith opens out into the rule of love, and this means that the faithfulness, applicability and intelligibility of Christian forms of life are never a cul de sac or a ghetto. A fuller reading of Lindbeck will insist upon going deeper into sacred texts, and the traditions of interpretation those texts generate, for God's sake *and* for the sake of the world. The simultaneity is critical, and it is this simultaneity that too many readers have passed over. There may be a danger of disordering love of God and neighbour; but this makes it all the more urgent that readers of Lindbeck correct and clarify how this relationship is understood so that the love of God and love of neighbour may be understood in trinitarian terms as ordinate and co-inherent (otherwise the neighbour is all too quickly displaced).[452] The rule of compassion, or charity, takes seriously the dominical mandate to 'love your neighbor as yourself', as part and parcel of the love of God. When reading Lindbeck, a rule of love aids the reader in interpreting him responsibly, and in a way that does justice to his overall vision.

When the scriptures are the basis for reasoning about our responsibility for shared problems in the world, and when this form of scriptural reasoning is subjected to public examination, Jews and Christians especially fulfil their responsibility to God to be a light to the nations. Emerging from this scriptural pragmatism is a political and ethical commitment to engage in public discourse with those who are different, making explicit the scriptural reasoning shaping such commitments. When Jews and Christians think together about the deepest reasons internal to their respective traditions, they are also called to a rule of compassion that makes this reasoning 'public' in response to pressing problems in the social body.

In closing, I want to let Lindbeck speak for himself in two passages that are particularly instructive about his vision. In both passages he expresses a conviction about how the scriptures are transformative, and how a return to scripture might change the world. Such passages make the charge of sectarianism ring false, and also indicate that the relationship that Lindbeck envisions between scripture and the world is much more dynamic (with reference to the Holy Spirit) than initial readings of *The Nature of Doctrine* have suggested. He writes in 1989 and 1997 respectively:

> Scripture permits and perhaps urges us to dream dreams and see visions. Barriers have been erased, retrieval has begun, and we can begin to imagine far more than was possible a mere generation ago ... God's guidance of the world and church history has sown the seeds for the rebirth of the written word, and it is for believers to pray, work and hope against hope that God will bring these seeds to fruition through the power of the Holy Spirit.[453]

> Seeking and praying for the welfare of the earthly cities in which Christians live cannot be separated from concern for the religions without which these societies could not in many cases survive. It is on how these religions sustain these societies that the worldwide diaspora of peoples of biblical faith is increasingly dependent for the peace without which they cannot freely and communally glorify and witness to the Name which is above every name. Thus helping other religions is imperative. The service of God and neighbor in this case intersects with communal self-interest.[454]

In the ancient practice of using clearer texts to help interpret obscurer ones, I propose readers of Lindbeck read *The Nature of Doctrine* in the light of such clear indications from Lindbeck that his work is as much 'for the healing of the nations' as it is for the church.[455]

# Notes

## Notes to the Preface, pp. ix–xiii

[1] Hans Frei, 'Epilogue: George Lindbeck and *The Nature of Doctrine*', in Bruce Marshall (ed.), *Theology and Dialogue: Essays in Conversation with George Lindbeck* (Notre Dame, IN: University of Notre Dame Press, 1990), p. 281 (emphasis in original).

[2] Interestingly, Peirce saw 'humanism' in 'generic agreement' to the original meaning of his 'pragmatism'. See Charles Peirce, 'What Pragmatism Is', *The Essential Peirce* (Bloomington, IN: Indiana University Press, 1998) 2.334. (Hereafter, *EP.*)

## Notes to the Introduction, pp. 1–12

[3] See David Ford, *Self and Salvation: Being Transformed* (Cambridge: Cambridge University Press, 1999).

[4] Lindbeck's work depends greatly on David Kelsey's *Proving Doctrine: The Uses of Scripture in Modern Theology* (Philadelphia, PA: Fortress Press, 1975) and on Hans Frei's two substantive books of the same period, *The Eclipse of Biblical Narrative: A Study in Eighteenth and Nineteenth Century Hermeneutics* (New Haven, CT: Yale University Press, 1974) and *The Identity of Jesus Christ: The Hermeneutical Bases of Dogmatic Theology* (Philadelphia, PA: Fortress Press, 1975). H. Richard Niebuhr, their revered teacher at Yale, has been quite understandably called the grandfather of Yale postliberalism. See Niebuhr's *The Meaning of Revelation* [New York: Macmillan, 1941].

[5] See Jeffrey Stout, *Democracy and Tradition* (Princeton, NJ: Princeton University Press, 2004), and compare the Eerdmans book series, 'Radical Traditions', that Hauerwas and Ochs edit.

[6] Students new to postliberal theology should begin by reading Lindbeck's *The Nature of Doctrine: Religion and Theology in a Postliberal Age* (Philadelphia, PA: Westminster Press, 1984 (hereafter *Doctrine*), in concert with the critical responses to that book which immediately followed in two important journals, *The Thomist*, especially issues 49.3 (July 1985) and 53 (1989), and *Modern Theology*, especially issues 4 (1987), 4.2 (1988), and 5 (1989). The assessments of postliberal theology in the 2nd and 3rd editions of *The Modern Theologians*, ed. David Ford (Oxford: Blackwell, 1997 and 2005) are also invaluable introductory resources.

117

[7] Frei and Lindbeck are best read together, as complementary halves of a whole. But I treat Lindbeck individually for pragmatic reasons, especially because his treatment of postliberal theology has arguably had the widest impact, primarily because of the pedagogical usefulness of *The Nature of Doctrine*. Interested readers, however, should examine Mike Higton's superb, *Christ, Providence and History: Hans Frei's Public Theology* (London: T&T Clark, 2004) as the elder brother and complement to this book.

[8] William Placher, 'Postliberal Theology', in Ford (ed.), *The Modern Theologians*, pp. 351–2.

[9] Jim Fodor, 'Postliberal Theology', in Ford (ed.), *The Modern Theologians*. Subsequent quotations from Fodor in this chapter are from this chapter.

[10] Charles Peirce first coined the term 'pragmatism' and defined it in various and technical ways. 'Practical consequences' was a common theme in his various definitions.

[11] Jim Fodor, 'Postliberal Theology'.

[12] David Tracy, 'Lindbeck's New Program for Theology: A Reflection', *The Thomist* 49.3 (July 1985): 470.

### Notes to Chapter 1: Lindbeck, pp. 13–36

[13] William Placher wrote in *The Thomist* that 'postliberal theology remains a minority position within Protestant theology; it has so far received little attention among Catholics', 49.3 (1985): 394. It is only fair to note that *The Nature of Doctrine* provoked the greatest intensity of debate in the United States (a debate considered in Chapter 2). But postliberalism found a positive and sympathetic reception in Britain as well, especially amongst theologians such as David Ford, Janet Soskice, Stephen Sykes, Nicholas Lash and Rowan Williams. Also significant has been the very positive recent reception of Lindbeck's work in Germany after the work was translated into German in 1994 by Markus Müller. See George Lindbeck, *Christliche Lehre als Grammatik des Glaubens. Religion und Theologie in postliberalen Zeitalter*, trans. Markus Müller; introduction Hans G. Ulrich and Reinhard Hütter (Gütersloh: Kaiser, 1994). French-language theology has only recently begun to appreciate postliberalism. See Marc Boss, Gilles Emery and Pierre Gisel (eds.), *Postlibéralisme? La théologie de George Lindbeck et sa réception* (Geneva: Labor et Fides, 2004).

[14] See William Placher, 'Revisionist and Postliberal Theologies and the Public Character of Theology', in *The Thomist* 49.3 (July 1985): 392–416.

[15] *Doctrine*, p. 7.

[16] George Lindbeck, 'Confession and Community: An Israel-like View of the Church', *The Christian Century*, 9 May 1990, p. 492.

[17] Lindbeck writes:

> In my childhood and youth, I encountered cultural and religious groups other than my own; later I would engage them theologically, in reverse order. The Chinese were the first I knew as different, then Jews, Roman Catholics and non-Lutheran Protestants, in that sequence. The latter engaged my theological attention first, and then the Roman Catholics and Jews. The Chinese I have yet to examine theologically, and now that I am in my 60s, perhaps I never will. Their tacit influence on my thinking, however, lies deepest and it is only gradually that I have become aware of how pervasive it has been.

See Lindbeck 'Confession and Community', p. 492.

[18] Sydney Ahlstrom, who wrote the definitive history of religion in America, taught here during this period before going on to Harvard and then Yale, as did George Lindbeck's future Yale colleague, Wittgensteinian philosopher Paul Holmer.

[19] *Doctrine*, p. 15.

[20] Lindbeck, 'Confession and Community', p. 493.

[21] Lindbeck, 'Confession and Community', p. 493.

[22] See the bibliography in Bruce Marshall (ed.), *Theology and Dialogue: Essays in Conversation with George Lindbeck* (Notre Dame, IN: University of Notre Dame Press, 1990), pp. 283ff.

[23] Cf. Jean-François Lyotard, *The Postmodern Condition: A Report on Knowledge* (Manchester: Manchester University Press, 1984). Lyotard's thesis about the postmodern condition was much discussed in academic circles during the time *The Nature of Doctrine* was being written. Lindbeck makes no reference to Lyotard (he refers only once to Derrida on p. 136, n. 5), nor are the similarities to Lyotard often acknowledged in literature on the context of Lindbeck's 'postliberalism', largely because Lindbeck explicitly distances himself from 'the deconstructionists'. However, the similarities and dissimilarities between them represent a common mood about the nature of knowledge that was emerging in both secular and non-secular contexts in Western intellectual culture in the last quarter of the twentieth century. Both books respond similarly to the loss of a coherent grand narrative in Western culture, and both promote 'performative' knowing as well as particularized 'small narratives' over and against grand ones (in Lyotard's case, even 'incredulity' towards them). Lyotard's book shows the way in which language games and the nature of knowledge generally require a pragmatic orientation (which I will treat in regard to Lindbeck below). To discuss the 'nature of doctrine' during this same period of recent intellectual history is (partly) to extend contemporary insights on the nature of knowledge to Christian knowledge (i.e. doctrine). Lyotard speaks of the 'use-value' of knowledge, 'performative' knowledge, 'narrative' knowledge, as well as legitimation and the legislation required to authorize normative rules. He shares with Lindbeck a dependence upon the Wittgensteinian insight that to know the meaning of a term, a phrase or a sentence is to attend to its use, how it functions in human interaction. Both books are tied to one particular theory of linguistic analysis (namely speech-act theory in the work of J.L. Austin). However, postliberal 'intratextuality' differs from deconstructionist claims in that it privileges a particular 'text-constituted' idiom and world. Lindbeck distances himself from Derrida, whom he (strangely) claims is an experiential-expressivist like Derrida's teacher, Paul Ricoeur (cf. *Doctrine*, p. 136, n. 5). But compare Ricoeur's emphasis upon 'the textuality of faith' in *Figuring the Sacred*, p. 218. And note David Tracy's comment that 'Lindbeck's long footnote (p. 136) on the Yale deconstructionists leads me to believe that he has not reflected very much on the rhetorical (hermeneutical and/or deconstructive) aspects of the question of interpretation of texts and thereby on how grammar and rhetoric (like code and use) inevitably interact in all concrete interpretations ...' in 'Lindbeck's New Program', *The Thomist* 49.3 (1985): 469. Unravelling this connection to the postmodern deconstructionists is useful to establish the intellectual context Lindbeck was working within. But it also may suggest that just as he implicitly shared many similarities with the deconstructionist thinkers he distanced himself from, he also might implicitly employ pragmatic categories while eschewing an explicit pragmatic philosophy, especially the kind he found prescribed by the neo-pragmatist Richard Rorty (cf. n. 18 below). One might also wonder if Derrida's more recent turns

towards Levinas, towards ethics, towards the Other, might be cause for Lindbeck (and his readers) to reflect more (as Tracy advises) on these questions of interpretation.

[24] Lindbeck, 'Confession and Community', p. 494.

[25] Lindbeck, 'Confession and Community', p. 494 (emphasis mine). Four creed-like statements become clear in Lindbeck's analysis of his 'integrating centre'. The first two are in the form of opposition (anathema-like) and the latter two are in the form of affirmation (belief-like). (1) Reformation Christianity is opposed to modern Protestantism (by which he also means something like culture-Protestantism); (2) Reformation Christianity is opposed to the conservative–liberal polarization that so distorts modern Protestantism; (3) Reformation Christianity is committed to a 'dogmatic' starting-point, from a communal confession of faith in Christ, expressed in the trinitarian and christological creeds; and (4) Reformation Christianity is committed to scripture, unconstrained by the conservative or liberal forms of modern Protestantism. From these four statements we can clearly see that the 'integrating centre' has mediatorial meaning, seeking relief from real, concrete problems experienced in a dyadic or polarized modern Protestantism. Thus the mediation is, also clearly, christological, trinitarian and scriptural.

[26] I take 'rule of faith' to be a fair summary of what Lindbeck is describing in the doctrine–scripture relationality. See his discussion of the 'interior rule of faith' in *Doctrine*, p. 79.

[27] The title of the book perhaps also recalls Gerhard Ebeling's *The Nature of Faith*, trans. Ronald Gregor Smith (Philadelphia, PA, 1967 [1st German edn, 1959]). See Lindbeck's review of Gerhard Ebeling, *Dogmatik des Christlichen Glaubens*, in *Journal of Religion* 61 (1981): 309–14 and his reference to it in *Doctrine*, pp. 119, ns 137–9. Lindbeck's interest in the Lutheran theologian is not insignificant, as Lindbeck considers Ebeling's experiential-expressive liberalism to be 'the most notable' attempt 'to understand the Reformation notion of the word of God in terms of an experiential "word event"' (*Doctrine*, p. 119). Ebeling had been an early proponent of relating developments in linguistic theory to doctrine and it is clear that Lindbeck sees the intratextuality of postliberalism developing this relationship in a very different way as 'new difficulties have arisen' (*Doctrine*, p. 119) Cf. Gerhard Ebeling, *Einfuhrung in Theologische Sprachlehre* (Tübingen: J.C.B. Mohr, 1971). This underscores the importance of understanding Lindbeck within the dialogue of his own Lutheran tradition.

[28] In the Foreword to the German translation, Lindbeck himself notes that there were significant differences between the book he wrote and the book critics read. And yet he rightly acknowledges (consistent with his pragmatic tendencies) that one cannot replace the other – 'the original text is basic in any attempt to understand the after-effects', George Lindbeck, *The Church in a Postliberal Age*, ed. James Buckley (London: SCM Press, 2002), p. 198.

[29] This is not at all to suggest that Lindbeck knew nothing of pragmatism. His colleague in philosophy at Yale, John E. Smith, was one of the major American pragmatists at this time (see Smith's *Purpose and Thought: The Meaning of Pragmatism* (Newhaven, CT: Yale University Press, 1978) for an excellent introduction to pragmatism written from a Peircean perspective). Yale was, owing to Smith's influence, second only to Columbia University in representing pragmatism in American universities. Smith trained pragmatists as diverse as Richard J. Bernstein, Peter Ochs, Murray Murphey and Richard Rorty. However, Lindbeck seems to know pragmatism somewhat singularly through the neo-pragmatism of Richard

Rorty, whom he notes 'illustrates this possibility of doing philosophy intratextually, but the inevitable vagueness of his canon of philosophical texts makes him verge on a philosophical version of deconstructionism' (*Doctrine*, p. 137, n. 20). Lindbeck refers here to Rorty's *Consequences of Pragmatism* (Minneapolis, MW: University of Minnesota Press, 1982). And he is right to see Rorty as he does, for Rorty is indeed indebted to Lyotard (cf. n. 11 above) and Derrida (and surprisingly, his thought does not much resemble the classical pragmatism of Charles Peirce). But perhaps Lindbeck is too quick to distance himself in an undifferentiated way from pragmatism. Pragmatism is a highly differentiated field, and Lindbeck's refusal of Rorty could be bolstered by a turn towards a Peircean pragmatism.

[30] I will use the technology of italicizing or using scare quotes around words or phrases which display the vague pragmatic tendencies, frequently leaving comment for future stages of my argument. Occasionally I will give hints of how this tendency can be made more explicit in a footnote, but my only purpose here is to prepare the reader for a development which will come in future chapters. David Tracy uniquely commented in 1985 that 'Lindbeck's position, as far as I can see, is one new linguistic version of one side of classical pragmatism' and he briefly examines in that article how a better understanding of a given pragmatist could help Lindbeck precisely on the issue of truth-claims (he sees Jamesian tendencies where I think Peircean ones will be more helpful). See 'Lindbeck's New Program', *The Thomist* 49.3 (1985): 470. Tracy's comments are unusually sensitive to the complexity of pragmatic philosophy, and it is curious that his line of clarification and correction was not taken much earlier in the community of Lindbeck readers – perhaps due to suspicions that pragmatism was not a fruitful line of enquiry for theological reflection, too often associated with its crudest contemporary forms (a suspicion Lindbeck seemed to have shared). My reading extends Tracy's good, though unexplored, instinct to examine the pragmatic tendencies in Lindbeck more deeply, opening up a potentially fruitful reading of Lindbeck.

[31] *Doctrine*, p. 7.

[32] We should note from the outset that this is a problem-solving enquiry that situates itself within a tradition (liberalism) and seeks to extend that tradition (postliberalism).

[33] *Doctrine*, p. 7 (emphasis mine). It is significant, however, that Lindbeck did not title his book 'The Function of Doctrine', but rather the 'The Nature of Doctrine', which suggests that he wants his pragmatism to be grounded in the ontologically real.

[34] *Doctrine*, p. 7. The mediatorial aspect seems, however, to mitigate against this claim.

[35] *Doctrine*, p. 8 (emphasis mine). I will later draw out the implications of Lindbeck's vague use of pragmatic categories. I intend to make a special connection between the pragmatic categories of 'usefulness' and fruitfulness' as they find their theological source in Augustine, and then effect the pragmatism of those such as Charles Peirce, Wittgenstein, George Lindbeck and the Jewish pragmatic philosophy of Peter Ochs.

[36] *Doctrine*, pp. 8–9.

[37] *Doctrine*, pp. 9–10. Lindbeck shares with pragmatism generally an interest in a non-foundationalist methodology, oriented towards removing 'anomalies' from 'living belief'.

[38] 'This claim of doctrinal neutrality is later tested at some length in reference to classic Trinitarian and Christological affirmations' (p. 9). 'It would be a mistake, however, to suppose that this attempt at doctrinal neutrality involves theological neutrality when theology is understood as the scholarly activity of second-order reflection on the data of religion (including doctrinal data) and of formulating

arguments for or against material positions (including doctrinal ones)' (p. 10). According to Lindbeck, the motives are more theological than theoretical, and he makes it clear that his commitment is the Christian one. 'All observation is theory-laden', Lindbeck admits, 'there is no neutral standpoint' (p. 11). The claim to doctrinal neutrality, however, is interesting as it displays a kind of cognitivism which places some trust in a scientific method, realistically construed towards a long-run goal or aim of a particular communal enquiry.

[39] *Doctrine*, p. 17. Accordingly, Karl Barth's realism called for a third way that was neither literal/ correspondential or symbolic/expressivist.

[40] *Doctrine*, p. 18.

[41] Cf. Smith, *Purpose and Thought*. Peirce, long before other linguistic pragmatists, believed that 'the "meaning" of a word is found in the way it might or would tend to mould the conduct of a person believing a proposition' (p. 134). For Peirce, 'truth consists in congruence with or conformity to an end' (p. 59).

[42] Cf. George Lindbeck, 'The Story-Shaped Church: Critical Exegesis and Theological Interpretation' in Garrett Green (ed.), *Scriptural Authority and Narrative Interpretation* (Philadelphia, PA: Fortress Press, 1987) pp. 161–78. This essay highlights the clarificatory importance of Hans Frei for Lindbeck's own work.

[43] George Hunsinger is partly right when he calls Lindbeck a 'neoliberal' rather than a postliberal, but for more reparative reasons than he suggests. See *Disruptive Grace: Studies in the Theology of Karl Barth* (Grand Rapids, MI: Eerdmans, 1999), Chapter 9.

[44] *Doctrine*, p. 112.

[45] *Doctrine*, p. 21. Karl Barth is thought to aid in this 'corrective' by avoiding the liberal 'turn to the subject' (p. 24). We can, perhaps, see in the appeal to Barth a certain retrieval of what matters most to those dismissed propositional model theologians, that is, a kind of realism that advocates that doctrines are truth-claims about objective realities. While disagreeing that doctrines are truth-claims about objective realities, Lindbeck does not dispute that doctrine can function as truth-claims about objective realities. Lindbeck is genuinely postliberal in calling for a different conception of the subject–object relation. The problem with the Kantian turn to the subject was not the subject, but the totalizing dichotomy of the subject–object relation (neo-Kantians were not wrong in pushing Kantian thought away from universalism and towards subjectivist relativism, this tendency was implicit in his thought). The genius of Charles Peirce was to attempt a correction of this totalizing tendency and to push Kant in a more realistic direction, equally attentive, simultaneously, to both subject and object in relation. Peirce's logic of relatives can be read as a postliberal repair and, I argue, can be read as a tendency similar to the one that we will see displayed in Lindbeck's argument.

[46] *Doctrine*, p. 21.

[47] I argue that Lindbeck more sensitively implies, via his postliberalism, that Kantian thought needs to rediscover its deeper logic(s) in scripture. See also Paul D. Murray, 'A Liberal Helping of Postliberalism Please', in Mark D. Chapman (ed.), *The Future of Liberal Theology*, (Aldershot: Ashgate, 2002), pp. 208–20.

[48] *Doctrine*, p. 30.

[49] *Doctrine*, p. 33.

[50] Cf. Peirce, 'What Pragmatism Is', in *EP*, 2.333. James names Peirce, but Peirce names Kant as the originator of the idea of 'pragmatism'. Peircean pragmatism can also be understood as a repair of Kantian pragmatism. But cf. Peter Ochs, *Peirce, Pragmatism and the Logic of Scripture* (Cambridge: Cambridge University Press,

1998), (hereafter *PPLS*), who not only sees Peirce as engaging in a repair of Kantian pragmatism, but sees the real roots of pragmatism in scripture. See also Smith, *Purpose and Thought*, p. 196. Smith notes the less assured and more marginal comment of Peirce, in a letter of 1903 to William James, that Berkeley has 'more right to be considered the introducer of pragmatism into philosophy than any other man' (citing H.S. Thayer, *Meaning and Action: A Critical History of Pragmatism* (Indianapolis, IN: Hackett, 1981), pp. 499ff. But it is fairly clear from his published work that Peirce sees figures like Berkeley and Hegel as belonging to this Kantian tradition of distinguishing between *praktisch* and *pragmatisch*, and sees himself as Kantian, despite being more realist than regulative in his thought. Something like *phronesis* (or *prudentia*, practical wisdom) is meant by *pragmatisch*.

51  Lindbeck's use of Wittgenstein might best be understood as representing an advance upon basically liberal tendencies, after Kant. One could say the relation of Wittgenstein to Kant is analogous to the relation of postliberalism to liberalism. And more to the point, Wittgenstein says that his 'life philosophy' sounded to him rather like 'pragmatism' (*On Certainty*, p. 422). Cited in Fergus Kerr, *Theology After Wittgenstein* (London: SPCK, 1997), p. 140.

52  Cf. Bruce Marshall, *Trinity and Truth* (Cambridge: Cambridge University Press, 1999). Marshall is the student of Lindbeck who has most thoroughly explored this concept philosophically in terms of recent analytical thought.

53  *Doctrine*, p. 51. Compare again the comment of Peirce, who believed that 'the "meaning" of a word is found in the way it might or would tend to mould the conduct of a person believing a proposition', cited in Smith, *Purpose and Thought*, p. 134.

54  *Doctrine*, p. 63.

55  I will later argue how this kind of 'performative' or 'dynamic correspondentialism' is, more precisely, a Peircean pragmatic tendency.

56  *Doctrine*, pp. 51–2 (emphasis mine).

57  *Doctrine*, p. 65.

58  This 'performative' emphasis translates into two practical categories of 'hearing' and 'learning' in his chapter on 'many religions and the one true faith'. Here Lindbeck wants to exclude the possibility of 'wholly implicit' faith either in propositional or experiential terms (p. 57). Using the Pauline phrase *fides ex auditu* (Romans 10.17) Lindbeck stresses that saving faith comes from hearing, that faith 'must be in some measure explicit' (p. 57). What should be apparent by now is the degree to which pragmatism goes to the heart of Lindbeck's concerns both about truth and meaning.

59  Cf. James Buckley, 'Doctrine in the Diaspora', *The Thomist* 49.3 (1985): 440–59. This corresponds to what Peirce called our 'mediatorial' interest in the function of language, and hints at the dynamically realistic orientation his pragmatism held. I will consider a specifically theological understanding of this in the third chapter on Augustinian semiotics.

60  *Doctrine*, p. 60. Cf. Augustine, *Confessions*, trans. Henry Chadwick (Oxford: Oxford University Press, 1998), 1:8. (Hereafter *Conf.*). Close to his mind, though, was Wittgenstein's treatment of that Augustinian text in *Philosophical Investigations* §1.

61  *Doctrine*, pp. 61–2 (emphasis mine).

62  *Doctrine*, p. 62.

63  *Doctrine*, p. 63 (emphasis mine). Lindbeck is also aware that his eschatological view has deep affinities with modern scientific cosmology (citing Teilhard de Chardin in particular), but worries about this connection for the potentially foundationalist

implications (why does he not explore the scriptural warrant for such an eschato-logical view?). See *Doctrine*, p. 71, n. 22. In my engagement with Charles Peirce and Peter Ochs I will later argue that such fears are unfounded, on scientific, philo-sophical and scriptural grounds.

[64] *Doctrine*, p. 78.

[65] *Doctrine*, p. 79 (emphasis mine).

[66] *Doctrine*, p. 80 (emphasis mine).

[67] *Doctrine*, p. 82. As we shall continue to observe, this is structurally similar to the logic of A- and B-Reasonings in Peircean philosophy, with A-Reasonings corre-sponding to the deeper grammars. This enables Lindbeck to maintain his commit-ments to a modest cognitivism that holds out for ontological truth.

[68] Cf. Smith, *Purpose and Thought*, Peirce's thought was totally coloured by the assumption of that more expansive time scale which is the hallmark of modern science and the rationalist in philosophy' (p. 75). Work needs to be done on how a theological notion of time might influence good theological method.

[69] *Doctrine*, p. 82. Peirce shared this worry. Cf. Smith, *Purpose and Thought*,

> long before the 'linguistic turn' in philosophy was taken, Peirce had worked out a framework within which the nature and function of languages, both natural and artificial, can be understood. On the other hand, it would be quite incorrect to think of him as in any sense a 'linguistic' philosopher, not only because of his philosophical realism and his insistence on beginning with experience and its funded result in commonsense, but in virtue of a declaration such as ... 'it is not the usage of language which we seek to learn, [but] what must be the description of fact in order that our ... categories ... may not only be true, but also have the utmost possible value...' (p. 136)

[70] *Doctrine*, p. 84.

[71] *Doctrine*, p. 87. As noted earlier, Peirce called these deeper grammars 'A-Reasonings', and believed that they guided the constant revision and testing of all our 'B-Reasonings', or in Lindbeck's terms, conditional grammars. Cf. Peter Ochs, *PPLS*, pp. 259–60.

[72] *Doctrine*, p. 91.

[73] Cf. Bernard Lonergan, *The Way to Nicea: The Dialectical Development of Trinitarian Theology*, trans. Conn O'Donovan (Philadelphia, PA: Westminster, 1976). Lonergan says that while the Nicene dogma was inevitable, it was also entirely new – the 'inevitable' and the 'new' represent, in Lindbeck's terms, the 'intertwining' of the variable and the invariable. Lonergan states that Nicaea

> marks a transition from multiplicity to unity: from a multiplicity of symbols, titles, predicates to the ultimate ground of all of these, namely, the Son's consubstan-tiality with the Father. Equally, it marks a transition from things as related to us to things as they are in themselves, from the relational concepts of God as supreme agent, Creator, Omnipotent Lord of all, to an ontological conception of the divine substance itself. (p. 136)

Further still, Lonergan states, it marks a transition (as the gospels themselves do) from the particular to the universal, from mere mystery to mystery truly revealed, and from 'a whole range of problems to a basic solution to those problems' (p. 137). Thus the entire process, for Lonergan, is seen as a movement 'from naïve realism, beyond Platonism, to dogmatic realism and in the direction of critical realism' (p. 137). All of this worked towards the solution of the trinitarian question which was finally given at Nicaea: an answer which 'laid the foundation on which, of its own accord, as it were, the whole systematisation of Catholic theology would arise' (p. 137). This consisted primarily in the formalization of the Athanasian rule which Lindbeck refers to, in relation to other *regula fidei*, as an ancient form of the regulative view. It also shows how the relationship between permanence and change works in one of Lindbeck's central interlocutors.

[74] *Doctrine*, p. 93. Lindbeck here uses 'truth claims' and 'rules' almost interchangeably.

[75] *Doctrine*, p. 93. Emphasis mine, in order to draw the reader's attention to Lindbeck's pragmatic tendency to assess concepts in terms of consequences.

[76] *Doctrine*, p. 94.

[77] *Doctrine*, p. 94. About the monotheistic principle, Lonergan says that there is really 'no need ... to speak of the importation of a hellenistic ontology' (*The Way To Nicea*, p. 130). He convincingly argues that a hellenistic ontology actually excluded thinkers from assent to Nicaea (because of an implicit rule about monotheism). Lonergan gives numerous examples of how dissenters from Nicaea had no other choice but to dissent because of their hellenistic ontology. The ontology, Lonergan suggests, implicit in Nicaea is not hellenistic – it is Jewish. But are these really the binaries before us? Or is there a more dynamic relationality of concepts involved?

[78] *Doctrine*, p. 94.

[79] *Doctrine*, p. 95. Cf. Lonergan, *The Way to Nicea*. Lonergan observes that in all of the historical debates about the development of doctrine, images are the first step in the process. Images are usually biblical images and they function by analogy. But images quickly move to concepts; the mind cannot help but make the shift (as concepts are more useful). Lonergan cites Maxwell's equations for the electromagnetic field as an example. His equations began with images, but the images quickly moved to concepts and the concepts demanded judgments, to the point that the images were entirely transcended. We can see this in the Athanasian rule as well: the images were not useful, so that the equation has now transcended image and has become conceptual judgment. This also corresponds to the 'A- and B-Reasoning' of Peircean logic that we will later explore.

[80] *Doctrine*, p. 96 (emphasis mine).

[81] *Doctrine*, p. 106.

[82] *Doctrine*, p. 106. This is a fascinating aside, especially given my argument in Chapter 2, which suggests the discovery of a new *vestigium trinitatis* in Augustine's scriptural semiotics (linking the Trinity and revelation in a way that Karl Barth, the original 'postliberal', would have recognized).

[83] *Doctrine*, p. 106.

[84] 'Peirce had a normative conception of truth rooted in an essentially realistic conception of things' (Smith, *Purpose and Thought*, p. 58). And though this pragmatically realistic theory of truth is bound up with method and test, with the long-run of enquiry, 'what must not be overlooked, however, is the essentially teleological presupposition at the root of the theory' (Smith, *Purpose and Thought*, p. 76). A Peircean theory of truth is bound up with eschatology, both realized and future. It is in some sense correspondential, but dynamic correspondence, which is fallible, deeply relational, deeply ethical, oriented more to practices and processes than to disembodied propositions; it is more sensitive to effects and consequences in the (short- and long-run) life of communities than it is to the powers and limitations of a thinking-self in isolation. This, I argue, is consistent with Lindbeck's own tendencies.

[85] Lindbeck does not cite Alasdair MacIntyre's arguments about 'tradition-constituted' rationality, but the similarities between them are difficult to miss. In my view, Lindbeck improves on MacIntyre by linking traditions to their root textual sources, and showing

the inherently hermeneutical function of traditions.

[86] *Doctrine*, p. 114. My concern here is with his sensitivity to semiotics and signification. I am going to propose that ontology, and other 'extratextual' concerns do matter – though not on 'extratextual' grounds, but because an intensified semiotics, or a 'theosemiotics', makes the act and being of God present through the play of signification in the communal reading of a text.

[87] *Doctrine*, p. 114. Some might say that this is itself an ontology, albeit an ontology of performance, making claims about the meaningfulness of reality. But this would be another way of talking about pragmatism, and Lindbeck indeed characteristically displays here a linguistic or semiotic pragmatism.

[88] *Doctrine*, p. 116 (emphasis mine). Notice Lindbeck's sensitivity to the structuralist semiotic language of 'encoding' in his more technical or formalized rule about how doctrines function in their relation to the logic of scripture. Cf. *Doctrine*, p. 136, n. 5. He has much more in common, however, with a Peircean semiotic than with any of the discussions in semiotic theory that were flourishing at the time.

[89] *Doctrine*, p. 116.

[90] *Doctrine*, p. 117. Such statements make it difficult to read Lindbeck as anything but a particular kind of realist, though this has not always been the way he has been read. For an assessment of those who have read Lindbeck through anti-realist eyes, see Jeffrey Hensley, 'Are Postliberals Necessarily Antirealists? Reexamining the Metaphysics of Lindbeck's Postliberal Theology', in T.R. Phillips and D.L. Okholm (eds), *The Nature of Confession* (Downers Grove: Intervarsity Press, 1996), pp. 69–80.

[91] *Doctrine*, p. 117. The well-known postliberal motto derives from: 'A scriptural world is thus able to absorb the universe.'

[92] *Doctrine*, p. 117.

[93] *Doctrine*, p. 118.

[94] *Doctrine*, p. 120.

[95] *Doctrine*, p. 120.

[96] Lindbeck is following Hans Frei, as well as David Kelsey's interpretation of Karl Barth here.

[97] *Doctrine*, p. 124 (emphasis mine). Clearly another instance of a pragmatic tendency in Lindbeck's argument.

[98] *Doctrine*, p. 125 (emphasis mine). In this rule of postliberalism especially we find a pragmatic tendency that shares more with the founder of pragmatism, Charles Peirce, than with any of the other pragmatists. I shall later argue, with the help of Peter Ochs, that Peirce is the pragmatist with whom Lindbeck's own tendencies flourish best, and whose pragmatism offers the most clarification and correction for the postliberal research programme.

[99] *Doctrine*, p. 128.

[100] *Doctrine*, p. 128.

[101] *Doctrine*, p. 131 (emphasis mine). Interestingly, Lindbeck is following the historian of science Thomas Kuhn on this point. The history of science was likewise crucial to Charles Peirce. Cf. Smith, *Purpose and Thought*: '[Peirce] differed from James in making the normative sciences – aesthetics, ethics and logic – basic, and deriving his conception of truth not so much from ordinary experience as from the history of science and the logic of inquiry' (p. 75).

[102] *Doctrine*, p. 131 (emphasis mine).

[103] *Doctrine*, p. 131.

[104] *Doctrine*, p. 132.

[105] The tentativeness of pragmatism is bordered by the ethical. Consider the comment of John Smith in *Purpose and Thought*:

> We are constantly forced to believe and to act – here and now – against the background of a knowledge which is not final; it will do us no good to pretend that the case is otherwise. Action does not require us to convert a tentative knowledge into an absolute certainty, but it does require us to 'make up our minds' as to what is relevant and what we must believe if we are to act at all. (p. 115)

[106] *Doctrine*, p. 132.

[107] *Doctrine*, p. 134.

[108] *Doctrine*, p. 134.

[109] In Peircean, pragmaticist terms, I have been arguing from abduction towards induction. Abduction is simply the process of hypothesis formation, it suggests what may be the case. It merely suggests; then the deductive can make predictions based upon it, which in turn can be tested only by induction, which tests whether the hypothesis actually is operative in the subject under examination. Cf. Charles Peirce, *Collected Papers of Charles Sanders Peirce*, ed. Charles Hartshorne, Paul Weiss and A. Burks (Cambridge, MA: Harvard University Press, 1935, 1958), 5.171 (hereafter *CP*). I will explore this further in Chapter 4. But for present purposes, it will suffice to describe this instance of hypothesis-formation as one which is aimed at deepening, or intensifying, enquiry. At this stage, however, all that is necessary is to have convinced the reader, by way of presumptive inference, that the observed facts show that the truth might be similar to the claims of my hypothesis. Testing the real probability of this thesis is the focus of the following chapters.

[110] Kerr, *Theology after Wittgenstein.*

[111] D.Z. Philips is probably most famous for his thoroughgoing use of Wittgenstein, but nearly all theologians now wrestle with Wittgenstein either implicitly or explicitly at some point in their work. I note just one recent example. See Sue Patterson, *Realist Christian Theology in a Postmodern Age* (Cambridge: Cambridge University Press, 1999). I share some sympathy with Patterson's thesis that Wittgenstein can be read as a kind of realist (akin to Hilary Putnam's internal realism), but continue to think that a retrieval of Wittgenstein is probably not the best way forward. I have doubts as to whether Wittgenstein is actually useful beyond the rather limited set of philosophical problems he set out to address. This can be seen clearly through Bruce Marshall's dependence upon the analytic tendency in Lindbeck, in *Trinity and Truth*, which has limited his own efforts to put forward a satisfying response to those who have expressed doubt about problems of truth and meaning in postliberalism.

[112] Such a comment ('theology as grammar') may owe more to William James and Karl Barth than Wittgenstein ever admitted. Cf. Neil B. MacDonald, *Karl Barth and the Strange New World within the Bible: Barth, Wittgenstein, and the Metadilemmas of the Enlightenment* (New York: Paternoster Press, 2000); and Russell Goodman, *Wittgenstein and William James* (Cambridge: Cambridge University Press, 2002).

[113] See David Tracy, 'Lindbeck's New Program for Theology: A Reflection', *The Thomist* 49.3 (July 1985).

[114] Russell B. Goodman, *Wittgenstein and William James* (Cambridge: Cambridge University Press, 2002), i.

[115] Cf. Goodman, *Wittgenstein and William James*, pp. 150–54.

[116] As I will suggest in the next chapter, he is more akin to Augustine than to Wittgenstein. The *Philosophical Investigations* famously open with a comment on Augustine's *Conf.* I.8. For a penetrating recent analysis of what Wittgenstein was

doing with Augustine (namely excluding his theological claims in connection to language) see M.F. Burnyeat, 'Wittgenstein and Augustine *De magistro*', in Garth B. Matthews (ed.), *The Augustinian Tradition* (Berkeley, CA: University of California Press, 1999), pp. 286–303; originally published in the *Proceedings of the Aristotelian Society*, supplementary vol. 61 (1987): 1–24. Wittgenstein's subversion of the theological in language learning and teaching has something to do with the translation he was using by Pusey, but was also a 'creative misprision' of Augustine crafted in such a way as to solve Augustine's problems without recourse to God (or the Platonic mind), that is, solved in 'naturalistic, purely human terms', p. 300.

[117]  Cf. Peter Ochs, 'Scriptural Logics: Towards a Postcritical Metaphysics', *Modern Theology* 11.1 (January 1995): 65–92. The article is dedicated, indeed, written '*for* George Lindbeck'. It was originally presented as a paper for the 'Yale Jewish Studies Tribute to George Lindbeck', in New Haven, December 1993.

[118]  There have, however, been consistent calls – usually deriving from a deep engagement with Charles Peirce – back to more realistic forms of pragmatism. To name just one example of a philosopher who has worked towards this end, see Nicholas Rescher, *Realistic Pragmatism: An Introduction to Pragmatic Philosophy* (Albany, NY: SUNY, 2000).

[119]  The classical pragmatists systematically eschewed 'coercive' argumentation in favour of 'hypothesis-formation' and the testing of hypotheses. The Yale pragmatic philosopher John E. Smith claims that this pragmatic tendency is theologically rooted in the Augustinian tradition of 'faith seeking understanding', *Purpose and Thought*, p. 165.

## Notes to Chapter 2: pp. 37–60

[120]  Lindbeck, *Doctrine*, p. 116.

[121]  Lindbeck's 1955 Yale doctorate, 'Is Duns Scotus an Essentialist?', was about the relation between Aquinas and Scotus, and argues for a 'participationist' metaphysic at the heart of the former's philosophical theology. As we shall see, this participationist approach is key to an understanding of Augustinian semiotics. Cf. *Doctrine*, p. 67.

[122]  Marshall, *Trinity and Truth*.

[123]  Eugene Rogers, *Thomas Aquinas and Karl Barth* (Notre Dame, IN: University of Notre Dame Press, 1995).

[124]  Karl Barth, like Augustine, concluded that 'the Word made flesh' constitutes 'the first, original and controlling sign of all signs', *Church Dogmatics* 2.1 (London: T&T Clark, 2004), p. 199, indicating how the structure of signification itself is central to our understanding of revelation.

[125]  Lindbeck, *Doctrine*, p. 79.

[126]  Lindbeck, *Doctrine*, p. 117.

[127]  Lindbeck, *Doctrine*, p. 134.

[128]  Lindbeck, *Doctrine*, p. 117. As we shall see, in agreement with Lindbeck, *De doctrina christiana* was just such an attempt, even though the hydraulic metaphor of 'absorption' does not adequately suit Augustine (and therefore may not adequately suit Lindbeck). I will later propose a more therapeutic metaphor to correct and clarify the hydraulic one. As already suggested, Augustine saw the scriptures as therapeutic.

[129]  Lindbeck himself notes that *The Nature of Doctrine* would have been helped by relating the 'project to the two theologians with whom I have been most in conversation over the years, Thomas Aquinas and Martin Luther' (Lindbeck in Buckley

[ed.], *The Church in a Postliberal Age*, p. 199). Both Aquinas and Luther are Augustinians, but Augustinians that represent precisely the church divisions that Lindbeck is trying to heal. By turning directly to the origins of these two figures' shared Augustinianism it is thought that resources will be brought to bear on our theological understanding of Lindbeck that will actually aid his overall ecumenical interests.

[130] Augustine is clearly not a postliberal, any more than Aquinas is a postliberal or Barth is a postliberal. Anachronism is avoided by the use of the word 'prototypical'. Where Augustine is fashioned towards postliberalism, it should be understood that this is a move that helps us to understand the meaning of postliberalism and not the other way round.

[131] See Graham Hughes, *Worship as Meaning: A Liturgical Theology for Late Modernity* (Cambridge: Cambridge University Press, 2003) for a concise comparison between Peirce and de Saussure.

[132] Tzvetan Todorov, *Theories of the Symbol* (Ithaca, NY: Cornell University Press, 1982), p. 40. I am indebted to Luigi Alici's introduction to Augustine, *Teaching Christianity: De Doctrina Christiana*, trans. Edmund Hill (Brooklyn, NY: New York City Press, 1991) ( Hereafter *De doct. chr.*), which first drew my attention to this important work.

[133] See Luigi Alici's comment on Eco in *De doct. chr.*, p. 50, n. 72. Also see U. Eco, R. Lambertini, C. Marmo and A. Taborroni, 'On Animal Language in the Medieval Classification of Signs', in  Umberto Eco and Costantino Marmo (eds), *On the Medieval Theory of Signs*, (Amsterdam: John Benjamins, 1989). Eco makes fascinating connections between Augustinian semiotics, and the medieval semiotics of Abelard and Aquinas, and shows how difficult it would be to assess any developments in semiotic theory without reference to Augustine.

[134] Brian Stock, *Augustine the Reader: Meditation, Self-Knowledge, and the Ethics of Interpretation* (Cambridge, MA: Belknap Press of Harvard University Press, 1996), p. 7. Though Stock is also dependent upon R.A. Markus and Luigi Alici (see above).

[135] Peirce, *Collected Papers*, 2.228.

[136] *De doct. chr.*, 2.1.

[137] 'What is a Sign?' in Peirce, *EP II*, 2.1.

[138] Alasdair MacIntyre, *After Virtue* (Notre Dame, IN: University of Notre Dame Press, 1981), pp. 1–2.

[139] R.A. Markus assesses Aristotle's discussion of signs in *Prior Analytics* II.27 as providing the 'broad terms for reference' in the debates between 'likeness' or 'image' and 'sign' or 'symbol', which Augustine would have been aware of from a variety of discourses he was familiar with – not least of which would have been debates about the Trinity and also scriptural interpretation. See R.A. Markus, 'St Augustine on Signs', *Phronesis* (1957): 62. Aristotle presents his sign theory, interestingly, in a work entitled *On Interpretation*, 'Spoken words are the symbols of mental experience and written words are the symbols of spoken words. Just as all men have not the same writing, so all men have not the same speech sounds, but the mental experiences, which these directly symbolize, are the same for all, as also are those things of which our experiences are the images', *On Interpretation*, 16a, in *The Works of Aristotle*, 12 vols, trans. and ed. W.D. Ross (Oxford: Clarendon Press, 1908–52). This displays Aristotle's tendency to think about words as representations, symbols of some mental experience of reality, and to think about the relationships between words, experience and reality.

[140] Stoic logic, or 'dialectics', was defined by Diogenes 'as the science "about signs and

things signified"'. See Markus, 'St Augustine on Signs', p. 62. According to the assessment of Sextus Empiricus, the Stoics insisted on the 'intervention of a conceptual intermediary' – a third thing 'between the sign and the thing signified in the sign-relation', namely that 'a sign signifies its object in virtue of a concept which applies to the object signified' (Markus, 'St Augustine on Signs', p. 63, citing Sextus Empiricus, *adv. Math.* VIII. 11–12). This conceptual or 'intellectualized' approach to mediation of the sign-relation is typical of Stoic logic that might also be called 'triadic' or dialectical (the concept between the 'third' in the relation between the sign and the signified). The theory of inference it accepts is one of 'elimination', following Aristotle. The Stoics distinguish three senses that lead a person to be convinced (in accordance with probability). First, there is the 'obvious' sense in which that which is true appears true. Then there is the 'specious' sense in which that which is false appears true. Thirdly, and most importantly for the Stoics, there is the 'general' or 'common' sense, which embraces both the first two senses and shows what is common to the truth and falsity of both, whilst leaving open the question of its own truth or falsity. (See David Sedley, 'On Signs', in Jonathan Barnes (ed.), *Signs and Speculation* (Cambridge: Cambridge University Press), p. 250.) This is descriptive of the overall logic of the Stoics, and shows the importance of their intellectualized third category (which might be described in Lindbeck's terms as a cognitive-propositional approach to sign theory).

[141] Brian Stock has written that

> it is difficult to generalize about [Augustine's] use of his sources. We are ill informed about the occasions on which he read many of the books at his disposal. Nor are we certain what he read. He knows some authors whom he does not quote; he quotes others ... selectively and interprets them as he wishes ... Augustine reshapes everything that he reads ... (*Augustine the Reader*, p. 4).

Apart from scripture, it is notoriously difficult to trace what Augustine read. According to Stock, between 391–413, the years in which his theory of signs developed, Augustine 'only extensively cited' scripture (*Augustine the Reader*, p. 4). While we can trace features of what Augustine might have received from the classical period – features which amount to a very basic but primarily Stoic theory of signs – we can also see that his own sign theory depends much more directly on what he received from the Alexandrian school of figural or typological interpretation, and from his reading of Scripture itself, as this changed his understanding of classical thinking on the subject. On this latter point, see David Dawson, 'Sign Theory, Allegorical Reading, and the Motions of the Soul in *De doctrina christiana*', in Duane Arnold and Pamela Bright (eds), *De doctrina christiana: A Classic of Western Culture* (Notre Dame, IN: University of Notre Dame Press, 1995).

[142] Augustine's Bible is roughly the same as the canon we have today; however, it was not bound as a single book, but as individual 'writings' or sometimes groups of writings such as the Psalms, the Gospels or the Pauline epistles. He documents his 'canon of Scripture,' in *De doct. chr.* 2.8.13, matching the canon of the Council of Hippo (397), as well as subsequent council decisions, and confirmed again at Trent in the sixteenth century.

[143] Ambrose hands over to Augustine a basically Alexandrian approach to the scriptures. And as Todorov notes: 'Not until Clement of Alexandria do we find, within the hermeneutic tradition itself, any effort in the direction of semiotics' (*Theories of the Symbol*, p. 32). Clement of Alexandria studies a great variety of symbol systems, including Egyptian hieroglyphics and the Hebrew scriptures, and initiates many distinctions in his theoretical contributions to a theory of sign and symbol, such as

direct and indirect, tropic and allegorical (which is, according to Todorov, 'the difference between two relations and three', *Theories of the Symbol*, p. 35) and the importance of the distinction between proper and transposed meaning. Clement fled persecution in Alexandria in 202, and when it was safe to return, Origen took his place as head of the Catechetical School, and continued this tradition. Clement and Origen represent well the kind of figural interpretation of the signs of scripture that Augustine was keen to teach in *De doctrina*. Augustine's theory of signs can be understood as an attempt at a hermeneutical method directly indebted to Clement and Origen, and those sympathetic to the Alexandrian School. But perhaps it is misleading to identify Augustine with Alexandria alone. What Augustine worked towards was a theory that eschewed oppositions between Antioch and Alexandria, between the literal and the figurative, between the proper and transposed meanings to be discovered in sacred scripture. Augustine was working towards a triunitary notion of the sign that affirmed both interpretive traditions.

[144] Markus, 'St Augustine on Signs', p. 66.

[145] Markus, 'St Augustine on Signs', p. 66.

[146] Michael Raposa originally applied the term 'theosemiotician' to Charles S. Peirce, but as Markus makes clear in his 1957 article 'St Augustine on Signs', the link between Augustine and Peirce is such that I believe, as apposite as it is for Peirce, it is an even more appropriate way of describing Augustine who is the most explicitly theological sign theorist. It is doubly significant, then, that he sits at the origins of modern sign theory.

[147] The phrase belongs to David Dawson, see 'Sign Theory, Allegorical Reading and the Motions of the Soul', in Arnold and Bright (eds), *De doctrina christiana*, p. 135.

[148] Stock, *Augustine the Reader*, p. 9. Stock is discussing Augustine's participationist view that 'signs and realities participate equally' in the beauty and eloquence of the universe. He refers to a number of discussions here, especially French commentators Maurice Pontet, *L'Exegese de s. Augustin predicateur* (Paris: Theologie 7, 1945) and C. Couturier, '"Sacramentum" et "mysterium" dans l'oevre de saint Augustin', in *Etudes augustiniennes* (1953): 161–332.

[149] Cf. *De doct. chr.* 1.13.12. Augustine argues that we are able to know God through wisdom precisely because wisdom came 'by the Word becoming flesh and dwelling amongst us … It is something like when we talk …' Augustine's theory of language, his sign theory, is itself a work which reflects an incarnational logic working itself out in a theory of human language, and if an incarnational logic, then also a trinitarian logic (in keeping with the text which is functioning as a rule here, namely Jn 1). Cf. James K.A. Smith, *Speech and Theology: Language and the Logic of Incarnation* (London: Routledge, 2002), pp. 114–29, who argues just this point about the 'incarnational logic' of Augustinian semiotics. He does not take the further step implicit in this incarnational logic, namely the trinitarian one that understands the purpose of communication in *De doct. chr.* 1.5.5 more broadly (i.e., as a vehicle or way of participation in the triune life of God). Smith's treatment of Augustine is excellent, especially in relation to Husserl and Derrida. His approach is weakened only by the fact that he seems to miss the place of scripture in the development of Augustinian semiotics. See my review of Smith in *Reviews in Religion and Theology* (June 2003): 289–91. Also see Takeshi Kato, 'Sonus et Verbum: *De doctrina christiana* 1.13.12', in Arnold and Bright (eds) *De doctrina christiana*, pp. 87–96.

[150] Edmund Hill has come down strongly in favour of reading 'doctrina' in pedagogical terms (thus his translation of *De doct. chr.* is 'Teaching Christianity'). But see Gerald A. Press, 'Augustine's *De doctrina christiana*', who rightly argues that Augustine

plays on the multiple meanings associated with *doctrina*. '*Doctrina* is a word with many meanings – teaching, instruction, education, knowledge, learning, culture – and of old and varied associations', p. 123. Press shows that it is fruitless to fix the meaning of the word *doctrina*, and much better to see the central point: Augustine is presenting a Christian '*doctrina*' that is worth having precisely because it promises to heal us – it is doctrine 'for our salvation', where *doctrina* is dedicated to discovering the Word of God in a redemptive relation to everything (sacred and secular).

[151] The tide does seem to be turning. But for example, Frederick van Fleteran still reflects the widespread assumption shared by many classical scholars in an otherwise excellent and very helpful article when he writes, 'Curiously, Augustine's semiotics stem from grammar and rhetoric, not the Bible, and in particular not the author of John's Gospel for whom sign was so significant', in 'Principles of Augustine's Hermeneutic: An Overview', in F. van Fleteran and J. C. Schnaubelt (eds), *Augustine: Biblical Exegete, Collectanea Augustiniana* (New York and Frankfurt: Peter Lang, 2001), p. 13. This opinion is probably drawn from the tendency in Augustinian studies to privilege unduly classical sources and to underestimate the deepest internal reasons for Augustine's hermeneutical decisions. Whenever Augustine 'absorbs' a theoretical point, whether it is from Philo, Plotinus or Tyconius, he 'repairs' it in a scriptural universe on theological grounds, and in doing so transforms the theory with the scriptures. When we think of Augustine as a 'synthetic thinker', as he is often called, it is important to recognize the direction of the synthetic relation (scripture absorbs and then repairs, ethically redirecting the world).

[152] Michael Cameron, 'Signs', in Allan D. Fitzgerald (ed.), *Augustine through the Ages: An Encyclopedia* (Grand Rapids, MI: Eermans, 1999), p. 795.

[153] Dawson, 'Sign Theory, p. 130.

[154] Dawson, 'Sign Theory', p. 131.

[155] *De doct. chr*. 2.5.6.

[156] The phrase belongs to David Dawson, see 'Sign Theory', p. 135.

[157] The Pauline teaching that 'faith comes from hearing' is every bit as crucial to Augustine as it is to Lindbeck.

[158] In *De doct. chr*., however, Augustine's principal concern with this 'faith that comes from hearing' is as an intratextual rule in relation to reading practices (as in his own experience, faith comes through reading the Word in a way that is intratextually consistent with the Word made flesh).

[159] Stock, *Augustine the Reader*, p. 54.

[160] Augustine, *Conf.* 6.3.4.

[161] This is a significant connection because Augustine is impressed that Ambrose reads silently. There is a profound link between hearing the word spoken aloud (preaching) and hearing the word silently, inside the mind as it were (reading). As we shall see, his earliest formative experience of Christian culture and language shapes his experience of the inner/outer distinction that reading/hearing instantiates.

[162] *Conf.* 6.4.6.

[163] It might be better to think of Augustine as 'post-Alexandrian', and 'post-Antiochan' in the sense that he seems to recognize that the debate about biblical interpretation between Antioch and Alexandria was now bridged, as we shall see in *De doct. chr*. especially. I take this as instructive for how I want to read the contemporary dyad 'Yale–Chicago'.

[164] *Conf.* 6.5.8. He further states that 'the authority of the Bible seemed the more to be venerated and more worthy of a holy faith on the ground that it was open to everyone to read, while keeping the dignity of its secret meaning for a profounder

interpretation'. The authority of scripture was due in part to its public and universal accessibility (unlike the philosophy of the Neoplatonists).

[165] *Conf.* 13.15.18.

[166] *Conf.* 13.18.22.

[167] *Conf.* 13.15.17. 'Fingers', suggesting that God has actually written, in some sense, the scriptures with human hands, and means to heal the world through this divine writing in the same way. Cf. *Conf.* 7.20.26, 'my wounds were healed by your gentle fingers', referring to the effect God's 'books' had upon him.

[168] *Conf.* 13.19.24. The text in Isaiah links reasoning with redemption and a transformed life of obedience to God poured out in service to the 'other' ('rescue the oppressed, defend the orphan, plead for the widow').

[169] *Conf.* 13.16.19.

[170] Erich Przywara, *An Augustine Synthesis* (London: Sheed and Ward, 1991), pp. 88–9.

[171] *Conf.* 7.20.26.

[172] *Conf.* 11.2.2–3. Scripture study, according to Augustine, is the central duty of a bishop in caring for his own strength and for the welfare of his flock. Here he is extensively citing the Psalms, and while Chadwick suggests that 'to meditate in your law' is a citation of Psalm 38.4, it is much better read as an echo of Psalm 119 (Ps. 118 in the Vulgate) where the phrase recurs a number of times and shows the point about inhabiting the scriptures in a fuller way.

[173] *Conf.* 11.2.2–3.

[174] This is especially true of the latter half of the work. James J. O'Donnell notes the shift that comes after Book 10, when the narrative changes its voice to the present tense, and seeks to involve the reader, through meditation in the scriptures and on the Holy Trinity. These latter books have been neglected because of this shift, and as a result, little attention has been paid to the place of scripture in these books (which is striking since Book 12 is devoted to the 'Word' and Book 13 has extended reflections on the Bible constituting God's heavenly firmament).

[175] *Conf.* 12.25.34–5. This, interestingly, is a point made in the context of promoting the public nature of truth (truth belongs to no one but is shared as a public possession). Earlier he writes that God is 'the truth presiding over all things', (*Conf.* 10.41.66).

[176] Cf. Plotinus, *The Enneads* (London: Penguin Press, 1991), 5.1.1.

[177] *Conf.* 7.9.13. Citing John 1, but aware of its resonance in Platonist thought concerning the illumination of the divine Reason (Logos). Cf. Augustine, *The Trinity: De Trinitate 1/5* (Brooklyn, NY: New York City Press, 1991), 4.4–6. (Hereafter *De trin.*)

[178] *Conf.* 7.9.13.

[179] *Conf.* 7.9.14 (emphasis mine).

[180] It is interesting to place this text about the Word made flesh and 'dwelling' or 'tenting' with us (*eskenosen / habitavit*) in conversation with his thoughts on scripture as a House of God, or as the firmament of authority, or as 'skin stretched over us', playing on both the notion of the 'skin' of parchment paper and the 'skin' of ancient tents (as he does in *Conf.* 13.15ff.).

[181] The text also meditates on Philippians 2.5–11, but it does so in an intertextual way that hermeneutically privileges John 1.1–14. See also James J. O'Donnell's (ed.), *Augustine: Commentary on the Confessions*, 3 vols (Oxford: Clarendon Press, 1992) for further insights on the structural importance of 7.9.13–14.

[182] This follows, as we shall see, his own insights on the received tradition concerning

the 'rule of faith', which is sometimes simply the canon of scripture itself and sometimes a rule about clearer passages being used to interpret, intratextually, more obscure ones. This is another case of Augustinian synthesis, where he combines diverse understandings of the rule of faith as a hermeneutical principle into a theological complex, being generated by the self-giving of God. The postliberal interest in 'habits' can be fruitfully reread in light of the *habitavit* of this rule for Christian scriptural pragmatism.

[183] Augustine, *The City of God: De civitate dei*, trans. Marcus Dods (New York: Random House, 1999), 10.29. (Hereafter *Civ. dei.*) Written from 413–26, one can see here the enduring attention Augustine pays to John 1.1–14, even two decades after the *Confessions* and *De doctrina christiana* were written.

[184] See *Conf.* 12.25. Cf. Cyril O'Regan, '*De doctrina christiana* and Modern Hermeneutics', in *De doctrina christiana: A Classic of Western Culture* (Notre Dame, IN: University of Notre Dame Press, 1995). O'Regan has noted that Augustine insists both on the need to read scripture well and the need to identify the rhetorical function of a text both inside and outside the Christian community. What is a text meant to *do* for reading communities?

[185] Augustine could not be charged with the same kind of sectarianism that some postliberal theologians get accused of today. Christianity for Augustine is always already a public affair, and this is as true before the Constantinian 'compromise' as it is ever after, always demanding a dynamic view of the church–world relation. It would be better to do away with anxieties over sectarianism in contemporary debates and focus instead on what the scriptures teach with regard to 'the neighbour'.

[186] *Conf.* 8.12. It is interesting that Augustine's own conversion, recounted in *Confessions*, is one in which he hears a child saying '*tolle lege*', 'pick up' and 'read.' These words were signs to him from God, and it is difficult to ignore this aspect of his autobiography when attending to the pattern of his development on signs – especially when one considers that Augustine receives first verbal signs, which then direct him to written signs. He later takes these two events in turn, semiotically, moving from verbal signs in *De magistro* (389) to written signs in *De doct. chr.* (396).

[187] Chadwick's translation offers a nice interpretation of *securitatis*: 'it was as if a light of relief from all anxiety flooded into my heart'. The effect of 'relief' is akin to a kind of peace and security. Augustine frequently links this kind of relief to 'peace' which only God can give through his Word, resonating biblically for him in such texts as Phil. 4.7, 'the peace which passes all understanding'.

[188] Cf. *Conf.* 3 and *Conf.* 8. 'Light' (*luce*) is a frequent metaphor used in scripture whenever discussing Israel's relation to the holy writ. Israel is to be a light to the Gentiles precisely in its observance of the Torah. Augustine also tends, as we see here, to refer to the scriptures in terms of light, and understands the Word as that which illuminates the world ('infuses' the world with light). He sometimes uses the language of ascent [which is biblical before it is platonic], imagining the world being 'taken up' into God's life through participation in the Word (there is clearly a link between Jacob's ladder and the Word of God). This overall sense could lead one to use 'hydraulic' metaphors for the word–world relation (as Lindbeck indeed does); however, the hydraulic metaphors might not do justice to the dynamism of what Augustine takes to be the purpose of such illumination or participation, namely the redemption of the world. And to be truer to the biblical metaphor, perhaps the dynamism has to do with a constant two-way flow of ascent and descent.

[189] As Dawson writes, 'scripture textually replicates the Incarnation', in 'Signs Theory', p. 135.

[190] Stock, *Augustine the Reader*, p. 61 (emphasis mine).

[191] Stock, *Augustine the Reader*, p. 64 (emphasis mine). See *Conf.* 6.4.6: 'And I was delighted to hear Ambrose in his sermons to the people saying, as if he were most carefully enunciating a principle of exegesis: "the letter kills, the Spirit gives life".' Augustine also links in this passage 'healing' with 'believing' that the scriptures ('the medicines of faith ... applied ... to the sicknesses of the world') are true.

[192] Gerald A. Press puts Augustine's point infelicitously as a new redemptive society with 'a religion based on a book'. His emphasis upon being 'based on a book' does not quite do justice to the subtly of Augustine's thought, and suggests both a foundationalism and a biblicism that does not ring true. See Press, 'The Subject and Structure of Augustine's *De doctrina christiana*', *Augustinian Studies*, 11 (1980): 121.

[193] Todorov places Augustine's initial reflections on signs even earlier, to 387, in *De dialectica* (*On Dialectics*). However, as this work has been disputed as genuine, I will leave it out of my treatment (as Markus does) despite the high probability that it was indeed written by Augustine. Todorov's treatment of *On Dialectics* is extensive, more extensive than his treatment of Augustine's other works, and his treatment would have been stronger had he placed as strong an emphasis upon the more secure (and developed) texts, such as *De doct. chr.* and *De trin.* (as does Brian Stock). What appears in *De doct. chr.* is a much more developed and applied version of the semiotic displayed in *On Dialectics*, which Todorov also compares with *The Teacher* (*De magistro*); see Todorov, *Theories of the Symbol*, pp. 36–40. Todorov fills a gap in the literature by treating *De dialectica*, and offers a strong case for a start to Augustinian semiotics in this text (nevertheless, he calls *De doctrina christiana* 'the first semiotic work'). However, both *De dialectica* and *De magistro* can give the impression that Augustine's sign theory is simply the result of his classical training in grammar and rhetoric. Attentiveness to his mature theology is essential for understanding his sign theory as it was received by subsequent generations.

[194] In *De magistro* he is interested in the meaning of the relationship between the sign and the signified. Cf. Augustine *The Teacher* (*De magistro*), trans. P. King (Indianapolis, IN: Hackett, 1995), 10.33, 132 (hereafter *De mag.*). Augustine sees that the power of the sign is not in itself, but in the relationships it mediates. Augustine says to Adeodatus, 'Most of all I'm trying to persuade you, if I'll be able to, that we don't learn anything by these signs called words. As I have stated, we learn the meaning of the word – that is, the signification hidden in the sound – once the thing signified is itself known, rather than our perceiving it by means of such signification' (*De mag.* 10.34, 155). The purpose of language learning, then, is to place the learner into a meaningful relationship with reality. In other words, language – the sign system – intends to transcend itself. This is where we begin to see that Augustine has developed a theological philosophy of language (generated by the scriptures) that sees that the play of signification is intended to teach us the wisdom of God for those who believe. Meditating on Isaiah 7.9, 'Unless you believe, you shall not understand', Augustine posits that it is Christ, 'the unchangeable power and everlasting wisdom of God', who dwells 'in the inner man' and teaches us (*De mag.* 11.38). We can see in *De mag.* the turn towards the incarnate Word as the source of 'meaning', or that that is unseen 'inner' in the external play of signification, but his reflections here do not yet lead him to the scriptural or semiotic pragmatism displayed in *De doct. chr.*

[195] Serge Lancel, *St Augustine*, trans. Antonia Nevill (London: SCM Press, 2002), p. 185. It is too early to tell if this dating by Lancel will hold, but an impressive case is made

reflecting research on new material. The traditional date given is 396, the year he begins work on *De Doct. chr.*

196  Cf. Marianne Djuth, 'The Royal Way: Augustine's Freedom of the Will and the Monastic Tradition', in van Fleteran and Schnaubelt (eds), *Augustine: Biblical Exegete*, pp. 129ff.

197  *De doct. chr.* Prologue, 1.

198  *De doct. chr.* Prologue, 8.

199  *De doct. chr.* Prologue, 8.

200  Roland Teske, 'The Good Samaritan (Lk 10.29–37) in Augustine's Exegesis', in van Fleteran and Schnaubelt, *Augustine*, p. 356.

201  Frederick van Fleteran, 'Principles of Augustine's Hermeneutic: An Overview', in van Fleteran and Schnaubelt, *Augustine*, p. 2. It is interesting to compare Augustine's *De doct. chr.* with Jean-Luc Marion, especially his fifth chapter 'Of the Eucharistic Site of Theology', in *God Without Being* (Chicago, IL: University of Chicago Press, 1991). Marion is reticent about Augustine in this work (against onto-theology). Yet the fifth chapter is, I believe, one of the best commentaries on *De doctrina christiana* written in recent years, even though Marion makes no mention of it at all. Even his reflections on the importance of the bishop as theologian *par excellence* seem not so subtly to veil reference to Augustine here. Cf. Mike Kraftson-Hogue, 'Predication Turning to Praise: Marion and Augustine on God and Hermeneutics', *Literature and Theology* 14.4 (2000): 399–411.

202  Augustine does not use the word *harmonia* in *De doct. chr.*, but I borrow from his theological use of it in *De trin.* 4.1.4, where he likens our participation in the Word made flesh (simultaneously partaking of both humanity and divinity) to the Greek idea of *harmonia,* clearly recalling his early work *De musica*, evidenced in his musical references to singing, tuning strings, tonometer, etc. With Catherine Pickstock I agree that Augustine actually offers a non-dualist account of reality (though I think it is the corrective pressure of the scriptures on his thought which prompt this development, owing especially to a christological and trinitarian reading). Cf. Pickstock, 'Soul, City and Cosmos after Augustine', in John Milbank, Catherine Pickstock and Graham Ward (eds), *Radical Orthodoxy* (London: Routledge, 1999), pp. 243–77.

203  *De doct. chr.* 1.1. Cf. William S. Babcock, '*Caritas* and Signification in *De doctrina christiana* 1–3', in Arnold and Bright (eds), *De doctrina christiana*, p. 145. As Babcock notes, Augustine says so much, it is easy to forget that this treatise is meant to serve one purpose: the *tractatio* (use or treatment) of the scriptures that best serves love of God and neighbour. The first three books deal with discovering the truth and meaning (the Word) of the scriptures, and the fourth book teaches how to communicate these discoveries to others in an attractive way. For greater depth on *tractatio* as the orienting concern of *De doct. chr.*, see Press, 'Augustine's *De doctrina christiana*', pp. 107–18. Press argues, with the textual evidence on his side but previous Augustinian scholarship against him, that the entirety of the work is oriented around *tractatio scripturarum* (and thus places all four books in the rhetorical tradition). Most commentators now seem to follow Press.

204  *De doct. chr.* 1.2.2. Charles Peirce will echo this over fourteen centuries later (1894) when he writes 'we think only in signs', in 'What is a Sign?', *EP*, 2.10.

205  *De doct. chr.* 1.2.2.

206  *Conf.* 10.43.69.

207  *De doct. chr.* 1.13.12.

208  This is implicit in linking the production of language with the incarnation of the Logos. Cf. *De trin.* 15.19,20 where he says 'the reason it [scripture] is called the word

of God is that it conveys divine not human teaching [he means both]. But the Word of God we are now seeking to see, however imperfectly, through this likeness, is the one of which it was said, The Word was God (Jn 1.1); of which it was said, All things were made through him (Jn 1.3); of which it was said, The Word became flesh (Jn 1.14) ...'

[209] For a comprehensive history of debates on the use–enjoyment distinction see Oliver O'Donovan's unsurpassed essay, '*Usus* and *Fruitio* in Augustine, *De doctrina christiana* I', *Journal of Theological Studies*, new series, 33.2 (1982): 361–97; also *The Problem of Self-Love in Augustine* (New Haven, CT: Yale University Press, 1980). Cf. John Burnaby, 'Amor in St Augustine', in C.W. Kegley (ed.), *The Philosophy and Theology of Anders Nygren* (Carbondale, IL: Southern Illinois University Press, 1970). Burnaby deals with earlier views from the 1930s, such as those of Anders Nygren and Gunnar Hultgren. Also see Ragner Holte, *Beatitude et sagesse: Saint Augustin et le problème de la fin d'homme dans la philosophie ancienne* (Paris: Etudes augustiniennes, 1962). O'Donovan ultimately rejects Holte's groundbreaking thesis on *uti–frui* (which made the distinction about practical and theoretical reasoning) in favour of Burnaby's view that there are multiple ways of understanding *uti–frui* in Augustine, but that the distinction is about the order of love. For the importance of this distinction in relation to *De trin.*, see my 'How Augustine Used the Trinity: Functionalism and the Development of Doctrine', *Anglican Theological Review* 85.1: 135–41, which stresses the anagogical and eschatological understanding of the distinction. My view now reflects an understanding of the distinction in terms of Augustine's scriptural pragmatism, with many implications (ontological, ethical, anagogical, eschatological, etc.).

[210] *De doct. chr.* 1.3.3.

[211] *De doct. chr.* 1.5.5.

[212] Stock has noted that for Augustine, 'the reading of scripture is the key element in the pursuit of wisdom' (*Augustine the Reader*, p. 9). Or it might be said that scripture locates our reading after wisdom. Augustine writes that wisdom has become for us a home, indeed, wisdom has 'made herself for us into the way home' (*De doct. chr.* 1.11.11). He writes similar things about Christ the Word as the way. The metaphor of travel is prominent in Augustine's thinking about signs (and very much bound up with his use–enjoyment distinction, and thus his scriptural pragmatism). Signs are thought of as 'vessels' or vehicles (the English word 'tractor' even comes from the Latin root *tracto*) which serve a mediatorial purpose, traversing distances, bridging gaps, directing, even pulling the intellect and will in a particular direction (i.e. eschatologically towards 'home', towards 'complete health', towards 'the love of God and neighbour').

[213] *De doct. chr.* 1.14.13 (emphasis mine).

[214] There are at least two reasons for this: (1) The structure and purpose of *De doct. chr.* are debated, and the many 'digressions' which occur in the treatise give readers the impression that the work is not unified; and (2) the healing metaphors which run throughout the work, but are especially linked in Book 1 with God's economy of healing are not read in any significant relation to the sign theory or the scriptural pragmatism it serves. Additionally, Augustine's frequent use of the word *tractatio*, and its medical connotations, are underappreciated. Hopefully Edmund Hill's new English translation will impact future interpretations, as his 'treatment' for *tractatio* retains the therapeutic and reparative aspect of the scriptures.

[215] *Conf.* 13.26.41, 'the fruit is the intention'. Cf. *De trin.* 15.31–5. Augustine looks to John 4.7 'Whoever does not love does not know God' as evidence that our enjoyment

of God must be made manifest in our love for the other. He looks also to Paul and Galatians 5.6, to commend us to a 'faith which works through love'. He continues a line of reasoning that takes the gift of God in Christ to be the Holy Spirit, and this divine gift-giving to be paradigmatic of Christian love for the other that he sees encoded in the story of the Good Samaritan. It is this gift of the Holy Spirit, which Augustine notes in Acts 10.44 was 'poured out among the nations also', which always ensures that the upward movement (love of God) enables the outward movement (towards the love of neighbour). The love of God enables the love of neighbour to be effective; it is the condition of the possibility of virtue.

[216] Dawson, 'Sign Theory', p. 125.

[217] Stock, *Augustine the Reader*, p. 12. Augustine's hermeneutical insights are always guided by this concern for the neighbour. See *De doct. chr.* 1.30.31, where the text before him is Luke 10.26ff. where Jesus asks the ultimate hermeneutical question 'What is written in the Torah and how do you read it?' This led Augustine directly into the ethical considerations of what it means to love the 'neighbour', which amounts to something like a theocentrically informed hermeneutic of ethical compassion to the other.

[218] *De doct. chr.* 1.39.35.

[219] *De doct. chr.* 1.38.34. Commenting on John 14.6, 'I am the way, the truth and the life', Augustine believes that the Word was made flesh so that we might have a way to the Father. Likewise, the Word in the scriptures is 'for our salvation'. Cf. *De doct. chr.* 2.6.5 where the scriptures heal 'the nations' who discover the divine will through them (by the inspiration of the Spirit).

[220] *De doct. chr.* 1.40.36.

[221] *De doct. chr.* 1.43.39 'But with them as a kind of scaffolding, such an impressive structure of faith and hope and charity has arisen ...' I am indebted to Ben Quash for enriching my reading of this text in an unpublished paper 'The Tent of Meeting and the Scaffolding of Wisdom', where he thinks of Jacob's ladder, and then scripture as a kind of scaffold with reparative implications (apparently unaware of this Augustinian reference).

[222] *De doct. chr.* 1.41.37. But cf. 1.43.39 where he entertains the possibility that the scaffold could be pushed away if the theological virtues were firmly set, as they would be in the event of a beatific vision (but this seems only a theoretical possibility throughout his life). But even if one could push away the scriptures for oneself, they would still need the scriptures 'for instructing others.' In *Conf.* 13.15.18 he suggests that only the angels have no need of the scriptures for God himself is a book to them, never closed or folded shut, but always open.

[223] *De doct. chr.* 1.28.27, where this follows comment upon Matthew 22.37–40 concerning the love of God and neighbour. Cf. *Civ. dei* 15.22, where Augustine comments on Canticles 2.4, 'Order love within me.' In *De doct. chr.* Augustine wants scripture rightly to order human love towards the other (broadly conceived as God and neighbour). He believes that if the scriptures are used properly they will reshape human will and intellect and effect 'justice' and 'complete health' in the world. This is an early case for 'restorative justice' following on from the wisdom gained through scripture study.

[224] Markus, 'Signs, Communication, and Communities in Augustine's *De doctrina christiana*', in Arnold and Bright (eds), *De doctrina christiana*, p. 103.

[225] *De doct. chr.* 2.3.2.

[226] *De doct. chr.* 2.4.3.

[227] *De doct. chr.* 2.5.4.

[228] *De doct. chr.* 2.5.4.

[229] *De doct. chr.* 2.6.5.

[230] *De doct. chr.* 2.6.5.

[231] *De doct. chr.* 2.9–11. Augustine describes a seven-stage search for wisdom (akin to 'faith seeking understanding'), wherein scripture study is mentioned in the third stage (*doctrina*). However, I think it is legitimate to understand the third stage not as 'the scripture stage' but as the stage of learning the inner logic of the scriptures, which is to love God and neighbour. I prefer, then, to read all seven stages as stages of scriptural reading, where the third stage is particularly important hermeneutically. The reader must begin seeking wisdom, the beginning of which is 'the fear of God'. The fear of God entails a transformation of human desire, so that the reader wishes 'to know his will, what he bids us seek and shun'. 'What is needed next is to grow modest with piety, and not to contradict the divine scripture ... we should rather think and believe that what is written there is better and truer, even if its meaning is hidden, than any good ideas we can think up for ourselves.' The next stage is knowledge of what the scriptures are about, namely love of God and love of neighbour. All of this enables the reader to recognize 'the authority of the sacred books', and the need for 'divine help' in reading. This is the beginning of the fourth stage, 'that of fortitude or courage, in which one is hungry and thirsty for justice'. The fifth stage is communal, it seeks 'counsel which goes with mercy', and at this stage you perfect your love of neighbour. In the sixth and penultimate stage is purgation and cleansing for purity of heart and a love of truth. And the seventh stage is wisdom, which is enjoyed 'in peace and tranquility'. The scriptures, it is true, are mentioned as part of this process, but they also frame the process, suggesting that each stage enables participation in the Word. At a minimum, we must conclude that *De doct. chr.* is primarily concerned with the parabolic movement from wisdom/Word to words to world (liberal arts), and from world to words to Word/wisdom, and that the interpretation of scripture plays a central part in this process of transformation.

[232] Mark D. Jordan, 'Words and Word: Incarnation and Signification in Augustine's *De doctrina christiana*', *Augustinian Studies*, 11 (1980): 178. Cf. *De doct. chr.* 1.14.13. See also Oliver Davies, 'The Sign Redeemed: A Study in Christian Fundamental Semiotics', *Modern Theology* 19.2 (April 2003): 226. Davies stresses the sacramental rite of the eucharist, where Augustine's sacramental semiotics are first more broadly theological and scriptural before they become recontextualized through liturgical performance.

[233] *De doct. chr.* 2.1.1.

[234] See the appendix to Markus, 'St Augustine on Signs'.

[235] Markus, 'Signs, Communication, and Communities', p. 103.

[236] Cf. *De doct. chr.* 2.19.29 concerning the building up of human institutions. Linking these thoughts, it becomes particularly apparent that the scriptural signs have a prominent role not only in the building up of communities of a Christian culture, but also in the building up of a shared or common culture through shared semiotic systems (the liberal arts).

[237] *De doct. chr.* 2.3.2.

[238] *De doct. chr.* 2.3.2.

[239] Charles Peirce calls this 'the logic of relatives'.

[240] *De doct. chr.* 2.3.2.

[241] *De doct. chr.* 2.10.15. 'Now there are two reasons why texts are not understood: if they are veiled in signs that are either unknown or ambiguous.'

242 *De doct. chr.* 3.2.2, 2–5.
243 *De doct. chr.* 3.2.5.
244 *De doct. chr.* 3.9.13.
245 *De doct. chr.* 3.9.13.
246 *De doct. chr.* 3.15.23.
247 This is the central similarity between Augustine and Peirce which has generated the hypothesis about a *vestigium trinitatis* in the logic of scriptural semiotics.

### Notes to Chapter 3, pp. 61–98

248 Though Ochs does not have them specifically in mind, I am especially concerned about the tendencies of those continental postmodern writers such as Alain Badiou, Gianni Vattimo and Slavoj Zizek who turn to the scriptures (especially to the Pauline epistles) in their critique of modernity, but offer philosophers and theologians no constructive way forward, only apocalyptic upheaval. See, e.g., Alain Badiou, *Ethics* (London: Verso, 2001) and Slavoj Zizek, *The Puppet and the Dwarf: The Perverse Core of Christianity* (Cambridge, MA: MIT Press, 2003). Ochs's postmodern return to the scriptures can be fruitfully contrasted with these continental postmodernisms that do not seem to offer either the rules for repair or the strategies for imaginative reconstruction that a Peircean, scriptural pragmatism does.
249 Ochs, *PPLS.*
250 Jim Fodor, review of *Peirce, Pragmatism and the Logic of Scripture* in *Pro Ecclesia* 10.4 (2002): 496.
251 *PPLS*, p. 36. Citing Peirce's pragmatic maxim.
252 Peter Ochs, 'The Logic of Indignity and the Logic of Redemption', The Center for Theological Inquiry, Consultation on Theological Anthropology (2003), p. 5.
253 I do not mean to suggest that a Jewish thinker like Peter Ochs is actually a Christian, after Augustine, but only that the strand of the Augustinian tradition identified in this thesis stresses a scriptural pragmatism that has recourse to God. It is this strand of the Augustinian tradition in which I find it helpful to place Ochs (partly due to his reliance on Peirce, whose logic is informed by this tradition).
254 See Louis Menand's *The Metaphysical Club* (London: Flamingo, 2002) for the significance of pragmatism in relation to the American Civil War, the bloodiest and most painful in American history.
255 *PPLS*, p. i.
256 *PPLS*, p. i.
257 Or rather a theo-logic that inscribes God's redemptive action in the workings (*oikonomia*) of the world.
258 See my, 'Radical Traditions and the Return to Scripture in Religion and Theology', *Reviews in Religion and Theology* 10.4 (September 2003). On the communitarian case for 'tradition-constituted' reasoning, see MacIntyre, *After Virtue*, 2nd edn (Notre Dame: University of Notre Dame Press, 1984) or Alisdair MacIntyre, *Three Rival Versions of Moral Enquiry* (London: Duckworth, 1990).
259 Ochs edits, with Stanley Hauerwas, a book series called 'Radical Traditions'. The series includes books by George Lindbeck and David Weiss Halivni, and in some ways can be understood to rely on the work of these two senior figures.
260 *PPLS*, p. 51.
261 *PPLS*, p. 35. For Ochs, the word 'return' is laden with its biblical Hebrew meaning, *teshuvah*, which means a return to faith in God, and to obedience to his word

inscribed in Torah. The 'return to sources' entails not just a return of the postmodern to the modern, or the modern to the scholastic, or the scholastic to patristic and rabbinical forms of scriptural theology but a return to the potential coherence of all these through a return to scripture as the foundation of all these traditions of enquiry.

[262] I am concerned that too many reviewers separate the first and second parts of *PPLS*, as if the Peircean aspects of the argument concerning philosophical traditions of reading could somehow be separated from its implications for religious traditions of reading. Those who suggest that the 'final chapter' can be taken separately miss, I think, the force of the whole book. This should be apparent from the simple fact that the final chapter, which some take as an arbitrary departure from the Peircean analysis, is in fact a practical test against each of the book's twelve hypotheses (which is, in fact, required for a pragmatic reading of pragmatism), proving through performance.

[263] *PPLS*, p. 35.

[264] I cannot claim to represent Peircean scholarship, but even a basic survey of reviews shows that Peirce scholars are still approaching this book with caution, despite its ability to bring insight and practical bearing upon a central issue (Peirce's intellectual development) within their field. The review by Richard Smyth, in *Transactions of the Charles Sanders Peirce Society* 35.2 (spring 1999), shows the reluctance of some Peircean scholars to think constructively about the interpretation of Peirce. Frequently the concern is that Ochs has misrepresented Peirce in some way, either at the level of logical analysis or at the level of 'authorial intention'. Some philosophers of religion worry explicitly that what Ochs offers is merely an account of rabbinic logic, loosely supported by the authority of Peirce (viz. Wayne Proudfoot's review in *Journal of Religion* 79.4 (October 1999). Such criticisms miss both the force and intention of Ochs's project, which is a dialogical enquiry in religious scriptural logics (both Jewish and Christian) and philosophical scriptural logics, understanding 'scripture' in terms of Peirce's logical graphs ('graphings' or 'engravings' or 'scriptures'). I read such dissent as resistance to interpretive innovation in Peirce scholarship, deriving from logical tendencies within analytic philosophy that restrict such innovation (it is telling that it is German philosophers within the continental tradition – such as Gadamer or Apel – who argue most passionately for the relevance of Peirce). However, not all traditional Peircean scholars are resistant in this way; see, e.g., the excellent review by Christopher Hookway in *Religious Studies* 35 (1999). Though Hookway tentatively acknowledges *PPLS* as 'well beyond the range of most secondary literature on Peirce', he also sees it as a bold and promising study that richly rewards careful attention.

[265] The Society of Textual Reasoning have engaged Ochs in conversation since the inception of the group as 'the Postmodern Jewish Philosophy Bitnetwork'; for a description see *PPLS*. Amongst Christian theologians, see the sympathetic reviews by David Burrell in *Modern Theology* 15.4 (1999), Jim Fodor in *Pro Ecclesia* 10.4 (autumn 2000), and Nicholas Adams in *Heythrop Journal* 42.3 (2001). Cf. David Ford, '"He is our peace": The Letter to the Ephesians and the Theology of Fulfillment – A Dialogue with Peter Ochs', http://etext.lib.virginia.edu/journals/ssr/issues/volume1/number1/ssr01-01-a01.html. Ford responds to Ochs through his treatment of Ephesians as well in 'A Messiah for the Third Millenium', *Modern Theology* 16.1 (2000). My own work is a contribution to the Christian reception and testing of Peter Ochs's theory of scriptural pragmatism, developing his assessment of Lindbeck and theologically supplementing it with a return to Augustinian semiotics.

266 It is worth noting that Ochs has been writing 'towards' this thesis for at least 25 years. To my knowledge the first mention of 'scriptural pragmatism' was in an article called 'Scriptural Pragmatism: Jewish Philosophy's Concept of Truth', in the *International Philosophical Quarterly* 26 (1986): 32–47. There he writes that in the Hebrew scriptures 'truth (*emet*) is a character of personal relationships', that 'truth is the bond of trust between persons and between God and Humanity' (p. 131). However, his interest, as he states in *PPLS*, goes back even further to his early interest in rabbinic logic, which led him to study Peirce at Yale in the late 1970s under John E. Smith, one of America's leading Peircean pragmatists at that time (could a strong Peircean presence at Yale have influenced Lindbeck?). I understand all of Ochs's theoretical work as a logical instantiation of the bond of trust between God and humanity, a redemptive relation he understands as truth, *emet*. This is not to understand the scriptures as 'truth' or even God as 'truth', but to understand truth as constitutive of human–divine relationality (itself a logic of repair). He writes:

> Truth, say the rabbis, is the seal of God. But to declare that God is truth is not yet to have received God's truth, which comes, ultimately, in the end of time, or piecemeal, at the end of each act of inquiry. It is, rather, to declare one's conviction that the failures we suffer are God's means of correcting our incomplete knowledge of His word and that by repairing our failures we come to know His word more deeply. (Ochs, 'Scriptural Pragmatism', p. 135)

267 *PPLS*, p. 36 citing Peirce, *CP* 5.402: 1893. Jesus provides here a criterion for judging 'the prophet,' the one who speaks for God, and therefore enscribes God's rule.

268 *PPLS*, p. 5.

269 *PPLS*, p. 9.

270 *PPLS*, p. 5.

271 *PPLS*, p. 5 (original emphasis).

272 *PPLS*, p. 305.

273 *PPLS*, pp. 6, 24.

274 *PPLS*, p. 6.

275 *PPLS*, p. 42.

276 *PPLS*, p. 9. There are stages to this method of reading, and Ochs suggests four of them: (1) 'collect the explicit texts' and map them semiotically (reference to sense) in order to assess the arguments; (2) 'reconstruct the texts … in a way that could conceivably separate the senses and references of the arguments' (e.g. hypotheses, problems, methods, leading tendencies); (3) 'distinguish between two kinds of leading tendency and … apply the working hypothesis that underlies the method of reading; (4) 'distinguish between the explicit Cartesian–Kantian text and the implicit text of which it is a sign. The explicit text defines itself as a definite and general (or indeterminate) sign of that possible world of which it makes some claim.' Three additional stages are given to 'interpretation'.

277 *PPLS*, p. 6.

278 *PPLS*, p. 20. This is not to suggest that sensitive Peircean scholars, like Richard Bernstein, Sandra Rosenthal or Murray Murphy, do not read him pragmatically. It is only to suggest that Ochs offers another level of insight by turning to the scriptural dimensions of his thought.

279 *PPLS*, p. 13. The emphasis upon the therapeutic in Ochs has (a Christian is tempted to say) messianic dimensions, continually drawing attention back to the source of the healing, the logic of scripture.

280 *PPLS*, p. 59.

[281] *PPLS*, p. 63.

[282] *PPLS*, p. 60.

[283] The phrase is Alasdair McIntyre's, but the list of thinkers is long, from Husserl and Wittgenstein to Thomas Kuhn and Charles Taylor.

[284] *PPLS*, p. 86. I am abstracting this text from its context, where is it being used to show tensions between Peirce's leading tendencies, simultaneously towards realism and conceptualism. But there is also a significant point to be made here about the ethical shape of logic.

[285] *PPLS*, p. 106.

[286] *PPLS*, pp. 106, 111, citing *CP* 5.130.

[287] *PPLS*, p. 113.

[288] See *PPLS*, p. 126.

[289] *PPLS*, p. 113.

[290] *PPLS*, p. 116, citing *CP* 5.28.

[291] *PPLS*, p. 114.

[292] *PPLS*, p. 126.

[293] *PPLS*, p. 114, citing *CP* 5.171.

[294] Peter Ochs, 'Scriptural Logic: Diagrams for a Postcritical Metaphysics', *Modern Theology* 11.1 (January 1995): 65.

[295] Ochs, 'Scriptural Logic', pp. 65–6.

[296] Ochs, 'Scriptural Logic', p. 68.

[297] Ochs, 'Scriptural Logic', p. 68.

[298] Ochs, 'Scriptural Logic', p. 68.

[299] Ochs, 'Scriptural Logic', p. 68.

[300] Ochs, 'Scriptural Logic', p. 69. This is a clear indication that the 'textualist' is George Lindbeck.

[301] Ochs, 'Scriptural Logic', pp. 69–70. I would add that the entire book, *Peirce, Pragmatism and the Logic of Scripture*, is an exercise in making these finer distinctions.

[302] Ochs, 'Scriptural Logic', p. 70.

[303] Ochs, 'Scriptural Logic', p. 70.

[304] Ochs, 'Scriptural Logic', p. 70.

[305] Ochs, 'Scriptural Logic', p. 70 (emphasis mine).

[306] Ochs, 'Scriptural Logic', p. 70.

[307] Ochs, 'Scriptural Logic', p. 70 (emphasis mine).

[308] Ochs, 'Scriptural Logic', p. 71, citing *CP* 2.189 (emphasis original).

[309] Ochs, 'Scriptural Logic', p. 72 (emphasis original).

[310] Ochs, 'Scriptural Logic', p. 74 (emphasis original).

[311] Cf. Ochs, 'Scriptural Logic', where he says 'postcritical theology emerges as a critique of the use of historicist, rationalist and emotivist modes of reasoning as modes of reading Scripture' (p. 75).

[312] Ochs, 'Scriptural Logic', p. 75.

[313] Ochs, 'Scriptural Logic', p. 75. Drawing on *CP* 4.552 and Peirce's discussion of the agency of scripture.

[314] Ochs, 'Scriptural Logic', p. 75.

[315] Ochs, 'Scriptural Logic', p. 75, citing *CP* 4.553.

[316] Ochs, 'Scriptural Logic', p. 85.

[317] Ochs, 'Scriptural Logic', p. 85.

[318] In a way that is logically similar to what might be taken to be a *vestigium trinitatis* in the scriptural semiotics of Augustine.

[319] Ochs, 'Scriptural Logic', p. 86.

[320] Ochs, 'Scriptural Logic', p. 86.

[321] *PPLS*, p. 275.

[322] *PPLS*, p. 275.

[323] *PPLS*, p. 275.

[324] *PPLS*, p. 275.

[325] *PPLS*, p. 276.

[326] *PPLS*, p. 285.

[327] *PPLS*, p. 285.

[328] *PPLS*, pp. 289–90.

[329] *PPLS*, p. 290.

[330] *PPLS*, p. 292.

[331] *PPLS*, p. 293.

[332] *PPLS*, p. 293.

[333] *PPLS*, p. 294.

[334] *PPLS*, p. 294, quoting Buber.

[335] *PPLS*, p. 294.

[336] *PPLS*, p. 296.

[337] *PPLS*, p. 296. The use of 'conjoin' here may recall the discussion of Augustinian semiotics in Chapter 2.

[338] *PPLS*, p. 296.

[339] *PPLS*, p. 296.

[340] *PPLS*, p. 296.

[341] *PPLS*, pp. 296–7.

[342] *PPLS*, p. 297. For further comment on the Song along these lines, see my 'The Readable City and the Rhetoric of Excess: A Reading of the Song of Songs', *Crosscurrents* 52.4 (winter 2003).

[343] *PPLS*, p. 298.

[344] *PPLS*, p. 298.

[345] *PPLS*, p. 298.

[346] *PPLS*, p. 299.

[347] *PPLS*, p. 299.

[348] *PPLS*, p. 299.

[349] *PPLS*, p. 300.

[350] *PPLS*, p. 300.

[351] *PPLS*, p. 302.

[352] *PPLS*, p. 302.

[353] *PPLS*, p. 303.

[354] *PPLS*, p. 303.

[355] *PPLS*, p. 303.

[356] *PPLS*, p. 304.

[357] *PPLS*, p. 304.

[358] *PPLS*, p. 304.

[359] *PPLS*, p. 305.

[360] *PPLS*, p. 305.

[361] *PPLS*, p. 305.

[362] For example, see Proudfoot's review of *Peirce, Pragmatism and the Logic of Scripture*, where he writes 'the claim for similarity [between Peirce and the rabbis] seems designed more to confer the authority of Peirce and pragmatism on the work

of postcritical scripturalists than to provide a resource for analysis of the logic of scripture' (p. 682). Such judgments are not only uncharitable but they betray inattentiveness to the dialogues that Ochs hosts in this book.

363 *PPLS*, p. 305.

364 David Weiss Halivni, *Revelation Restored: Divine Writ and Critical Responses* (London: SCM Press, 2001), p. 76.

365 Halivni, *Revelation Restored*, p. 85.

366 Halivni, *Revelation Restored*, p. 45.

367 Peter Ochs and Nancy Levene (eds), *Textual Reasonings* (London: SCM Press, 2002).

368 Ochs and Levene (eds), *Textual Reasonings*, p. 120.

369 Ochs and Levene (eds), *Textual Reasonings*, p. 121.

370 Though on one level *peshat* and *derash* can be seen as corresponding to B-Reasonings and A-Reasonings respectively (through the Ochs–Halivni exchange especially) it is better to understand both as mutually correcting and clarifying B-Reasonings; through their interpretive co-inherence that they reach towards A-Reasoning, i.e. the logic of Scripture.

371 Ochs and Levene (eds), *Textual Reasonings*, p. 121.

372 Ochs and Levene (eds), *Textual Reasonings*, p. 121.

373 Ochs and Levene (eds), *Textual Reasonings*, p. 124.

374 Ochs and Levene (eds), *Textual Reasonings*, p. 124.

375 *PPLS*, p. 270.

376 *PPLS*, p. 270.

377 *PPLS*, p. 308.

378 *PPLS*, p. 309.

379 *PPLS*, p. 309, citing Frei's understanding of Lindbeck.

380 *PPLS*, p. 309.

381 *PPLS*, p. 309. Alluding to Lindbeck's claim that in cognitive-propositionalist terms Christianity would be like one single giant proposition, and truth would necessarily need to be a lived reality.

382 *PPLS*, p. 309.

383 Frei, 'Epilogue: George Lindbeck and *The Nature of Doctrine*', p. 277.

384 *PPLS*, p. 270.

385 *PPLS*, p. 310.

386 *PPLS*, p. 310.

387 *PPLS*, p. 310.

388 *PPLS*, p. 275.

389 *PPLS*, p. 275.

390 *PPLS*, p. 275.

391 *PPLS*, p. 275.

392 *PPLS*, p. 310.

393 *PPLS*, p. 276.

394 *PPLS*, p. 282.

395 *PPLS*, p. 276.

396 *PPLS*, p. 270.

397 James Buckley presents one of the wisest early interpretations of postliberalism when he writes that Lindbeck presents us with a 'soteriology of language'. See 'Doctrine in the Diaspora'.

398 *PPLS*, p. 310.

399 *PPLS*, pp. 310–11.

400 See Lindbeck's essay on Luther and Kadushin in Buckley (ed.) *The Church in a Postliberal Age* (London: SCM Press, 2002), pp. 21–37.

[401] *PPLS*, p. 311.

[402] *PPLS*, p. 311.

[403] *PPLS*, p. 312.

[404] *PPLS*, p. 312.

[405] *PPLS*, pp. 313–14 for the citations in this paragraph.

[406] *PPLS*, p. 314.

[407] *PPLS*, p. 314.

[408] *PPLS*, p. 315.

[409] *PPLS*, p. 315 (emphasis in original).

[410] *PPLS*, p. 315.

[411] *PPLS*, p. 315.

## Notes to Conclusion, pp. 99–116

[412] Augustine, *Conf.* 7.18.24.

[413] This is apparent even in Niebuhr's early work. See *Moral Relativism and the Christian Ethic* (Pamphlet of the International Missionary Council, 1929).

[414] Marshall, *Trinity and Truth*.

[415] George Hunsinger moves in a more fruitful direction with Lindbeck on truth when he seeks to transform what he calls Lindbeck's 'neoliberal' categories into more 'postliberal' hermeneutical ones, to draw him into an even closer alliance with Hans Frei. See Chapters 9 and 13 in Hunsinger, *Disruptive Grace*.

[416] Marshall, *Trinity and Truth*, p. 103.

[417] Lindbeck prefers to understand truth-claims in intrasystematic and performative terms, not excluding propositional or ontological truth-claims, but incorporating them into a larger vision of life.

[418] Cf. Hans-Georg Gadamer, *Truth and Method*, 2nd edn (London: Sheed & Ward, 2001).

[419] This comment was inspired by Jeffrey Stout, *Democracy and Tradition* (Princeton, NJ: Princeton University Press, 2004). See especially Chapter 7, 'Between Example and Doctrine'.

[420] These insights are partly inspired by Jeff Stout's pragmatist understanding of a nonrelativist account of truth, juxtaposed against contextualist accounts of justification. See both Jeffrey Stout, *Ethics after Babel*, 2nd edn (Princeton, NJ: Princeton University Press, 2002) and the development of the argument in Stout, *Democracy and Tradition*, Chapter 10.

[421] There is the sense in Lindbeck, logically similar to the Barthian understanding of the relationship between dogmatics and apologetics, that good anthropology will be good christology in the end, reversing the liberal tendency to do just the opposite – to turn christology into anthropology.

[422] It is very difficult to say where the metaphor came from. Eugene Rogers suggested to me that it may come from Alasdair MacIntyre (personal correspondence). But I would have thought Karl Barth would be a better candidate. See *Church Dogmatics* 1.2: 792–3, and Barth's insight that the Word of God challenges us to understand that 'dogmatics itself is ethics; and ethics is also dogmatics'. Barth uses the absorption metaphor in this passage, stating that 'only the doer of the Word is its real hearer, for it is the Word of the living God addressed to the living man absorbed in the work and action of his life'. This tempts me to suggest that Lindbeck's 'absorption' metaphor ultimately derives from Barth, who uses it liberally in this regard. The

metaphor is not used in Augustine, whom he cites as actually perfoming the Word–world absorption.

[423] Bruce Marshall, 'Absorbing the World: Christianity and the Universe of Truths', in Marshall (ed.) *Theology and Dialogue*, pp. 69–104.

[424] Milbank's approach is to dismiss the analytic tendencies in Lindbeck, and extol his own continental tendencies in a post-Lindbeck way (in a sense, to attend to the post-structural concerns that Lindbeck intentionally avoided because they did not privilege 'whatever counts as holy writ', see *Doctrine*, p. 136). The effect is that readers may be directed to Milbank's metanarrative rather than something that is scripturally attentive. The effect is that readers may be directed to Milbank's metanarrative rather than something that is scripturally attentive. Milbank misses an implicit assumption in Lindbeck, that the rules instantiated in communities of interpretation are histori-cally (liturgically) embedded *and* generated by the logic of scripture (cf. the discussion of A- and B-Reasonings in Chapter 3).

[425] John Milbank, *Theology and Social Theory: Beyond Secular Reason* (Oxford: Blackwell, 1993), p. 382. The final chapter of that book is the first attempt I know of to juxtapose Lindbeck and Augustine, yet there is very little in the way of an engaged conversation hosted between the two. Lindbeck is praised but then summarily displaced by Milbank's Augustine. I have attempted a different juxtaposition.

[426] Milbank, *Theology and Social Theory*, p. 382.

[427] As Milbank admits, the phrase was originally used by Ken Surin to describe John Milbank. See *Theology and Social Theory*, p. 434, n. 5.

[428] Oliver Davies performs this in *A Theology of Compassion: Metaphysics of Difference and the Renewal of Tradition* (London: SCM Press, 2001).

[429] It may be found that, in the end, the word 'ontology' simply functions differently for Milbank than it did for Lindbeck. Since 'ontology' for Lindbeck is a category used primarily with reference to the performance of a way of life, it is always already an ethical category. This would be more or less true for Augustine to the extent that he remains Neoplatonist or transforms Neoplatonist categories into scriptural ones.

[430] Stout, *Democracy & Tradition*, p. 13.

[431] Stout, *Democracy & Tradition*, p. 59.

[432] See Ochs and Levene (eds), *Textual Reasonings*. See especially George Lindbeck's contribution, pp. 252–8, where he notes the logical similarity between Jewish and Christian 'textual reasoning'.

[433] George Lindbeck, *The Church in a Postliberal Age*, p. 197.

[434] George Lindbeck, *The Church in a Postliberal Age*, p. 200.

[435] Lindbeck was particularly prone to 'sectarian' rhetoric in his earlier work. See, e.g., George Lindbeck, 'The Sectarian Future of the Church', in Joseph Whelan (ed.), *The God Experience* (New York: Newman Press, 1971), pp. 226–43. In *The Nature of Doctrine* Lindbeck will use rhetorically useful language that sounds 'sectarian', but readers should be very careful in assessing the project as a whole in the light of rhetoric that is intended as a defence for a minority position in theology and religion (it should be added that his rhetorical strategies were very effective). But Lindbeck himself seems always aware that his rhetoric is also putting his project at risk. Just to take an example, 'yet this approach, as was noted in earlier chapters, need not confine the theological study of religion to an intellectual ghetto, but can free it for closer contact with other disciplines' (*Doctrine*, p. 129). Such sentences should be highlighted in any reading of Lindbeck so as to avoid misreadings. I have sometimes found it helpful to distinguish between sectarian 'withdrawal' and sectarian 'engagement,' to prevent the postliberal use of sectarian rhetoric from being read in

terms of withdrawal from social, political and ethical responsibility for the common good.

[436] Cf. Augustine on the use–enjoyment distinction in Chapter 2, or Lindbeck's own thoughts on the faith–works relationship. The phrase 'journey of intensification' belongs to David Tracy.

[437] 'Another reformation' is the title of a forthcoming book by Peter Ochs, which specifically treats Lindbeck's thought on the church–Israel relation.

[438] *Doctrine*, pp. 70–71.

[439] Such a hypothesis is currently being tested by the Society of Scriptural Reasoning, a sister society to the Society of Textual Reasoning referred to in Chapter 3.

[440] A number of descriptions of this work, in addition to this one, are available online at http:///www.depts.drew.edu/ssr/nationalssr/. A number of forthcoming publications promise further descriptions. See especially Nicholas Adams, *Habermas, Theology and Scripture* (Cambridge: Cambridge University Press, 2005) and his eleventh chapter on 'Scriptural Difference and Scriptural Reasoning'. For ways in which this work intersects with contemporary issues in political theology, see my article 'Democracy and the Politics of the Word: Stout and Hauerwas on Democracy and Scripture', *Scottish Journal of Theology* 58.2 (May 2005), and Jeff Stout's response in the same issue.

[441] See Augustine, *The Enchiridion on Faith, Hope, and Love: The Augustine Catechism*, trans. B. Harbert (Brooklyn, NY: New City Press, 1999). Recall Lindbeck's suggestion that 'the postliberal method ... resembles ancient catechesis more than modern translation', *Doctrine*, p. 132.

[442] Lindbeck acknowledges this proximity when he states that his was not an isolated work even when it first appeared. He writes, 'Alasdair MacIntyre and Stanley Hauerwas were already producing philosophical and theological works with affinity to this one' (*The Church in a Postliberal Age*, p. 199).

[443] Augustine, *The Enchiridion on Faith, Hope, and Love*, p. 91.

[444] Cf. Matthew Levering's *Scripture and Metaphysics: Aquinas and the Renewal of Trinitarian Theology* (Oxford: Blackwell, 2004). The same point made with regard to Augustine also applies to Aquinas. As Levering writes, 'in seeking contemplative ends, we attain practical ends as well' (p. 238).

[445] Lindbeck later discusses the 'rule of faith' as articulating 'the liturgically embedded Christological and Trinitarian reading of the Hebrew Scriptures'. In this sense, Lindbeck sees scripture and the church in a trinitarian way, as 'co-inherent' (*The Church in a Postliberal Age*, p. 204).

[446] *Doctrine*, p. 125.

[447] *Doctrine*, p. 126.

[448] *Doctrine*, p. 127.

[449] *Doctrine*, p. 128 (emphasis mine).

[450] *Doctrine*, p. 133.

[451] *Doctrine*, p. 134.

[452] Lk. 10.29.

[453] *The Church in a Postliberal Age*, p. 222.

[454] *The Church in a Postliberal Age*, p. 252.

[455] See Rev. 22.2, 'and the leaves of the tree are for the healing of the nations'.

# Bibliography

The scripture quotations contained herein are from the *New Revised Standard Version Bible*, copyright © 1989 by the Division of Christian Education of the National Council of the Churches of Christ in the USA. Used by permission. All rights reserved.

The *Patrologia Cursus Completus, Series Latina*, ed. J.P. Migne, 221 vols (Paris: 1844–64) was consulted for all of the texts in the Augustinian corpus. Unless otherwise stated, all translations depend upon the English version of the text listed below.

Adams, Nicholas with Charles Elliott, 'Ethnography is Dogmatics: Making Description Central to Systematic Theology', *Scottish Journal of Theology* 50.4 (autumn 2000): 410–25.

Adams, Nicholas, review of *Peirce, Pragmatism and the Logic of Scripture*, in *Heythrop Journal* 42.3 (2001).

Arendt, Hannah, *Love and Saint Augustine*. (Chicago, IL: University of Chicago Press, 1996).

Arnold, Duane and Pamela Bright (eds), *De doctrina christiana: A Classic of Western Culture*, Christianity and Judaism in Antiquity, Vol. 9 (Notre Dame, IN: University of Notre Dame Press, 1995).

Aristotle, *The Works of Aristotle Translated into English*, 12 vols, ed. W.D. Ross (Oxford: The Clarendon Press, 1908–52).

Augustine, *De dialectica*, trans. B.D. Jackson (Dordrecht and Boston: Synthese Historical Library, 1975).

——, *The Trinity: De trinitate*, trans. Edmund Hill (Brooklyn, NY: New City Press, 1991).

——, *Against the Academicians and The Teacher*, trans. P. King (Indianapolis, IN: Hackett, 1995).

——, *Teaching Christianity: De doctrina christiana*, trans. Edmund Hill (Brooklyn, NY: New City Press, 1996).

——, *Confessions*, trans. Henry Chadwick (Oxford: Oxford University Press, 1998).

——, *The City of God*, trans. Marcus Dods (New York: Random House, 1999).

——, *Enchiridion on Faith, Hope, and Love: The Augustine Catechism*, trans. B. Harbert (Brooklyn, NY: New City Press, 1999).

Babcock, William S., '*Caritas* and Signification in *De doctrina christiana* 1–3', in Arnold and Bright (eds) *De doctrina christiana: A Classic of Western Culture* (Notre Dame, IN: University of Notre Dame Press, 1995).

Badiou, Alain, *Ethics* (London: Verso, 2001).

Balthasar, Hans Urs von, *Love Alone: The Way of Revelation* (London: Sheed and Ward, 1977).

Barrett, Lee C., 'Theology as Grammar: Regulative Principles or Paradigms and Practices', *Modern Theology* 4 (1988): 155–72.

Barth, Karl, *Church Dogmatics* 1.1 (London: T&T Clark, 2004).

——, *Church Dogmatics* 2.1 (London: T&T Clark, 2004).

Behrens, Georg, 'Schleiermacher *contra* Lindbeck on the Status of Doctrinal Sentences', *Religious Studies* 30 (1994): 399–417.

Boss, Marc, Emery Gilles and Pierre Gisel (eds), *Postlibéralisme? La Théologie de George Lindbeck et sa réception* (Geneva: Labor et Fides, 2004).

Bryant, David J., 'Christian Identity and Historical Change: Postliberals and Historicity', *Journal of Religion* 73.1 (1993): 31–42.

Buckley, James, 'Doctrine in the Diaspora', *The Thomist* 49.3 (July 1985): 440–59.

——, *Seeking the Humanity of God: Practices, Doctrines, and Catholic Theology* (Collegeville, MN: Liturgical Press, 1992).

Burnaby, John, 'Amor in St Augustine', in *The Philosophy and Theology of Anders Nygren*, (ed.) C.W. Kegley (Carbondale, IL: Southern Illinois University Press, 1970).

Burnyeat, M.F., 'Wittgenstein and Augustine *De magistro*', in Gareth B. Matthews (ed.), *The Augustinian Tradition* (Berkeley and Los Angeles, CA: University of California Press, 1999).

Burrell, David, review of *Peirce, Pragmatism and the Logic of Scripture*, in *Modern Theology* 15.4 (1999).

Cameron, Michael, 'Signs', in Allan D. Fitzgerald (ed.) *Augustine through the Ages: An Encyclopedia* (Grand Rapids, MI: Eerdmans, 1999).

Cavadini, John C., 'The Quest for Truth in Augustine's *De trinitate*', *Theological Studies* 58 (1997): 429–45.

Cohen, Jeremy, *Living Letters: Ideas of the Jew in Medieval Christianity* (Berkeley, CA: University of California Press, 1999).

Couturier, C., '"Sacramentum" et "mysterium" dans l'oevre de saint Augustin', in *Etudes augustiniennes* (1953): 161–332.

Davidson, Donald, *Inquiries into Truth and Interpretation*, 2nd edn (Oxford: Clarendon Press, 2001).

Davies, Oliver, *A Theology of Compassion: The Metaphysics of Difference and the Renewal of Tradition* (London: SCM Press, 2002).

——, 'The Sign Redeemed: A Study in Christian Fundamental Semiotics', *Modern Theology* 19.2 (April 2003): 219–41.

Dawson, David, 'Sign Theory, Allegorical Reading, and the Motions of the Soul in *De doctrina christiana*', in Arnold and Bright (eds), *De doctrina christiana: A Classic of Western Culture* (Notre Dame, IN: University of Notre Dame Press, 1995).

de Lubac, Henri, *Medieval Exegesis Vols 1–2: The Four Senses of Scripture*, trans. M. Sebanc (Edinburgh: T&T Clark, 1998).

——, *Scripture in the Tradition*, trans. L. O' Neill (New York: Herder & Herder, 2000).

——, *Augustinianism and Modern Theology*, trans. L. Sheppard. (New York: Herder & Herder, 2000).

Djuth, Marianne, 'The Royal Way: Augustine's Freedom of the Will and the Monastic Tradition', in F. Van Fleteran and J.C. Schnaubelt (eds), *Augustine: Biblical Exegete, Collectanea Augustiniana* (Peter Lang, 2001).

Ebeling, Gerhard, *The Nature of Faith*, trans. Ronald Gregor Smith (Philadelphia, PA: Westminster, 1967).

——, *Einführung in Theologische Sprachlehre* (Tübingen: J.C.B. Mohr, 1971).

Eco, Umberto, *Semiotics and the Philosophy of Language* (Bloomington, IN: Indiana University Press, 1984).

Eco, Umberto, Roberto Lambertini, Constantino Marmo and Andrea Taborroni 'On Animal Language in the Medieval Classification of Signs', in Umberto Eco and Costantino Marmo (eds), *On the Medieval Theory of Signs* (Amsterdam: John Benjamins, 1989).

Eco, Umberto and Costantino Marmo (eds), *On the Medieval Theory of Signs* (Amsterdam: John Benjamins, 1989).

Fergusson, David. 'Meaning, Truth, and Realism in Bultmann and Lindbeck', *Religious Studies* 26 (1990): 183–98.

Fodor, Jim, review of *Peirce, Pragmatism and the Logic of Scripture*, in *Pro Ecclesia* 10.4 (2002): 496.

Ford, David, *Self and Salvation: Being Transformed* (Cambridge:

Cambridge University Press, 1999).

——, 'A Messiah for the Third Millennium,' *Modern Theology* 16.1 (January 2000): 75–90.

Ford, David (ed), *The Modern Theologians: An Introduction to Christian Theology in the Twentieth Century*, 2nd edn (Oxford: Blackwell, 2005).

Ford, David and Rachel Muers (eds), *The Modern Theologians: An Introduction to Christian Theology since 1918*, 3rd edn (Oxford: Blackwell, 2005).

Frei, Hans W., *The Eclipse of Biblical Narrative: A Study in Eighteenth and Nineteenth Century Hermeneutics* (New Haven, CT: Yale University Press, 1974).

——, *The Identity of Jesus Christ: The Hermeneutical Bases of Dogmatic Theology* (Philadelphia, PA: Fortress Press, 1975).

——, 'Epilogue: George Lindbeck and *The Nature of Doctrine*', in Bruce Marshall (ed), *Theology and Dialogue: Essays in Conversation with George Lindbeck* (Notre Dame, IN: University of Notre Dame Press, 1990).

——, *Types of Christian Theology* (New Haven, CT: Yale University Press, 1992).

Gadamer, Hans-Georg, *Truth and Method*, 2nd edn (London: Sheed and Ward, 2001).

Green, Garrett (ed.), *Scriptural Authority and Narrative Interpretation* (Philadelphia, PA: Fortress Press: 1987).

Goodman, Russell B., *Wittgenstein and William James* (Cambridge: Cambridge University Press, 2002).

Halivni, David Weiss, *Revelation Restored: Divine Writ and Critical Responses* (London: SCM Press, 2001).

Hardy, Daniel W., *God's Ways with the World* (Edinburgh: T&T Clark, 1996).

——, *Finding the Church* (London: SCM Press, 2003).

Hensley, Jeffrey, 'Are Postliberals Necessarily Antirealists? Reexamining the Metaphysics of Lindbeck's Postliberal Theology', in T.R. Phillips and D.L. Okholm (eds), *The Nature of Confession*, (Downers Grove: Intervarsity Press, 1996).

Higton, Michael, *Christ, Providence and History: Hans Frei's Public Theology* (London: T&T Clark, 2004).

Holte, Ragnar, *Béatitude et sagesse: Saint Augustin et le problème de la fin de l'homme dans la philosophie ancienne* (Paris: Etudes augustiniennes, 1962).

Hookway, Christopher, review of *Peirce, Pragmatism and the Logic of*

*Scripture*, in *Religious Studies* 35 (1999).

Hughes, Graham, *Worship as Meaning: A Liturgical Theology for Late Modernity* (Cambridge: Cambridge University Press, 2003).

Hunsinger, George, *How to Read Karl Barth: The Shape of his Theology* (Oxford: Oxford University Press, 1991).

——, 'Truth as Self-Involving: Barth and Lindbeck on the Cognitive and Performative Aspects of Truth in Theological Discourse', *Journal of the American Academy of Religion* 61.1 (1993): 41–56.

——, *Disruptive Grace: Studies in the Theology of Karl Barth* (Grand Rapids, MI: Eerdmans, 2000).

James, William, *Pragmatism* (New York: Dover, 1995).

——, 'What Pragmatism Means', in *Selected Writings* (New York: BOTMC, 1997).

Jordan, Mark D., 'Words and Word: Incarnation and Signification in Augustine's *De doctrina christiana*', *Augustinian Studies*, 11 (1980): 175–95.

Kato, Takeshi, '*Sonus et Verbum: De doctrina christiana* 1.13.12', in Arnold and Bright (eds), *De doctrina christiana: A Classic of Western Culture* (Notre Dame, IN: University of Notre Dame Press, 1995).

Kelsey, David H., *Proving Doctrine: The Uses of Scripture in Modern Theology* (Harrisburg, NY: Trinity Press, 1999).

Kerr, Fergus, *Theology After Wittgenstein*, 2nd edn (London: SPCK, 1997).

Kirwan, Christopher, *Augustine, Arguments of the Philosophers* (New York: Routledge, 1991).

Kraftson-Hogue, Michael, 'Predication Turning to Praise: Marion and Augustine on God and Hermeneutics', *Literature and Theology* 14.4 (2000): 399–411.

Kuhn, Thomas, *The Structure of Scientific Revolutions* (Chicago, IL: University of Chicago Press, 1967).

Kuklick, Bruce, *A History of Philosophy in America 1720–2000* (Oxford: Oxford University Press, 2001).

Lancel, Serge, *St Augustine*, trans. Antonia Nevill. (London: SCM Press, 2002).

Levering, Matthew, *Scriptures and Metaphysics: Aquinas and the Renewal of Trinitarian Theology* (Oxford: Blackwell, 2004).

Lindbeck, George, 'Is Duns Scotus an Essentialist?' unpublished PhD dissertation, Yale University, 1955.

——, 'The Sectarian Future of the Church', in Joseph Whelan (ed.), *The God Experience* (New York: Newman Press, 1971).

——, *The Nature of Doctrine: Religion and Theology in a Postliberal Age* (Philadelphia, PA: Westminster, 1984).

——, 'The Story-Shaped Church' in Garrett Green (ed.), *Scriptural Authority and Narrative Interpretation* (Philadelphia, PA: Fortress Press, 1987).

——, 'Confession and Community: An Israel-like View of the Church', *The Christian Century* 107 (6 May 1990): 492–6.

——, *Christliche Lehre als Grammatik des Glaubens. Religion und Theologie in postliberalen Zeitalter*, trans. Markus Müller; intro. Hans G. Ulrich and Reinhard Hütter (Gütersloh: Kaiser, 1994).

——, *The Church in a Postliberal Age* (ed.) James Buckley (London: SCM Press, 2002).

Lints, Richard, 'The Postpositivist Choice: Tracy or Lindbeck?' *Journal of the American Academy of Religion* 61.4 (1993): 655–77.

Lonergan, Bernard, *The Way to Nicea: The Dialectical Development of Trinitarian Theology*, trans. Conn O'Donovan (Philadelphia, PA: Westminster, 1976).

Lyotard, Jean-François, *The Postmodern Condition: A Report on Knowledge* (Manchester: Manchester University Press, 1984).

MacDonald, Neil B., *Karl Barth and the Strange New World within the Bible: Barth, Wittgenstein and the Metadilemmas of the Enlightenment* (New York: Paternoster Press, 2000).

MacIntyre, Alasdair, *After Virtue* (Notre Dame, IN: University of Notre Dame Press, 1981).

——, *Three Rival Versions of Moral Enquiry* (London: Duckworth, 1990).

Manetti, Giovanni (ed.), *Knowledge Through Signs: Ancient Semiotic Theories and Practices*, (Bologna: Brepols, 1996).

Marion, Jean-Luc, *God Without Being* (Chicago, IL: University of Chicago Press, 1991).

Markus, R.A., 'St Augustine on Signs', *Phronesis* (1957): 61–91.

——, *Saeculum: History and Society in the Theology of Saint Augustine*, 2nd edn (Cambridge: Cambridge University Press, 1988).

——, 'Sign, Communication, and Communities in Augustine's *De doctrina christiana*', in Arnold and Bright (eds), *De doctrina christiana: A Classic of Western Culture* (Notre Dame, IN: University of Notre Dame Press, 1995).

Marsden, George, *The Soul of the American University: From Protestant Establishment to Established Non-Belief* (Oxford: Oxford University Press, 1994).

Marshall, Bruce (ed.), *Theology and Dialogue: Essays in Conversation with George Lindbeck* (Notre Dame, IN: University of Notre Dame Press, 1990).

——, *Trinity and Truth* (Cambridge: Cambridge University Press, 1999).

Matthews, Gareth B. (ed.), *The Augustinian Tradition* (Berkeley and Los Angeles, CA: University of California Press, 1999).

Menand, Louis, *The Metaphysical Club* (London: Flamingo, 2001).

Michaelson, Gordon E., 'The Response to Lindbeck', *Modern Theology* 4 (1988): 107–20.

Milbank, John, 'Theology without Substance: Christianity, Signs, Origins', *Literature and Theology* 2 (1988): 3–21.

——, *Theology and Social Theory: Beyond Secular Reason* (Oxford: Blackwell, 1993).

Milbank, John, Catherine Pickstock and Graham Ward (eds), *Radical Orthodoxy* (London: Routledge, 1999).

Misak, Cheryl J., *Truth and the End of Inquiry: A Peircean Account of Truth* (Oxford: Oxford University Press, 1991).

Murray, Paul D., 'A Liberal Helping of Postliberalism Please', in Mark D. Chapman (ed.), *The Future of Liberal Theology* (Aldershot: Ashgate, 2002), pp. 208–20.

Neibuhr, H. Richard, *Moral Relativism and the Christian Ethic* (London: International Missionary Council, 1929).

——, *The Meaning of Revelation* (New York: Macmillan, 1941).

——, *Christ and Culture* (New York: Harper & Row, 1951).

——, *The Kingdom of God in America* (New York: Harper & Row, 1959).

——, *The Responsible Self: An Essay in Christian Moral Philosophy* (New York: Harper & Row, 1963).

——, *Theology, History, and Culture: Major Unpublished Writings*, ed. William Stacy Johnson (New Haven, CT: Yale University Press, 1996).

Niebuhr, Reinhold, *Christian Realism and Political Problems* (London: Faber & Faber, 1954).

——, *Moral Man and Immoral Society: A Study of Ethics and Politics* (Philadelphia, PA: Westminster / John Knox Press, 2002).

Ochs, Peter. 'Scriptural Pragmatism: Jewish Philosophy's Concept of Truth', in the *International Philosophical Quarterly* 26.2 (1986): 32–47.

——, 'Scriptural Logics: Towards a Postcritical Metaphysics', *Modern Theology* 11.1 (January 1995): 65–92.

Ochs, Peter, *Peirce, Pragmatism and the Logic of Scripture* (Cambridge: Cambridge University Press, 1998).

——, 'The Logic of Indignity and the Logic of Redemption', unpublished Paper for the Center for Theological Inquiry, consultation on theological anthropology (Princeton, NJ: Center for Theological Inquiry, 2003).

Ochs, Peter and Nancy Levene (eds), *Textual Reasonings* (London: SCM Press, 2002).

O'Donnell, James J. (ed.), *Augustine: Commentary on the Confessions*, 3 vols (Oxford: Clarendon, 1992).

O'Donovan, Oliver, *The Problem of Self-Love in Augustine* (New Haven, CT: Yale University Press, 1980).

——, '*Usus* and *Fruitio* in Augustine, *De Doctrina Christiana I*', *Journal of Theological Studies* (new series), 33.2 (1982): 361–97.

O'Neill, Colman E., 'The Rule Theory of Doctrine and Propositional Truth', *The Thomist* 49.3 (July 1985): 417–42.

O'Regan, Cyril, '*De doctrina christiana* and Modern Hermeneutics', in *De doctrina christiana: A Classic of Western Culture* (Notre Dame, IN: University of Notre Dame Press, 1995).

Patterson, Sue, *Realist Christian Theology in a Postmodern Age* (Cambridge: Cambridge University Press, 1999).

Pecknold, C.C., review of James K.A. Smith's *Speech and Theology: Language and the Logic of the Incarnation*, in *Reviews in Religion and Theology* 10.3 (June 2003).

——, '*Radical Traditions* and the Return to Scripture in Religion and Theology', *Reviews in Religion and Theology* 10.4 (September 2003): 373–8.

——, 'How Augustine Used the Trinity: Functionalism and the Development of Doctrine', *Anglican Theological Review* 85.1 (winter 2003): 127–41.

——, 'The Readable City and the Rhetoric of Excess: A Reading of the Song of Songs', *Crosscurrents* 52.4 (winter 2003): 516–20.

——, 'Democracy and the Politics of the Word: Stout and Hauerwas on Democracy and Scripture', *Scottish Journal of Theology* 58.2 (May 2005): forthcoming.

Peirce, Charles, *Collected Papers of Charles Sanders Peirce*, ed. Charles Hartshorne, Paul Weiss and A. Burks (Cambridge, MA: Harvard University Press, 1935, 1958).

——, *The Essential Peirce*, 2 vols (Bloomington, IN: Indiana University Press, 1998).

Percy, Walker, *Signposts in a Strange Land* (New York: Noonday, 1991).

Phillips, D.Z., 'Lindbeck's Audience', *Modern Theology* 4.2 (1988): 133–54.

Phillips, Timothy R. and Dennis L. Okholm (eds), *The Nature of Confession: Evangelicals and Postliberals in Conversation* (Downers Grove: Intervarsity Press, 1996).

Pickstock, Catherine, 'Soul, City and Cosmos after Augustine', in John Milbank, Catherine Pickstock and Graham Ward (eds), *Radical Orthodoxy* (London: Routledge, 1999).

Placher, William C., 'Revisionist and Postliberal Theologies and the Public Character of Theology', *The Thomist* 49.3 (July 1985): 392–416.

——, 'Paul Ricoeur and Postliberal Theology: A Conflict of Interpretations', *Modern Theology* 4 (1987): 35–52.

Plotinus, *The Enneads* (London: Penguin, 1991).

Pontet, Maurice, *L'Exegese de s. Augustin predicateur* (Paris: Theologie 7, 1945).

Press, Gerald A., 'The Subject and Structure of Augustine's *De doctrina christiana*,' *Augustinian Studies*, 11 (1980): 107–21.

Proudfoot, Wayne, review of *Peirce, Pragmatism and the Logic of Scripture*, in *The Journal of Religion* 79.4 (October 1999).

Przywara, Erich, *An Augustine Synthesis* (London: Sheed & Ward, 1991).

Raposa, Michael, *Peirce's Philosophy of Religion*, Peirce Studies, No. 5 (Bloomington, IN: Indiana University Press, 1989).

Rescher, Nicholas, *Realistic Pragmatism* (Albany, NY: SUNY Press, 2001).

Ricoeur, Paul, *Figuring the Sacred: Religion, Narrative and Imagination* (Philadelphia, PA: Fortress Press, 1995).

Rogers, Eugene, *Thomas Aquinas and Karl Barth* (Notre Dame, IN: University of Notre Dame Press, 1995).

Rorty, Richard, *Consequences of Pragmatism* (Minneapolis, MN: University of Minnesota Press, 1982).

Sedley, David, 'On Signs', in Jonathan Barnes (ed), *Science and Speculation* (Cambridge: Cambridge University Press, 1982), pp. 239–72.

Smith, James K.A., *Speech and Theology: Language and the Logic of Incarnation* (London: Routledge, 2002).

Smith, John E., *Purpose and Thought: The Meaning of Pragmatism* (New Haven, CT: Yale University Press, 1978).

Smyth, Richard, review of *Peirce, Pragmatism and the Logic of Scripture*, in *Transactions of the Charles Sanders Peirce Society* 35.2 (spring 1999).

Stell, Stephen L., 'Hermeneutics in Theology and the Theology of Hermeneutics: Beyond Lindbeck and Tracy', *Journal of the American Academy of Religion* 61.4 (1993): 679–702.

Stock, Brian, *Augustine the Reader: Meditation, Self-Knowledge, and the Ethics of Interpretation* (Cambridge, MA: Belknap Press of Harvard University Press, 1996).

Stout, Jeffrey, *Ethics after Babel*, 2nd edn (Princeton, NJ: Princeton University Press, 2002).

——, *Democracy and Tradition* (Princeton, NJ: Princeton University Press, 2004).

Stump, Eleanore and Norman Kretzmann (eds), *The Cambridge Companion to Augustine* (Cambridge: Cambridge University Press, 2001).

Surin, Kenneth, 'Many Religions and the One True Faith: An Examination of Lindbeck's Chapter Three', *Modern Theology* 4.2 (1988): 187–209.

TeSelle, Eugene, *Augustine the Theologian* (New York: Herder & Herder, 1970).

Teske, Roland, 'The Good Samaritan (Lk. 10.29–37) in Augustine's Exegesis', in *Augustine: Biblical Exegete* (New York and Frankfurt: Peter Lang, 2001).

Thayer, H.S., *Meaning and Action: A Critical History of Pragmatism* (Indianapolis, IN: Hackett, 1981).

Tilley, Terrence W., 'Incommensurability, Intratextuality, and Fideism', *Modern Theology* 5 (1989): 87–111.

Todorov, Tzvetan, *Theories of the Symbol* (Ithaca, NY: Cornell University Press, 1982).

Tracy, David, 'Lindbeck's New Program for Theology: A Reflection', *The Thomist* 49.3 (July 1985): 460–72.

Van Fleteran, Frederick, 'Principles of Augustine's Hermeneutic: An Overview', in *Augustine: Biblical Exegete* (New York and Frankfurt: Peter Lang, 2001).

Wainwright, Geoffrey, 'Ecumenical Dimensions of Lindbeck's Nature of Doctrine', *Modern Theology* 4.2 (1988): 121–32.

Werpehowski, William, 'Ad Hoc Apologetics', *Journal of Religion* 66.3 (1986): 282–301.

Williams, Rowan, 'Language, Reality and Desire in Augustine's De doctrina', *Literature and Theology* 3 (1989): 138–50.

Williams, Stephen, 'Lindbeck's Regulative Christology', *Modern Theology* 4.2 (1988): 173–86.

Wittgenstein, Ludwig, *The Philosophical Investigations* (Oxford: Basil Blackwell, 1958).

Zizek, Slavoj, *The Puppet and the Dwarf: The Perverse Core of Christianity* (Cambridge, MA: MIT Press, 2003).

Zorn, Hans, 'Grammar, Doctrines, and Practice', *Journal of Religion* 75.4 (1995): 509–22.

# Index